Praise for *Freddie Steinmark*

"The authors . . . capture Freddie's cheerful essence, vividly recreate key games and posit his life against the canvas of history . . . a deeply informed and proper tribute to the little Texas Longhorn with Heart."
— *The Austin American-Statesman*

"What makes the new book unique is the access Yousse and Cryan had to the story. . . . The authors offer a fleshed-out picture of Steinmark's early life—his natural athletic ability, his dedication to Catholicism, the way he inspired his friends and teammates with a positive attitude at a very young age, the way he looked after his little brother, Sammy, his focus on schoolwork and love of football. . . . These details give a better sense of the person Steinmark was before he became a poster boy for cancer in the early 1970s. *Freddie Steinmark* is definitely worth a read."
— *Houston Chronicle*

"So few athletes have a lasting legacy, and even fewer leave the world a better place than they found it. Now, in the hands of born storytellers Bower Yousse and Thomas Cryan, the legend of Freddie Steinmark will continue to do his good work."
—Susan Fornoff, author of *"Lady in the Locker Room"*

"On and off the field, Freddie always lit it up."
—Fred Akers, Broadcaster, Head Football Coach, University of Texas (1977–1986), and Defensive Backs Coach, University of Texas (1966–1974)

"The 1969 Champion Texas Longhorns were a special team for many reasons, but the biggest one was the remarkable, unforgettable relationship between Coach Royal and *his* All-American, Safety Freddie Steinmark."
—Aaron Eckhart, actor, "Coach Royal" in the movie *My All American*

FREDDIE STEINMARK

Faith, Family, Football

BOWER YOUSSE AND
THOMAS J. CRYAN

University of Texas Press
Austin

Frontispiece: When asked by reporters for his reaction after the Cotton Bowl game, Freddie Steinmark replied, "It was the greatest day of my life."

Single capital letters indicate photos in the first unnumbered section. Double capital letters indicate photos in the second unnumbered section. Frontispiece (page ii) created by the *Daily Texan*, Prints and Photographs Collection, di_05224, the Dolph Briscoe Center for American History, the University of Texas at Austin. Photos A–S, FF, II–KK, PP–TT, courtesy of the Steinmark family. Photos AA–EE, GG–HH, LL–OO, VV, courtesy of the University of Texas at Austin. Photo UU courtesy of Roger Balettie.

Copyright © 2015 by FJS Productions Inc.
All rights reserved
Printed in the United States of America
First edition, 2015
First paperback printing, 2017

Requests for permission to reproduce material from this work should be sent to:
Permissions
University of Texas Press
P.O. Box 7819
Austin, TX 78713-7819
http://utpress.utexas.edu/index.php/rp-form

♾ The paper used in this book meets the minimum requirements of
ANSI/NISO Z39.48-1992 (R1997) (Permanence of Paper).

LIBRARY OF CONGRESS CATALOGING-IN-PUBLICATION DATA
Yousse, Bower, author.
Freddie Steinmark : faith, family, football / Bower Yousse and Thomas J. Cryan. —
First edition.
pages   cm
Includes bibliographical references and index.
ISBN 978-1-4773-1215-5 (paper)
ISBN 978-1-4773-0822-6 (library e-book)
ISBN 978-1-4773-0823-3 (non-library e-book)
1. Steinmark, Freddie. 2. Football players—United States—Biography. 3. Cancer—
Patients—United States—Biography. I. Cryan, Thomas J., author. II. Title.
GV939.S74Y68 2015
796.332092—dc23   2015004079
doi:10.7560/308219

To the enduring spirit of Freddie Joe Steinmark,
still lighting it up.

My heart leaps up when I behold
A rainbow in the sky:
So was it when my life began;
So is it now I am a man;
So be it when I shall grow old,
Or let me die!
The Child is father of the Man;
And I could wish my days to be
Bound each to each by natural piety.

WILLIAM WORDSWORTH

Contents

AUTHORS' NOTE

IN AUGUST 1967, A SOFT-SPOKEN, UNDERSIZED eighteen-year-old athlete from Wheat Ridge, Colorado, arrived in Austin, Texas, to pursue a college degree and play football for the University of Texas Longhorns. Two years later, he competed in the national championship game against the University of Arkansas, performing in great pain. Six days after the game, doctors removed his cancer-ridden left leg. This young man met that challenge with bravery, grace, and dignity. His name was Freddie Steinmark.

Today, Freddie occupies a singular place in the history and rich tradition of the Longhorns. He endures as an inspiration for football players as they stream through the tunnel into Darrell K Royal–Texas Memorial Stadium and the thunderous embrace of a hundred thousand burnt-orange-clad fans. His name adorns the stadium scoreboard.

This book is an exploration of how Freddie rose to become such a symbol of perseverance and how he continues to stand for hope and strength in the face of obstacles and tribulations. We have attempted to capture his true essence. While some of Freddie's story may be familiar to the Longhorn nation and to devoted college football fans, much of his journey has remained, until now, unspoken. Freddie's time on earth was brief but catalytic, and you may find that a deeper understanding of the way he lived his life reveals many truths. His is a story of determination, passion, and faith. It is a story encompassing a time in our country's history fraught with upheaval and despair. It is a story of a family's bond, unbroken for decades. It is a story of how one prepares for and addresses the ultimate. And most especially, it is a story of love.

Freddie and I (Bower Yousse) were friends. We grew up together in Denver, in the shadow of the Rocky Mountains. Our families' lives were intertwined, revolving around sports. Freddie's father, "Big Fred," was our baseball and football coach for many of the years we were teammates. The Steinmarks are a second family to me.

Additionally, my coauthor, Thomas Cryan, has been a close associate of the Steinmarks for more than twenty years. He too is intimately acquainted with aspects of Freddie's life not known to the general public.

We feel that our unrestricted and unprecedented access to documents associated with Freddie, and our personal knowledge of him, have enabled us to provide precise insight into his character. We have been able to examine how he touched the collective consciousness of a nation and to explore the still-rippling effects of his life.

We don't claim to be unbiased or impartial in this rendering of Freddie's life. What we do claim is to present an authentic story distilled from our relationships with Freddie, his family, his friends, his teammates, and his coaches. At crucial junctures in this narrative, when it seems justified, I speculate on Freddie's thoughts and feelings, something that previous accounts of Freddie have not done. These attempts are based on either what he communicated to me or how I knew him to be. In the pages that follow, we present a narrative that begins with the childhoods of Freddie's parents, Gloria Marchitti and Fred Steinmark (Big Fred), how they met, their marriage, and the birth of their first child, Freddie Joe, because an understanding of Freddie cannot be achieved separate from that of his family.

When I attended Freddie's funeral in 1971, I was twenty-two years old and in shock. We all were. It was incomprehensible that

Freddie was no longer with us. In the Steinmark home afterward, a man who was there as President Nixon's representative pulled Freddie's mother aside and asked whether there was anything the president could do to comfort her. Gloria made one request: "Tell him to fight cancer just as he would fight any other war."

It was shortly thereafter that Congress went to work crafting legislation for the National Cancer Act. This bill, which marked the start of President Nixon's "War on Cancer," was signed into law on December 23, 1971.

But that is just part of the journey that was Freddie Joe Steinmark's life.

This is the rest of his story.

BOWER YOUSSE

THOMAS J. CRYAN

PART ONE
1929–1967

*I will play the game hard and clean
and never be a quitter. What matters
is courage. It is no disgrace to be
beaten; the great disgrace is to quit
or turn yellow.*

THE ROUGH RIDERS' CREED

CHAPTER 1

THE ALL-AMERICAN BOY

THE THIRD TIME JOE DUNCAN SNAPPED OPEN the newspaper, Gloria Marchitti stirred from her deep sleep. She lay in her twin bed, in the pink bedroom that she shared with her sister Lena. Her soon-to-be brother-in-law stood alongside the bed, continuing to rustle the newspaper. She glared at him over her right shoulder. It was eight on a summer morning. Teenage Gloria had wanted to sleep in.

"Hey," Joe said cheerfully, peering over the top of the *Rocky Mountain News*. A cigarette bounced on his lip. "Look at this, Gloria." He held the tabloid in front of her face. "See this guy? This is the guy you gotta date when you start North High School." A handsome young man grinned on the newspaper page. The headline read: "Steinmark Selected All-American Boy." The subhead added: "North Side Youngster Picked Unanimously." Gloria rolled over, away from Joe. "I don't know anything about him."

"I'm telling you, Gloria, this guy is swell . . . real swell." Gloria feigned sleep, stared at the wall, and pictured in her mind the handsome boy in the photograph.

BARELY A YEAR HAD PASSED SINCE THE END OF WORLD War II. The joy that came from victory in the war and the return of troops from overseas gave everybody a boost. Baseball fans re-

3

joiced that star players such as Ted Williams had returned from active duty, and the game reasserted itself as America's pastime.

Like Williams, Joe Duncan was a navy man, home from the war. Unlike Williams, Joe was merely a fan. On the morning he woke up his future sister-in-law by reading from the Denver sports page, he was visiting his fiancée, Lena Marchitti, at her mother's home in North Denver. The wedding was four weeks away. Joe sat at the breakfast table, half listening to Lena's wedding concerns as he sipped coffee and read the sports section. Lena's oldest brother, Dominick, would give her away. Her three sisters, Marie, Lucille, and Gloria, were the bridesmaids. Two hundred guests had been invited to the wedding at St. Catherine's, with the reception to follow in her mother's beautiful yard. And there was the matter of preparing all that food. A big Italian wedding had to include a big Italian feast.

Lena asked Joe whether he was listening. He nodded without looking up. The Steinmark article had completely captured his attention. He wasn't the only one—baseball fans all over Denver effused about their own, newly proclaimed all-American boy. The article read:

Fred Steinmark, a 16-year-old broad-shouldered shortstop from North Denver, is Colorado's All-American baseball boy for 1946. He was unanimously voted the honor last night by a five-man selection board after two days of tryouts, including a regulation game, at Merchants Park. The judges, all major league scouts, each voted Steinmark five points for first place in balloting for the five boys they thought were outstanding in the field of 57 candidates from Colorado and Cheyenne, Wyoming. Steinmark's victory earns him an all-expense trip to Chicago and participation in Esquire's third annual All-American Boys Game on Aug. 10 at Wrigley Field. He will be a member of the West squad, coached and managed by Ty Cobb, which will meet an all-star aggregation from East of the Mississippi River and which will be tutored by Honus Wagner. The husky, strong-armed lad, who will be a senior at North High next school year, was the most decisive winner in the three years of balloting for the honor.

The article added that Steinmark's selection had been based on "the individual trials of Friday, in which his hitting, fielding, and throwing drew applause from all onlookers," as well as on Saturday's game: "He went 2-for-4 at the plate, and handled five chances cleanly in the field. . . . His shoestring stab of a liner in the fifth inning was the fielding highlight in the eyes of the judges."

Joe might have been thinking that Fred Steinmark could have any girl at school, but it also crossed his mind that Lena's very cute, very popular sister Gloria was the perfect girl for an all-American boy. If Joe had any worries that Fred might have a large ego, which would have been unfortunate, they vanished when he read that "Steinmark's selection was a popular choice with rival players and fans." When even opponents say they like you, Joe must have figured, you have to be a pretty good guy.

FRED STEINMARK HAD THICK SANDY HAIR, GREEN EYES, and a square jaw that made every girl swoon, and his athletic exploits made every boy want to be his friend. Teachers at North High liked him because in addition to being a straight-A student, he was respectful and polite. The baseball, basketball, and football coaches liked him because he was a stellar athlete gifted with uncommon natural ability and outstanding leadership skills, a rare combination for anyone his age. He made a coach's job easier because his "field sense" and intuition essentially allowed him to function as both a player and a coach on the field. With him in the game, a team had a good chance to win. He set the bar high for himself, and pulled the performance of his teammates up to a higher level. Despite accolades from every corner, he remained humble.

Fred's athletic prowess was genetic and God given, but his humility was grounded in his upbringing. He had more or less been on his own since the age of eleven. One day after baseball practice, he came home to discover that he had been abandoned. His mother, Viola, had fled with Fred's six-month-old baby sister, Sandra. She was desperate to avoid another confrontation with Fred's tough German father, Friedrich, a minor league baseball player who frequently came home stumbling and swinging after whiskey-fueled benders. Fred didn't mind when his father wasn't around—even preferred it that way. He liked that his father played professional baseball, but he hated the drinking. He prayed his dad would be better to his mother. The absence of his mother was something new. She had moved everything out, and it seemed clear she didn't intend to return. Yet Fred remained calm—a character trait that others would remark on throughout his life.

The next morning, Fred got up and went to school and then to practice. He did the same thing on the following day. On the third day, his coach brought him back to his own house. Viola, who had moved to the other side of town, had contacted the coach and asked him to look after Fred until she could get on her feet. The coach and his wife gave Fred a cot to sleep on in the converted porch at the back of their house, and he slept there for the next three years. He got a job washing dishes at a nearby restaurant so that he could eat.

Athletics became Fred's sanctuary and foundry. There he escaped the difficulties of his childhood and, at the same time, forged and hammered himself into a fearless, formidable, punishing competitor. At thirteen, he was playing shortstop, the most skill-intensive position on the baseball diamond, for the Kansas City Life team in American Legion ball. His teammates and the boys he played against were three years older than he was. But Fred had been forced to grow up fast, and his maturity showed in all he did. He was, everyone agreed, a "can't miss" young man destined for great things.

GLORIA AND HER BEST FRIEND, LIZ BERRY, COULD HARDLY wait for their sophomore year to begin at North High. With three junior high schools feeding into North, the sophomore class would number upward of eight hundred. Gloria expected it to be a continuation, on a larger stage, of the fun she had had at Skinner Junior High, where she had been the popular head girl. She was a petite auburn-haired beauty with mischievous brown eyes, a big smile, an infectious laugh, a sharp wit, and a singing voice that her junior high school music teacher felt confident could take her places. Boys liked her, she knew, but her life was crowded with a large family, an abundance of friends, and many social and singing commitments. She would talk to boys, but that was as far as she would allow it to go.

A born performer, and often necessarily left alone at home as a little girl, Gloria sang to herself as she played with her dolls. Neighbors looked in on her when the singing stopped, which wasn't often, and made it a point to tell Gloria's mother, Frances, how beautifully her child sang.

She grew up in the Bottoms, a predominantly Italian and Mexican housing area along the South Platte River where, today, the Colorado Rockies baseball stadium sits. "My mother worked eighteen-hour days," Gloria recalls.

> She was alone too. My father died when I was four. Mother was a business owner who had to get up at four o'clock in the morning to bake thirty loaves of bread for her store and small restaurant. She prepared all the food, pickled and canned and preserved fruits and meats and vegetables, made cheese, and fed the homeless. She washed, ironed, and starched all the linens. She sewed. She spoke Italian, Spanish, and English, so she was always translating for someone. She was the community nursemaid and midwife, and served on the Denver City Council. Mother had a lot of people to take care of, not just me.

By the time she was fourteen, Gloria's singing and dancing had earned plaudits and attracted widespread attention. She occasionally sang patriotic songs for troops stationed at Fort Logan, Lowry Air Force Base, and Buckley Air Base in Aurora, east of Denver. Riding the bus across town by herself to Mrs. Friedman's big house, where she would join the other performers going to the bases, and then riding back home alone at midnight made the job a challenge, but in Gloria's mind, the joy of performing trumped everything. "Besides," she says, "I wasn't ever afraid." Gloria has an unshakable faith in God, and always felt Jesus would be there if she needed help. She sometimes performed for wealthy women at backyard luncheons or evening socials, and once she took part in a program to entertain prisoners at the city jail. She recalls, "You should have heard the racket all those metal cups made going back and forth across the bars."

Skinner Junior High's departing students were asked to evaluate their classes and identify the course that they had learned the most in. Gloria felt she had learned the most in social science, since she had learned more about music in her outside activities than at school. Gloria's honest evaluation, however, hit a sour note with the music teacher, who shared it with the music teacher at North High.

"Liz and I were so excited for our first day at North," Gloria recalls. "It was so big, and there were so many kids. I was scared to death." She wasn't looking for the all-American boy, the one Joe said she should date. "I hadn't even thought about him."

When Gloria walked into the music room, she was surprised at how cold the teacher was to her. More confusing still, instead of placing Gloria in the a cappella group with other top vocalists, the teacher ushered her into the choir. Gloria questioned this, saying she was sure she was supposed to be in a cappella. The teacher responded icily that Gloria was where she was supposed to be. Gloria didn't understand why the music teacher was treating her so poorly, but after resigning herself to being in the choir, she lost interest in performing.

The newness of North High wore off after a few weeks, and Gloria settled into a regular routine of getting to school early with Liz to walk the halls. "It's what everybody did," she recalled. "You wanted to see what people were wearing, who was walking together, and things like that." They also sat outside on the wide cement steps in front of the school—which explains why the boys, including Fred Steinmark, always congregated on the grassy area below the steps, where they would try to steal a glance up at the girls, who all wore skirts.

The first time Gloria remembers hearing Fred's name at North High was at a football game. She was sitting in the bleachers with Liz; neither one of them knew much about the game. It seemed to them that the public-address announcer said Fred Steinmark's name after every play. When Fred, wearing number 1 in the Vikings' purple and gold, carried the ball yet again, Gloria blurted, "Why don't they let someone else have the ball once in a while?"

What Gloria didn't know was that Fred had spotted her on the cement steps before school one morning and had been keeping his eye on her for weeks. Her first clue came one evening when she and Liz were sitting in the Marchittis' music room. Liz liked to come over and play on the piano—she couldn't really play, but liked to try. The piano was in a large corner room at the front of the house. Two of the walls had four windows each. The oldest of the Marchitti children, Dominick, fifteen years older than Gloria, was an accomplished pianist and performer in demand all over the city. He practiced day and night. On warm evenings, he would open all the windows while he practiced, and the neighbors would come out of their homes, sit on their front steps, and listen to him.

As Liz plunked away, the neighbors knew it wasn't "Dom" playing that night. Fred Steinmark and his buddy Bob Jump drove back and forth in front of the Marchitti house. "There's a black car that keeps driving past," Gloria recalls Liz saying. So they sat quietly and watched for it. When it came around the block again, the driver pulled to the curb and shut off the engine. With the windows of the music room open, and the windows of the car rolled down, they could hear the conversation inside the car: "Well, if you want to meet her, go ring the damn doorbell." With that, the engine started and the car drove away.

The next night, the car returned. Fred sat idling with his hands on the steering wheel, looking at the impressive, Mediterranean-style home. The walls were reddish-brown brick with large arched windows. It had a red tile roof. Columns supported the roof over the front porch. An elegant wrought-iron fence enclosed trees and shrubs in the immaculately landscaped yard.

In the Highlands area of North Denver, the Marchitti home was the newest house on the block. At the corner of Grove and Clyde Place, it was only a few miles up the hill from the Bottoms, where Gloria had lived as a child. It may as well have been a world away. The Bottoms was adjacent to Union Station. Gloria remembers lying in her mother's bed at night and listening to the constant comings and goings of trains. She remembers the perils of rain, too. If a thunderstorm descended over the Rockies and stayed for a few days, the river would rise rapidly and inundate everything in its path, including Union Station and the Bottoms. Gloria knew what it was like to be awakened during the night with waist-deep water in her house.

The doorbell rang, but Gloria wasn't expecting anyone. "I opened the door," she recalls, "and who's standing there? Freddie Steinmark." He was wearing his letter sweater and had a big smile on his face. There was no introduction. "He knew who I was, and I knew who he was. Everyone knew who he was." He asked whether she wanted to go get a Coke. She said, "Yeah, I'll get a Coke with you." He walked her to his car and opened her door. She liked that he was a gentleman.

Her mind was racing during the short drive to The Scotchman, a motor restaurant popular with teens. She was a sophomore; he was a senior. Every girl at North, maybe every teenage girl in the city, wanted to be with him. He really was the all-American boy. As they sat in his car sipping their Cokes and talking, she was conscious of the scrutinizing. The girls didn't look happy. When he took her home and walked her to her front door, he thanked her for coming out and didn't try to kiss her.

Gloria's expectation for a fun-filled sophomore year ran aground after she was seen with Fred at The Scotchman. She heard the whispers when students were in the hallways moving to their next classes. "What does he see in her?" And, "She's a sophomore!" There were icy glares and cold shoulders, many from girls she thought were friends. Even teachers fond of Fred seemed annoyed with her.

They got together again on a chilly night in late October when they both were invited to a Halloween party. Even though it had snowed earlier in the week, the snow was mostly gone, so the party's hostess went ahead with a planned scavenger hunt. The idea was for teams consisting of a boy and girl to take off running and bring back in one hour as many of the items on the scavenger list as possible. To make up the teams, each boy pulled a girl's name from a hat. Fred drew Gloria's name. The giddiness of being picked by Fred sent Gloria charging into the hunt the instant she heard the hostess yell, "Go!"

She shot across the street with Fred in pursuit, but just as she reached the curb on the other side, she heard Fred fall. He was wearing loafers and had slipped on a patch of ice. She turned to see him sprawled on his back in the middle of the street. He didn't pop back up the way he did on the football field. She walked back and stood over him, looking down at his face. "Are you okay?" she asked. He nodded sheepishly. "I slipped." She nodded in agreement. "I can see that. I thought you were supposed to be some kind of great athlete or something."

Although Gloria had fun with Fred during the few times they were together, she was enduring plenty of shunning for being with him. Fred was a celebrity, not just at North High, but also in Denver. When Fred took Gloria to The Scotchman, kids, even those from the other schools, wanted to shake his hand and say hello. He was always polite, and made it a point to introduce Gloria, but she could feel their rejection. Fred belonged to them, not her.

She had given up trying to regain favor with the music teacher, and she wasn't having much luck with other teachers either. One afternoon in study hall, sitting at the back of the room and whispering back and forth with her funny friend Tony, she had to stifle a giggle. The teacher called out her name and told her to pack up and leave. Tony could stay. While walking to her locker, she spotted Fred standing at his open locker. Feeling chagrined about being thrown out of study hall, she hoped she could get past him unseen. When she was almost in the clear, he called to her. "Can't you talk?"

She stopped and looked at him. "Yeah, I can talk. What do you want to talk about?"

He huffed and said, "Come here and I'll tell you."

Standing before him at his locker, Gloria thought he seemed bigger than ever. She sensed he was up to something, and he was. "You want to wear my letter sweater?" he asked.

This was serious business. If she wore that sweater, it meant they were going together. She looked it over. Fred's *D* (for "Denver") had more things pinned to it than any letter at any school in the city. "It's kinda big, isn't it? It would fit me like a dress." He laughed, took it off, and helped her into it. The shoulders were at her elbows. The bottom touched her knees. The sleeves had to be rolled up five times so that she could use her hands. He called it a perfect fit. It was official now: Fred Steinmark and Gloria Marchitti were going together.

She went to her next class, music, and immediately was accosted by an angry girl, seething about the sweater: "Where'd you get that sweater? Who gave it to you?"

Gloria smirked and said flippantly, "The guy it belongs to gave it to me." She pushed past her attacker and realized in that moment that being the girlfriend of the most popular boy in school meant she would be the most unpopular girl in school. She weighed this new reality and concluded that being Fred's girl, and having Liz for a best friend, maybe her only friend, was good enough. Fred was right: what other people thought just didn't matter.

Gloria's mother liked Fred. He was two years older, yes, but Gloria was mature for her age. In Frances's mind, two years was nothing. She herself had been a fifteen-year-old bride in an arranged marriage to Joseph Marchitti, age thirty-seven. A successful businessman, he courted her properly, in the Italian tradition. Joseph and Frances had seven children. After the first six—Dominick, Nick, Marie, Lucille, John, and Lena—Frances teased Joseph that he was too old to produce any more. He bet her that he could, and promised to build her a big, beautiful, Mediterranean-style house on his property up the hill, in the Highlands, if she had another child. Gloria was their seventh child. The house she lived in now was the payoff for the bet that had brought her into the world sixteen years earlier.

FRED WAS BACKED AGAINST THE WROUGHT-IRON RAILing in a corner of the porch, away from the front door. Gloria was thinking it was time to say good night and go inside. They had been to The Scotchman for a Coke and had talked about how a consequence of being his girlfriend was that she had lost friends and created enemies. He told her again that it didn't matter what other people thought, then opened his arms wide and said, "Come here."

"Boy, he was a good kisser," she recalls. "And that first kiss was awesome. It was the first kiss that ever made me feel that tingle from the top of my head to the tip of my toes. I knew as he was kissing me that something was going to happen with him. I had never been kissed like that, and I knew I wasn't going to get over that feeling. I didn't know what was happening yet, but I knew something was."

By spring of 1947, Fred and Gloria were almost inseparable, but it was baseball season, and he was the focus of much attention. Sports reporters, professional scouts, and college coaches were regularly in the bleachers to watch Fred play. She had learned to live with the constant presence of people wanting to talk to him, but she was taken aback one night when Fred called to say he had agreed to take out the daughter of the East High football coach, Pat Panek. Coach Panek was very fond of Fred, and knew Fred was going places, and when he dropped a hint about having a daughter worthy of the all-American boy's attention, Fred didn't want to disappoint him. Gloria thought about it. "Just go ahead and go," she said. "Get it out of your system." Fred promised he would call as soon as the date was over. She recalls that the date lasted about an hour, and then "he was back at my house, ringing the doorbell."

She got another surprise one morning before school when her brother John, who was living at the house, read to her a small item in the *Rocky Mountain News* sports section. It said that during his senior year, Fred had signed a professional baseball contract to play for the Cleveland Indians, and that as soon as school was out he planned to report to their farm team in Green Bay, Wisconsin. Fred hadn't mentioned the contract to her.

"Lots of people were happy for him, because that was his dream. He wanted to play pro ball. His teachers wanted him to go to college first, and he easily could have, because he had scholarship offers from just about everybody—athletic and academic." Fred didn't share much with Gloria about his family. She knew he lived with his mother and sister in an apartment above a barbershop, and guessed that one of the reasons he wanted to play professional baseball was to get money to help his mother. Gloria wished that he would go to college and get a degree first, but she understood and supported his decision.

Their relationship did not end with the last day of school and Fred's departure for the minors. Gloria's emotions were mixed: she was sad that he was leaving, yet happy that he was pursuing his dream. Yes, she told him, she still wanted to go steady even though he wouldn't be there. He promised that he would call and write as often as he could. At Union Station he boarded his train, sat by a window, and waved to her as the train pulled away. "It really was what they say about parting," she recalls. "Sweet sorrow."

BASEBALL AT THE PROFESSIONAL LEVEL IS NOT AND NEVER has been the paradise that young boys might imagine. Minor-league ball, in particular, has always been a rough existence. It is dog-eat-dog and endless sunbaked days. It is long bus rides and little sleep and less money. It is aches and pains, many you have to tend to yourself. And if you ever falter, unable to play for even one day, there are legions of players lined up right behind you—if the next guy gets his chance, your career can be gone with the wind like so much dandelion fluff. Minor league baseball is a meat grinder: young players go in, and a few come out the other end as major leaguers.

The odds of making it are astronomical even if a player is talented enough to get a contract. In reality, entire minor-league teams exist so that one genuine prospect has a place to play. Of Fred's ninety-seven teammates, on four minor-league teams, only four men ever made an appearance in the majors.

Fred left Denver as the all-American boy, the star athlete, the can't-miss kid, the one boy everybody knew would make it. It was only a matter of time. What he encountered upon his arrival in faraway Wisconsin, home of the Cleveland-affiliated Class D farm team the Green Bay Blue Jays, was very different from what he imagined it would be. There was no glitz or glamour. The playing surfaces were not as good as the field at North High School. There were uncouth players and jeering fans—if there were fans at all. Brawls were not uncommon. There were nights of going to bed hungry. The players on Fred's team were around his age, eighteen to twenty-five, though most were rookies, and each one was determined to succeed against the wishes of the others.

In Fred's rookie year, 1947, Class D alone had twenty leagues, comprising 178 teams. The Green Bay Blue Jays were one of them. Class C, the next step up, had fifteen leagues and 108 teams. Class B, nine leagues and 68 teams. Class A, three leagues and 22 teams. Double-A, two leagues and 16 teams. And the uppermost stratum of minor-league baseball, Triple-A, had three leagues and 24 teams. As a conservative estimate, there were twenty-five players on each of these 416 professional teams at any given time, or 10,400 young men, all vying to get to the big leagues in the frantic postwar revival of America's pastime.

FRED LOVED PLAYING BASEBALL, BUT HE WAS FAR FROM home and he missed Gloria. He underperformed in his first year, but looked forward to spending time with Gloria in the off-season, confident that his second season would be better.

His second year, which began with the Class C Burlington Indians, in Iowa, would end with him on the roster of the Class B Meridian Peps, in Mississippi, but his play wasn't appreciably better. The long-distance relationship with Gloria affected his ability to perform, and he knew he had to do something about it. In May he made a quick trip to Denver.

It was Color Day at North High, and school spirit soared. A picnic was planned for later in the day. Gloria, whose popularity had improved with Fred gone, intended to go to the picnic accompanied by a boy whose letter sweater she had just started wearing. During the morning, she was summoned to the principal's office to take an urgent telephone call from her mother. What Gloria heard shocked her. Her mother said, "Gloria, guess who's in town? Fred." Gloria knew Fred would come to the school, so she hastily returned the letter sweater and backed out of the picnic. It was, she recalls, "one of the worst days of my life." She told Fred about the picnic and invited him to take her to it, which he did, reluctantly, but he didn't want to go to the Color Day dance.

What Fred wanted was to get married. She was seventeen. He was nineteen. Gloria thought she should finish school before getting married. Fred was persuasive. His aunt and uncle met them at the courthouse in Golden, Colorado, and stood up for them. The marriage was recorded, but wouldn't be blessed in a church until March of the following year, after Fred had taken classes required by the Catholic Church.

Fred did not play baseball for the next two years. On the way to apply for an off-season job at the coal company, in a new car belonging to Gloria's brother Johnny, Fred was hit head-on by a coal truck. Sportswriters who wrote about the accident said the injuries to Fred's knee and throwing arm were serious enough to end his dream of playing major-league baseball.

The new couple lived in Gloria's bedroom in Frances's house when their first child was born, on January 27, 1949. They named him Freddie Joe. As soon as Freddie Joe was strong enough to sit in a corner without falling over, Fred put a catcher's mask on his son and rolled balls to him, explaining to Gloria that this way, Freddie Joe would never be afraid of the ball. Sports had been good to Fred. He was sure they would be good to Freddie Joe too.

Fred worked hard to rehab his injured arm. With the arrival

of the 1951 baseball season, he pronounced himself ready to play again. But two years out of action is an eternity in professional sports, and he had a hard time getting anyone interested enough to give him a tryout. Oklahoma's Enid Buffaloes were an unaffiliated team in the Western Association, and when they agreed to give Fred a uniform, he couldn't have been happier, or more determined to make it to the big leagues.

When Gloria gave birth to their second child, Gloria Gene, on June 7, 1951, Fred was batting .361, an average much more in line with what had been expected of him before the accident. He had heard rumors that he might be "moving up," and he called Gloria to give her the good news. But Gloria didn't share his enthusiasm. In fact, she had lost interest in his baseball career altogether. She was living in her mother's basement with two babies to take care of, and she felt strongly that Freddie Joe needed his father. Fred knew all too well what it was like for a boy to grow up without his father, so he made the decision in that moment to let go of his dream. The all-American boy headed home to begin his new life as the all-American dad.

CHAPTER 2

ROUGH RIDERS
AND FARMERS

THERE WAS A FAMOUS SPOCK BEFORE THE
Vulcan who served under Captain James T. Kirk on the
starship *Enterprise*. Dr. Benjamin Spock may not have
been known throughout the galaxy, but he became a household
name across America in the early 1950s as his book *Baby and
Child Care* flew off the shelves. The book's message to mothers was
basically "you know more than you think you do." Spock told parents to treat their children as individuals and to be flexible and
affectionate with them.

"I wouldn't have had time to read that book even if I had it,"
Gloria laughs. "Are you kidding me? I was busy day and night."
She and Fred were kids who had kids. In many ways, they had
never had the chance to be just a couple. Yet here they were, living
in a basement and raising their two-year-old son and six-month-
old daughter. Still, Spock was right: Gloria was a young mother
who *did* know more about the job than she thought. "When they're
hungry, they let you know. When they need their diapers changed,
they let you know. If they're sick, they cry. They like to be held, and
they like to hear your voice singing to them." Instinctively, she let
Freddie Joe and Gloria Gene "GiGi" amuse each other. "They were
just happy babies. Freddie Joe was a little angel—always so quiet.
So was GiGi. They were close. And when Fred got home—he was

always working, you know—he'd pick them up and make faces and sing to them. I loved to hear Fred sing. If Fred started singing 'Ballerina,' you'd think it was Vaughn Monroe on the radio." Monroe's "Ballerina" hit number 1 on the music charts in 1948.

Fred dove into his full-time role as a father with the enthusiasm and commitment that had helped him excel at sports. If, after a hard day at work, he was so tired that all he wanted to do at home was to collapse, he would still find the energy to spend time with his children. "Sometimes it meant putting Freddie Joe in the bathtub with him," Gloria says.

One wonders whether Big Fred might have considered all the chance circumstances, all the dominoes that had to fall, in order for them all to be there together, for him to be holding his own son named Freddie there on Clyde Place after those long days at work. Parents wonder about these things when they see their children and feel the responsibility that their own parents perhaps once felt. All the inextricable events of the past become apparent then, all having moved toward this one singular moment.

IN MARCH 1908, THE 450-FOOT IMPERIAL MAIL STEAM-ship RPD *Seydlitz* set sail from Bremen, Germany, to New York, carrying 1,906 passengers. Traveling in third-class steerage were thirty-year-old Friedrich Steinmark and his new bride, Elizabeth Stoll Steinmark, along with several other Germans who had left their home behind, the village of Doenhoff, in the Volga River region of Russia. Upon landing in New York, the Steinmarks and their German companions went westward.

That journey across the Atlantic was the continuation of an odyssey that had begun for the Steinmark family some 120 years earlier as part of an exodus from Germany after the devastation of the Seven Years' War (1756–1763). Many Germans who had been reduced to living in poverty looked for ways to start a new life, and the Steinmarks found opportunities in Catherine the Great's Russia. (Catherine, originally a princess from the German region Pomerania, offered immigrants special privileges if they settled in southeastern Russia.) They flourished in Doenhoff for the next century.

In the late 1800s, the young Friedrich Steinmark came to know the Stoll family, who were fellow Lutherans. The story goes that Friedrich courted and married the oldest Stoll daughter, Maria. Shortly after the wedding, however, Maria's left leg began to hurt, and over the course of a year, her thigh, for no apparent reason, withered away to almost nothing. The mysteriously diseased limb became infected and one night it fell off. Her screams were heard all over the village. Maria bled to death. After a suitable amount of time had passed, the Stoll family patriarch suggested that Friedrich consider marrying his younger daughter, Elizabeth. The two of them started to keep company together, fell in love, and were soon married.

Tsar Alexander II (ruled 1855–1881) systematically revoked the privileges formerly enjoyed by the German immigrants. Friedrich and Elizabeth were eventually forced to look for new horizons in America. After their voyage on the *Seydlitz*, they traveled to the small town of Sedgwick, Colorado, as part of a mass migration of German Russians to the Great Plains and western Canada. Eventually, they moved to the little settlement called Globeville on the South Platte River, just north of Denver, Colorado, where Steinmark served as the Lutheran pastor.

A year later, on November 28, 1909, Elizabeth gave birth to a son, whom they named Friedrich. To him, they passed on their hopes and aspirations, but also their genes, including the one that had likely resulted in the mysterious disease that killed Elizabeth's older sister. The young Friedrich grew up fast, drank too much, and married Viola Ford when he was twenty years old. On October 20, 1929, they had their first child, a boy, whom they named Freddie Gene. I would come to know him as Big Fred.

NANA MARCHITTI'S HOUSE WAS BIG ENOUGH TO BE A small hotel, and much of the time it seemed like one. Gloria and Fred and their two kids lived in the basement. Gloria's two sisters, their husbands, and their eight children lived upstairs. And from time to time, other brothers and sisters and their kids would drop in. While growing up in this environment, Freddie developed special friendships with his cousins, especially Loretta, Janet, Gregg, and Johnnyboy.

When it came to athletics, Freddie was a chip off the old block. "You could see it from the start," Gloria says. After Big Fred quit professional baseball, he continued to play and coach semipro ball and softball around the Denver area. The competition scratched a certain itch, and if he ever regretted his decision to leave the minor leagues, he never told anyone. One day when Freddie was still in diapers, Big Fred came home with a baseball and placed it in his son's hands. "It looked like he was holding a basketball, he was so little," Gloria says. "He started kicking and carrying on, he was so excited about that thing. 'He's going to be a ballplayer,' Fred told me."

Fred, Gloria, and the kids moved out of Nana's when they were finally able to afford it. For a while, they shared a duplex with Joe and Lena and their two kids, Janet and Gregg. Freddie and Gregg were the same age and would eventually become childhood teammates, then high school competitors. From the duplex, the Steinmarks moved into an apartment owned by Pete Ciancio, a friend of Gloria's brother. These North Denver Italians were a tight-knit community. Paisanos were paisanos, friends for life. Big Fred adapted, Gloria says. "Fred had to grow into the Italian culture. Being Italian, you kiss people all the time. He said one day, 'If you keep letting all those people kiss you, you're going to get hoof and mouth disease.'"

They might have stayed in the apartment longer had it not been for Gloria's sister Betty contracting tuberculosis. Betty, her husband, John, and their kids were still living at Nana's at the time. Because Betty had to be quarantined in a sanitarium, John needed help with his children, and so back to Nana's went Gloria, Big Fred, and their children. John and Betty's son Johnny, "Johnnyboy" to everyone, had been born with a weak left side and a left leg shorter than the right, which forced him to walk on the ball of his foot with his knee turned in. Surgeries had tried to correct this "handicap," as it was termed, and his leg required daily massaging.

"Everybody has storms in their life," Gloria says. "It's what you make of it in the end. You either go through it, or you walk away from it. God helps you get through it all. You go through the suffering and you learn from it. I don't know how else to explain it."

Johnnyboy, now nearly seventy years old, is still "Johnnyboy" to everyone. When he talks about Freddie there is affection in his voice that comes from someplace deep down: "Freddie had a great impact on my life. We grew up in the same house, so we were like brothers. I was a little older, but he was like my best friend. We did everything together."

Johnnyboy tells of the big lot on the side of Nana's house, where he and Freddie rounded up the cousins and neighborhood kids to play games. "We turned Nana's beautiful grass into bare dirt pretty fast, but she didn't care. I guess she figured the grass would grow back, but kids aren't around forever."

Those childhood games provided early, good-natured proving grounds for Freddie. According to Johnnyboy, "When it was time to go back inside, if Freddie's team was winning our game, he'd say the game was over, but if his team was losing, he'd say it was just halftime." Johnnyboy laughs, remembering Freddie's competitive spirit, there from the very beginning. "I had a bad leg, and I limped, but that didn't stop Freddie from wanting to beat me in our races. Boy, he was fast. He'd always give me a half-a-block head start." That competitive drive came from Big Fred, Johnnyboy affirms.

"Fred's [semipro and softball] games were our entertainment," Gloria explains. "Fred loved having Freddie Joe at the ball field with him, of course. When Freddie Joe was five, he was the bat boy at City Park for Fred's games."

Fred and Gloria lived in Nana's basement for another four years and had two more children during that time. Paula Kay, "P.K.," was born in 1954. Sammy Scott arrived in 1956. "I got what I wanted,"

Gloria says. "Two boys and two girls. We didn't have any money to do anything, but we had a lot of love."

WHEN FREDDIE JOE WAS SEVEN, GLORIA, BARELY ABLE to see over the steering wheel, took him to the park where the Rough Riders of the Young America League were practicing. Fred had just been hired by the Denver Police Department, so it fell to Gloria to get Freddie Joe started in organized football. Muzzy Vecchiarelli and Harry Risoli were the Rough Riders' coaches. They were tough, but they were Fred's friends. "I told Muzzy, 'Fred says Freddie Joe is ready to play with the Rough Riders.' Muzzy looked at him—Freddie Joe was a little undersized—and he said, 'Okay. If Fred says he's ready, he's ready.' I said, 'Freddie Joe, this is Mr. Vecchiarelli. He's your coach. Do what he says.'"

Freddie took the Rough Rider pledge, which he never forgot—and which I heard many times—and his life in football was off and running: "I will play the game hard and clean and never be a quitter. What matters most is courage. It is no disgrace to be beaten; the great disgrace is to quit or turn yellow."

Fred had taught Freddie Joe so much about playing football that it was hard to believe he was only seven years old. Freddie's cousin Gregg, who was on that team, remembers that Muzzy turned Freddie into the punisher. "If you screwed up in the drills, Muzzy would shove the football in your stomach and make you try to get past Freddie. *Nobody* wanted to do that, Freddie tackled so hard."

The only time Muzzy ever got mad at Freddie was during a game in which Freddie tried to dodge a tackler on the way to the goal line and got caught from behind. At halftime, Muzzy screamed at him to run in a straight line and use his speed. Confused, Freddie responded, "My dad said to dodge 'em."

Muzzy exploded: "When you're playing for me, you run straight! When you're playing for your dad, you can dodge 'em!"

It was an important lesson. Freddie kept it in mind during the next five years while playing, always, on two teams—Muzzy's, in North Denver, and a team in Wheat Ridge (a western suburb of

Denver), coached by his dad. A glorious October night awaited them in the future when, spellbound along with ten thousand others, they would watch Freddie do just what they first coached him to do—both running straight and dodging in one long, magnificent run.

But on the football fields and baseball diamonds of Denver, a young boy didn't have to think about anything but what he was doing at the moment. If you were Freddie, you were doing it half the time under the observant eyes of a coach who was your father. One of those diamonds was where I first met Freddie. I played for his father, and this was when the boys on the team began to call him "Big Fred." Big Fred didn't miss a thing. If you weren't fully "in the game," he would notice and you would pay a price. Lenny Losasso recalls losing a baseball game because he misjudged a fly ball in centerfield and Freddie made an error at shortstop. Big Fred made both of them stay after the game, and for an hour he hit fly balls to Lenny and hard grounders to Freddie.

My experience with Big Fred's coaching style was a little different. I was a pretty fair right-handed pitcher, but I was the worst hitter on our team, too. I dreaded having to bat because I always struck out. Unlike Freddie, who wanted to be the guy who could win the game with a hit, I prayed I wouldn't be the guy in the batter's box who could win it, or lose it.

On my way to the plate one Saturday, I was that guy, and I would rather have been anywhere else. Big Fred called time-out and approached me. "Bat left-handed," he said. I protested. I knew how to hit only right-handed. "I know that," he said, his hands on my shoulders. "Just do it. You can do it."

I stepped up to the wrong side of the plate. My father thought so, too, and he stood up behind the backstop, shouting to remind me that I wasn't a lefty.

I watched the first pitch, a perfect strike. I didn't move a muscle, but I saw the ball like I never had before. I could see the actual stitches on the baseball, standing out, red against white.

Amazed, I glanced at Big Fred. He was grinning. "Hit the one you like!" he shouted.

I hit the next pitch over the right-field fence, the game winner. As I rounded third and headed for home, he clapped me on the back and ran beside me, shouting, "How come you didn't tell me you can't see out of your left eye?"

THE STEINMARK FAMILY HAD MOVED TO WHEAT RIDGE when Freddie was ten, after Fred became a K-9 policeman. Fred's German Shepherd partner, Duke, was the kids' playmate when he was off-duty, and Freddie loved throwing balls for him to fetch. But the move was initially one of the unhappiest moments of Freddie Joe's young life. He had wanted to be an altar boy at St. Catherine's Catholic Church, near Nana's house, but that was no longer possible after they left the parish. Gloria doesn't remember Freddie crying much as a boy, "But he cried so much about that. It was really sad." It was also at this time that Freddie had to step up and begin looking after Sammy, because both Big Fred and Gloria were working.

It was hard to make ends meet on Fred's salary. The financial pressure reached a breaking point when Freddie was thirteen. Big Fred was considering relocating the family to Richmond, California, where his mother and sister lived and where policemen were better paid. In anticipation of the move, the family sent Freddie to California early to live with his grandmother; that way, he wouldn't miss basketball season. Meanwhile, though, Big Fred's fortunes improved, when he landed a third job working security. Soon he was able to bring Freddie home, and the West Coast move was averted.

Upon his return, Freddie had to play one year at Manning Junior High rather than at Wheat Ridge, when the family moved into the Manning school district. At about the same time, Fred was promoted to detective with the vice division. It was odd to play against Freddie when we had played beside him for years. He helped Manning's football team considerably—in fact, the only game Freddie lost that season was against us, at Wheat Ridge. But we learned, as others had, that Freddie did not bring friendships onto the field or the basketball court or the baseball diamond. It was you against him, and you had better know going in that he was determined to beat you.

"The way you guys talked about Freddie Steinmark, I couldn't believe somebody could be that good," recalls Kent Cluck, who would become one of Freddie's closest friends. "I didn't know him, because I didn't start going to public school until ninth grade at Wheat Ridge, and Freddie was at Manning that year. I remember when we played Manning in basketball. Coach Linnenberger said to me before the game, 'Now, Kent, you'll be playing man-to-man against Freddie Steinmark. He's sneaky fast, so watch him close. If the ball comes to you, get rid of it as fast as you can, because he'll steal it.'" Cluck also recalls that Freddie always was the banker when the family played Monopoly, and the game was not over until Freddie owned everything.

Freddie went to Wheat Ridge High as a sophomore (Manning Junior High was a feeder school for Wheat Ridge High) and was happy to reunite with us all. He picked up right where he left off, excelling in sports and in the classroom. But away from school, it was a year marred by Freddie's first real encounter with mortality, among other moments of emotional strife.

While playing basketball in a neighbor's driveway one afternoon, Freddie's close friend Frankie Sanzalone took a hard fall. He did not realize he had ruptured his liver. On the way home, Frankie collapsed. When Freddie got home from his own practice, Gloria told him that Frankie was in the hospital. Freddie put his books down and ran to the hospital, almost two miles away. When he got there, he wasn't allowed to see Frankie. He went back home, and Gloria told him a phone call had come with very sad news: Frankie had died. "Freddie and Frankie were really close," GiGi says. "[Freddie] went to his room and got on his knees and started praying for Frankie. He was so heartbroken."

The year also introduced complicated emotions into the Steinmark home, threatening to unravel their tight family bond. Fred's work with the vice squad brought him face-to-face with depraved lives and unspeakable acts, drugs and alcohol, hopelessness and despair. If a person, even an honest cop with a family at home, saw enough of it night after night, week after week, it might become too much to bear, too much to forget at the end of a shift. A deep desire to escape the constant grimness and an abhorrence of bringing it home might cause errors in judgment that on some level seemed justifiable.

Every evening, no matter what, the family ate together at five sharp. It was Fred's rule. But suddenly, Big Fred wasn't there one evening, and Gloria carried on without her husband. Freddie and his siblings were confused. When Fred wasn't home for dinner for the next several nights, and then the next several weeks, it became clear that he had done something, and for a time, he wasn't welcome in Gloria's house. The children knew that a mistake had been made, but they wouldn't pry or press. They waited, prayed, and hoped that things might be repaired. And Gloria did eventually invite Fred home, but things weren't quite the same. Another lesson was learned: actions have consequences, and even after forgiveness, things can remain different.

Freddie had problems of his own. His classmates had elected him part of the homecoming court, but he couldn't afford the expense of taking a date to the dance. His cousin Loretta, who was our classmate and always seemed to be there when Freddie needed her, solved the problem: they went to homecoming together.

A broken leg caused Freddie to miss half the football season in his junior year at Wheat Ridge. This was of great concern to Big Fred because Freddie needed a scholarship in order to go to college. Since he was undersized, if it appeared to scouts that he might be prone to injuries, it might be too much for them to overlook. He had to get a scholarship.

Near the end of the school year, Jack Jost, an assistant varsity football coach and history teacher, put the word out that he wanted all boys who planned to go out for football in the fall to come to his room after school. "I think we all had a pretty good idea what it was going to be about," Stan Politano says. "Something about a little party the previous weekend? Yeah, that was it. The kegger up in Clear Creek Canyon." One by one we began filing into Jost's room, and sat quietly. From the front of the room, Jost looked at us, at the door, at his watch. He had a flattop haircut that was probably a half inch too long, wore black horn-rims, and had on a white short-sleeve shirt and a narrow black tie that with another two inches would have been close to his belt. There was a degree of discomfort in the room. We sensed an impending chewing out. When Jost had finally waited long enough, he pulled the door shut.

"Gentlemen," he said. "Something has come to my attention that we need to talk about."

Politano leaned toward me and nodded. *Knew it.*

"You will have a new football coach this fall."

We were struck silent.

"I can't tell you who he is yet because it isn't official, but I can tell you this: he'd be awfully disappointed to hear about that beer party last weekend. Frankly, I'm disappointed. You guys have a chance to do something really special with this new coach, but if you don't get it together before you leave this room, it won't happen. I'm not going to tell you everything I've been told—things some of you have been doing—you know who you are. I won't embarrass you. So I'm going to leave now, and I'm going to pull this door shut, and I don't care if it takes you until midnight, settle your differences and come out of this room a team. Promise yourself that you'll put your best foot forward from now on."

We all knew there was only one guy in the room who had been doing this all along: Freddie. And you can be sure he wasn't at that kegger.

CHAPTER 3

HE'S MY BROTHER

B OYS HOPING TO MAKE THE WHEAT RIDGE
Farmers football team in 1966 anticipated that things
would be different under new head coach John W. "Red"
Coats. Expectations were that under Coats, a Texan and former Marine, Wheat Ridge would finally beat rival Lakewood. The Farmers'
losing streak versus Lakewood had become an embarrassment.

Coats had three successful seasons at Arapahoe High in that
school's first three years of operation. Arapahoe was one of the
new schools in the rapidly growing Littleton area south of Denver, and Coats had been a winner with nothing but underclassmen
thrown together through school district realignment. His method
was simple and straightforward: discipline and hard work. Before
coaching at Arapahoe, he led a high school team in El Paso, Texas, to six district championships in seven seasons. When he left,
mourning fans showed their appreciation by giving him a new
Buick. Before El Paso, he had been the head coach at Odessa Junior College for two years, and in one of them was named junior
college coach of the year. Coats's penchant for winning got the attention of Wheat Ridge principal Donald Solem, who for more
than a year had been under heavy pressure from players' parents
to get a new coach. It wasn't a matter of the Farmers not winning;
they won often enough to finish second or third in the Jefferson
County League's final standings every year. The problem was what

had become the predictable annual loss to Lakewood, a loss that the whole community felt because Wheat Ridge High School, like suburban and rural high schools everywhere, was a cornerstone of our community's pride.

More than just an embarrassment, the losses to Lakewood had become a stumbling block for Wheat Ridge football players hoping to earn athletic scholarships. College coaches and scouts were ever present at Lakewood's games. The Tigers' great coach, Tom Hancock, consistently produced fundamentally sound, hard-hitting players who were taught how to win. If a college recruiter with a scholarship to offer had to choose between two kids of identical size, speed, grades, and intangibles, one from Lakewood and the other not, the Lakewood kid would get it every time.

So losing to Lakewood depressed everyone—parents, players, younger siblings, students, teachers, school bus drivers, restaurateurs, and shop owners. Big Fred's frustration with Lakewood's dominance reached critical mass following the 1965 loss. Looking grim, he came into the locker room and found Freddie and me removing our uniforms. Through barely moving lips he said, "That's it. You guys are going to Lakewood next year." He looked both of us in the eye as he always did when he wanted to be certain he had made himself clear, and then he wheeled and left. It might have been gnawing at him that Freddie could have been playing for Lakewood already. Hancock had tried hard to persuade the Steinmarks to move into the Lakewood school district after Freddie's ninth-grade year at Manning Junior High. Big Fred had been in favor of doing it, because he felt there would be more recruiter interest in Freddie if he were wearing a Lakewood jersey than a Wheat Ridge jersey. But he let Freddie make the decision. Freddie chose Wheat Ridge, along with the friends and teammates he had grown up with. I was certainly glad for Freddie's choice.

At breakfast on the morning after Big Fred's pronouncement, I told my father that I guessed I would be going to Lakewood for my senior year. He snorted and went right on reading the newspaper. Losing to Lakewood made everyone irritable.

A LOOSELY ORGANIZED CABAL OF PARENTS ASKED FOR A meeting with Principal Solem soon after the season ended. Their request was blunt: end the mediocrity. They felt that their children and the whole community deserved a coach who could beat Lakewood, boost school pride, and give their kids the best possible opportunity to showcase their talents.

Solem wanted the best of everything for Wheat Ridge. In a newspaper story, he declared, "We want the best, whether it's football, chemistry, English or dramatics. Our community is so proud." It helped that he was a big sports fan. "A good sports program can add so much to a school. Kids need things they can go to and get attached to. The behavior is better and the spirit is better. It's an intangible thing."

Solem had his work cut out for him. Finding a coach that could beat Lakewood was not going to be an easy task. The orange-and-black-clad Tigers were in the hunt for the state championship year in and year out. Their winning tradition had started in 1955 when Hancock arrived at his first Lakewood practice and told the players, "There was a time when Lakewood went on the field and other teams feared them." He was determined to restore that fearsome attitude and reputation, and by 1966 he had built the program to such dominance that when the *Jefferson Sentinel* newspaper published the county's football schedule each fall, players at the league's other six schools checked to see when they would have to face Lakewood. In our senior year, Wheat Ridge and Lakewood would meet in the fourth game—Lakewood's homecoming.

So Solem and his hiring committee found Red Coats. Coats's winning record spoke for itself, but it still must have felt like a momentous decision when Solem made the job offer and Coats accepted. A new era was about to begin at Wheat Ridge, and the community hoped it would bring the much sought-after football success.

When it was officially announced that Red Coats would be the new coach, a contingent of players led by Stan Politano volunteered to help the Coats family move their furniture and belongings from

South Denver to their new home in the upscale Applewood Country Club area in the rolling hills at the base of the Front Range. Although it was against the rules for coaches to work with players before the season officially started, helping the coach move didn't qualify as an "organized practice." On moving day, however, the volunteer movers did have an opportunity to watch a few minutes of film of Arapahoe High games and got a glimpse of the pro-set, spread offense the new coach would be bringing to Wheat Ridge. This fueled considerable excitement among the players, and a little anxiety too. A new system and a new coach meant that everybody would be starting from scratch and would have to earn a position.

As he did every summer, Freddie played baseball, worked out hard to stay in shape, and held down a full-time job. The summer before his senior year, he worked construction as a hoddie for his Uncle Al, who was a house builder. A hoddie carried bricks and mortar to masons. It was dirty, backbreaking work, but Freddie saw it as a good way to build muscles, especially leg muscles. The hod was a three-sided wooden box mounted on a pole. He carried it on his shoulder and had to balance it while hustling up inclined planks to reach bricklayers perched on scaffolding. He carried up to twelve five-pound bricks at a time to the mason, who typically laid a thousand bricks a day. Between loads of bricks he carried unwieldy dumps of heavy mortar, timing the trips so that the mason always had enough mortar and enough bricks to maintain the rhythm of his work. From time to time it would become necessary to wet down the mortarboards to prevent cement from sticking to them, so Freddie had to haul buckets of water up the planks, too. On an average day he moved nearly three tons of bricks from pallets on the ground to masons on the scaffolding.

One week when Uncle Al didn't need Freddie, my father's construction company required extra help with tearing out the McDougals' driveway. Freddie joined a laborer and me in the task, glad that he wouldn't have to lose a week of pay. At the end of every summer, Freddie took Sammy shopping for school clothes and paid for them out of his earnings. It was getting expensive, because

Freddie liked to dress well and Sammy wanted to dress just like his brother. If Freddie got roughout cowboy boots, Sammy wanted a pair. If madras shirts were that year's "thing," Sammy had to have madras shirts too.

Breaking up a big slab of concrete held together by steel mesh and rebar is hard work, especially when the tools at hand are sledgehammers and hacksaws instead of pneumatic jackhammers and cutting torches. Always one to look on the bright side, Freddie considered the work as good as lifting weights. The job held a bonus too, or at least we thought so at the outset: Karen McDougal was a classmate, and we hoped to catch her sunbathing in the backyard. That wish evaporated when we learned she had a summer job and wouldn't be there. We talked about the new football coach and new offense while we worked. At the end of the day, my father offered us a cold can of Coors as a reward for our hard labor. Freddie passed. Breaking training was anathema to him. He believed that if you broke training once, it was easier to do a second time, and easier still after that.

ONE EVENING A FEW WEEKS BEFORE FOOTBALL SEASON got under way, Freddie, Sammy, and I were working out on the high school practice field. We had done it many times during the summer. A car drove up and parked in the lot overlooking the field. The driver watched us for a moment and then retrieved a large, Santa Claus–style bag from his trunk. He descended the stairs and came toward us. "That's Bob Scarpitto, the Denver Broncos' punter!" Freddie said excitedly. Scarpitto, we would learn, lived only a few blocks from the school. He introduced himself, noted that we were "hitting it pretty hard," and asked whether we would mind sharing the field. He asked what positions we played and wished us luck with the new coach, then headed for the west end zone with the big bag of footballs slung over his shoulder. Freddie called to him, "I'm our punt returner!" Scarpitto turned and walked backward, yelling that he would kick some to us. "I'm our punter too!" Freddie yelled. Scarpitto, still walking backward, laughed and shouted, "Great! Kick 'em back!"

For the next hour we fielded the high, spiraling punts of the Broncos' kicker, who was about to have his best year as a pro and be named to the Pro Bowl team. To paraphrase what Tom Robbins wrote in *Still Life With Woodpecker*, everything is connected. Six months later, at the Colorado Sports Hall of Fame annual dinner, Scarpitto was one of the nominees for special recognition as Colorado's professional athlete of the year. Freddie was at the dinner, too, nominated along with George Washington's Rick Fisher and Thomas Jefferson's Matt Sterling for special recognition as Colorado's high school athlete of the year. Freddie won.

We ran each punt back five to ten yards at full speed in order to simulate game action. That was what Big Fred had coached us to do long ago. He said it didn't do any good to practice at one speed and play at another speed. At the end of the workout, Scarpitto complimented Freddie on his kicking, which Freddie said could have been better. He offered us a ride home, but Freddie told him that running home was part of the workout. As we walked off the field, Scarpitto asked Freddie where he wanted to play college ball. "Notre Dame," Freddie said. Scarpitto gave him a friendly punch on the arm. Notre Dame was Scarpitto's alma mater. Before leaving, he told us that he would try to work out about the same time every day and that he hoped to see us again. But we never got to repeat the experience. Someone—we figured it was probably someone from Lakewood—reported us for practicing on school property before the season began. Apparently, that was against the rules.

THE 1966 SEASON BEGAN ON MONDAY, AUGUST 22. THERE were three weeks of practice before the first game, against Denver's Lincoln High School. Lincoln was hoping to avenge the previous year's loss to Wheat Ridge. Freddie's cousin Gregg Duncan played for Lincoln, so the game held extra interest for the Steinmark and Marchitti families. It was Gregg's father, Joe, who had rustled the newspaper twenty years earlier to awaken Gloria and urge her to date the all-American boy Fred Steinmark when she got to North High.

There were two practices each day for the first two weeks, with heavy emphasis on conditioning. How tough the new coach would be was on everyone's mind, as was the timed mile run that had always marked the beginning of the season. To make the team, linemen had to run the mile in less than six minutes, and backs had to do it in five and a half. Nobody liked running the mile.

Coats, at forty-three, had the weathered look that came from spending many years in the intense Texas sun, and the swagger of a bowlegged old pro. He wore shorts and a T-shirt, a navy blue ball cap with a yellow *W* on it, midcalf white socks, and polished black shoes. A whistle on a string hung around his neck. He had a big, friendly grin, spoke with a Texas accent, and had the air of someone truly enjoying himself. The apprehension that players had felt on the first day of practice in previous years quickly was replaced by the high spirits of a ship's crew about to set sail. A hundred boys had come out for football, but only fifty or so would make the varsity roster. After shoulder pads and helmets were issued to everyone, Coats and his assistants herded the squad a quarter mile to the practice field.

"Gather 'round!" Coats barked as the last of the players reached the grass. The team pushed in around him. He introduced himself and his assistant coaches, and acknowledged that his job was to beat Lakewood and then everyone else. He started to explain how things would be different from the way they had been in the past, but stopped midsentence, distracted by Sammy, who was flipping a football and watching from the sideline. Sammy was ten and small for his age, so he looked even younger.

"Does anyone know who that kid is over there?" Coats asked. Everyone looked. When half the team said, "Sammy," Sammy fumbled the ball and chased after it awkwardly as it bounced away. Coats turned back to the team.

"Who?"

Freddie's voice surfaced from the middle of the pack of blue helmets. "He's my brother, Coach." Coats craned to see whose name was taped on the front of the helmet.

"Well who's watching him, Steinmark?"

"I am, sir," Freddie said. Coats grimaced and glanced at his assistants, then said, "Aw hell, man." He pronounced "hell," "hail."

The coach resumed his speech and told the players that they were a bunch of no-good mullets and that he understood it had been the custom in years past to run a mile within "some silly amount of time" to make the team. His jab at the previous coach jarred a few players who were fond of the former coach, but everyone broke into laughter when Coats said, "Hell, man, if you can't catch 'em in a hundred yards, there's no point running any farther." He assured the team that there would be plenty of running, just not the mile.

There was considerable curiosity about Coats within the community, and scores of onlookers showed up to watch the first practice. With twelve lettermen returning, and new offensive and defensive schemes that might finally get the Farmers past Lakewood, Wheat Ridge football was generating some excitement. Big Fred and my father were among the crowd watching from the parking lot.

After the coaches led the team through warm-up exercises, linemen and backs broke into groups. The linemen pushed blocking sleds while the backs took turns throwing and catching passes, and kicking and punting. Coats walked among the groups, observing everyone's skill level. Near the end of practice, he gathered the team together and said the afternoon would begin with a weigh-in, and advised us to not eat too much lunch for fear of fouling the football field. He said it with a sly grin. Then he ordered everyone to the goal line for wind sprints.

A Coats tenet was that the team in the best shape in the fourth quarter would usually win. This belief had always been part of Big Fred's coaching philosophy, too, and Freddie always had been a sterling example of its validity. Exhausted opponents had been victimized many times by Freddie's spare tank of gas and fourth-quarter heroics. Coats got his first look at this Steinmark trait during a dozen fifty-yard wind sprints he made the team run. Each time the backs ran, Freddie led the pack, and his lead at the end

of each sprint was wider than it had been in the previous one. After the sixth sprint, Coats gave everyone a minute to catch their
breath. Stan Politano, Kent Cluck, Bob Himes, Dave Dirks, and
Mike VanMaarth, stalwarts of the offensive line, were bent over,
gasping for air. Freddie, apparently not all that winded, was standing near them, hands on his waist. Politano looked at him and
turned to Cluck.

"Doesn't he ever get tired?"

Cluck shook his head. "No. When he gets tired, we'll already be
dead."

Stan glanced at Freddie and dropped his head, deflated. "I'm
gonna die."

Freddie stifled a laugh and said, "Don't die. Sammy and I need
a ride home."

THE ATMOSPHERE IN THE LOCKER ROOM AT THE BEGIN-
ning of the afternoon practice was more serious than it had been
in the morning. Freddie spoke to Coats about Sammy, explaining that his parents, who worked, didn't want Sammy to be home
alone. Sammy would have to be with Freddie at every practice,
even when school started. Coats was worried that Sammy might
get in the way and get hurt. "He's been around sports his whole
life, Coach," Freddie said. "He'll be okay, and I'll keep an eye on
him." At that moment, Sammy was in the trainer's room, helping
the team managers put rolls of adhesive tape into the medicine kit.

As the players formed a line for the weigh-in, they were told several boys had already quit the team, and the coaches expected that
more would quit after the afternoon wind sprints. Freddie was
the one guy in the locker room who would have preferred running
wind sprints to getting weighed.

As each player stepped onto the scale and voiced his name,
Coats, standing beside the scale, adjusted the two sliding weights
on the balance arm and then called out the player's weight. The top
balance arm was calibrated in fifty-pound increments; the lower
arm, in one-pound differentials. Assistant coach Jack Jost kept
track of the figures on a clipboard. It pleased Coats when players

weighed more than two hundred pounds. You could hear it in the way he called out the weights. Bobby Mitchell, a running back who had moved to Wheat Ridge from California before our junior year, especially pleased Coats. At two hundred pounds, Bobby was bigger than most of the linemen. As Freddie started to step onto the scale, Coats moved the weight on the top arm to the left.

"How much do you weigh, Steinmark?"

"One hundred fifty-two. About," Freddie said.

"How much would you like to weigh?" Coats asked.

"One sixty-five."

"One sixty-five it is then," Coats said.

The new offense was introduced during the afternoon practice, and each player was given a playbook in a three-ring binder. By the end of the first week, when no contact was permitted, the Farmers were fairly efficiently running the Dallas Cowboys' offense. Coats, along with a few other coaches from around the country, had once spent a week with the Cowboys as an observer. Sidelined for good, finally, was the stale, run-focused wing-T offense the Farmers had deployed for years. However, 200-pound Bobby Mitchell and "165"-pound Freddie Steinmark now played the same position.

It wasn't just a different offense and defense that Coats brought to Wheat Ridge. He brought a different attitude, different terminology, and an entirely different approach to playing football. He was tough, but made practice fun. Coats demanded discipline and told us that anyone who broke training rules would be caught and would have hell to pay. Four co-captains—Freddie, Bob Mitchell, Stan Politano, and Dave Dirks—were Coats's eyes and ears. Being a captain on his team was a special honor, Coats said, but it was a responsibility too. He let the team know that his captains would do "spot checks"—random phone calls to see whether someone was home or out past the 8:30 p.m. curfew. He neglected to say that he, too, would be making those random calls.

During the second week of two-a-days, we were running the offense so well that Coats couldn't keep from grinning. He was killing us with conditioning, which often included running up and down the steep, weedy embankment that separated the practice field from the upper parking lot, known as The Hill, and we were killing each other with hard hitting. Yet everyone sensed something special was happening: the Farmers were being transformed into what we had never been before—champions.

Big Fred and my father parked next to each other almost every day and watched the afternoon practices. They both were between their day jobs and their night jobs at that time of day, so they hardly ever missed a practice. It was enough for my father to see that I was on the starting team. Big Fred, on the other hand, watched every move Freddie made and kept a mental notebook of his observations. These he would discuss with Freddie over supper with the family, before he left home for his night job as a Denver policeman. Big Fred was enthusiastic about the new offense. It opened up the field and allowed Freddie to display his talent and speed. But Big Fred didn't miss much while watching those practices, and it is likely he was beginning to see something that concerned him.

With two-a-days almost over, the team was in high spirits. The fall semester would commence in a few days, and the culmination of the first week back at school would be a pep rally and the Friday-night contest against Lincoln. At one of the last morning practices, Coats emerged from his office with an uncharacteristically sour expression on his face. He walked through the locker room to the outside exit without speaking to anyone, not even acknowledging those of us who greeted him. Something was obviously amiss, and we hurriedly got into our pads and hustled to the practice field. Whatever was eating Coats, we knew that keeping him waiting would only make him angrier.

The team was going through its usual warm-up when Coats, agitated, blew his whistle sharply and ordered everyone to the goal line at the east end of the field. We moved toward it too slowly, like a herd of nervous cattle, and he shouted at us to pick it up. This was a side of Coats we hadn't yet seen, and it was jolting. From one side of the field to the other, we stood silently, shoulder to shoulder, facing him. He looked at us as if we were suspects in a police lineup.

"One of you mullets broke curfew last night," Coats seethed. "I guess you forgot I'd be making calls too. Step forward so we can see who you are." Nobody moved. Coats waited. "Okay," he said, "y'all can pay the price." Shockingly, Freddie started to step forward, but Bob Mitchell stepped out and said, "It's me." Whatever Coats said after that got lost in the confusion of the moment. It appeared Freddie had been willing to take the fall for the one who committed the infraction. It even seemed possible that Mitchell, Coats, and Freddie had staged the whole thing as part of some Sun Tzu–like motivational tactic. But Coats's anger with Mitchell put that notion to rest. Mitchell ran wind sprints until he puked, and then had to run more. Everyone had to stand there and watch, and it was hard to do. When Coats decided Mitchell had run enough, practice restarted as if nothing had happened. But the message was clear: there were no sacred cows on the team. Everyone would be held accountable.

The new-look Wheat Ridge Farmers were introduced to Colorado sportswriters on Friday, September 9, in a rematch against Lincoln. Freddie's cousin Gregg was the starting center for the Lancers. Knowing that Freddie and the Farmers were going to be a tough opponent, he advised his teammates, "My cousin is really fast, so don't let him get outside or he'll be gone." It didn't take long for Gregg's teammates to see the proof: Freddie fielded the opening kickoff at our fifteen-yard line and raced it back eighty-five yards for a touchdown. Ten seconds into the season, Freddie and the Farmers were on the scoreboard. Ten seconds into the season, Freddie's moves were already turning heads. Sportswriters statewide soon observed, "Steinmark is gifted with a sixth sense when it comes to eluding would-be tacklers." When asked about his rising star, Coach Coats replied, "He has an instinct about making a cut early enough that he can recover if the opposing player doesn't go for the fake."

Freddie scored another touchdown on a long scamper later in the game. Mitchell also scored twice. The final score was 52–25, and the whole community celebrated the win. Stan Politano's parents were so giddy that they invited the Farmers' coaches and lettermen to a spaghetti dinner in their home on Sunday night. They put on such a feast that the players and coaches didn't stop raving about it until Mr. and Mrs. Politano promised everyone a return visit each time the Farmers won a game. "It seemed like a good idea at the time," Stan says now, shaking his head.

A week later the Farmers traveled by bus to southern Colorado to take on the steel-town-tough defending state champions, the Pueblo Central Wildcats. Pueblo's city stadium had the ominous nickname the "Snakepit." Coats got the team there three hours early and persuaded the security guards to let the Farmers into the stadium to see the field. "You mullets go feel that grass under your feet," he said. "It's just like the grass we play on and practice on back home. We aren't going to have many friends in this stadium tonight, but we'll sure as hell know we can play on this grass." He was right about the crowd. It was plenty loud, and menacing; some old Farmers later recalled it as "the Oakland Raiders crowd of high school football." Despite the Snakepit, the Farmers took down the Wildcats 19–7. The minute the game was over, Coats grabbed Sammy's hand and hurried everyone to the team bus. "They don't like to lose down here," he said. A few rocks bounced off the roof of the bus as the Farmers pulled away.

One week later, Wheat Ridge met the Alameda Pirates in the first league contest and sank them 33–0. Three games, three wins. But nobody was really thinking about that.

Our next opponent was Lakewood.

CHAPTER 4

THE MOST IMPORTANT GAME OF OUR LIVES

FROM THE START IT WAS UNLIKELY THAT RED Coats and Tom Hancock would become friends. Coats's primary mission was to beat Hancock, who had terrorized the Wheat Ridge football team for years. Coats came from a Marine Corps tradition where drill instructors taught him to believe, and to never forget, that there is "no better friend than a Marine, no worse enemy." Coats might have traded in his combat boots for a coach's whistle, but in the world of gridirons and ground attacks, Hancock was more than just an average opponent; he was an enemy.

The first time they spoke to each other, the story goes, Hancock telephoned Coats during the August two-a-days, ostensibly to welcome him to the Jefferson County League. Hancock was probably happy that the Coats-coached Farmers would provide a little more competition for the Tigers than past Wheat Ridge teams. The Tigers' yearly waltz through the league schedule didn't help them prepare for the more challenging foes they faced in the state playoffs. "Wheat Ridge was always our toughest *league* opponent," recalls Mike Schnitker, a former University of Colorado and Denver Broncos starter, and Lakewood's great end on their '63 state championship team, "but we sure liked playing 'em—because we always kicked their asses! It was a good rivalry, though. We tried to steal their girls; they tried to steal ours. You know. All that great high school stuff."

When Hancock's call rang in, Coats was sitting at his office desk, chatting with a few players and coaches. Although the players could hear only Coats's part of the short conversation, it was easy enough to figure out the rest. After Coats said, "Hello?" and the caller identified himself, a "shit-eating grin" broke across Coats's face, and he said, elongating the caller's name in feigned perplexity, "*T-o-o-o-o-o-m*? Tom *who*? I don't know any Tom." Whether it really happened that way, or happened at all, didn't matter. The story spread through the locker room like a flashflood in the desert: *Coach just put down Hancock!* HANCOCK!

If Coats had been looking for a way to slay Lakewood's intimidation factor—a monster under Wheat Ridge's bed—the story of the phone call did it. He had snubbed the king, and the people were free. From then on, Lakewood was just another opponent on the nine-week Wheat Ridge schedule. Of course, Wheat Ridge versus Lakewood involved more than just a game between a bunch of great kids on two high school football teams. It was a contest of communities, one older and slowing down, the other hitting its stride and pushing its boundaries ever farther to accommodate a growing population. Wheat Ridge had been a farming community for most of its life, and once was known as the Carnation Capital of the World. The high school was founded in 1868. Lakewood, sixty years younger, had an energetic commercial corridor running through its heart—Colfax Avenue, also known as US 40. When people seeing the USA in their Chevrolets passed through Colorado headed east or west, they drove on Colfax. Lakewood had nightspots and bright lights and lots of choices for fine dining. Nothing in Wheat Ridge compared with Lakewood's great afterdark venues such as the Tally Ho Restaurant and Taylor's Supper Club.

The arrival of Red Coats changed everything about the Wheat Ridge–Lakewood rivalry. His track record of winning gave Wheat Ridge's entire community the hope that beating Lakewood was a real possibility. His cockiness and swagger imbued everyone with a degree of confidence. And because Coats had a flair for show-manship and loved recognition for himself and his star players, he took delight in fueling fan frenzy and attracting media coverage. We were always glad to see sportswriters in his office or waiting for him on the practice field, since press attention amused him and he would share his good mood with the team. We knew we were still mullets, but we also knew Coats was having a lot of fun coaching us.

Perhaps the only person who wasn't *completely* thrilled with Coats was Big Fred. Some supper table discussions in recent weeks had touched on how many times a game Freddie was carrying the ball compared with Bob Mitchell, or who was finding the end zone most often and from how far out. These were things Freddie would have preferred not hearing about. Even if they mattered to him, he wouldn't say so. Statistics and "ink" were for others to be con-cerned about. Freddie tried to stay focused on doing his all-out best whether he was carrying the ball, making a tackle, or running a wind sprint.

Sometime during the two weeks between the Alameda game and the Lakewood game, Big Fred went to the school to have a talk with Coats. Coats had two offices, one in the locker room and one in the cafeteria. GiGi, who happened to be in the cafeteria, saw her dad go into Coats's office. Shocked, she moved close enough to eavesdrop and heard Big Fred telling Coats how important it was for Freddie to get an athletic scholarship. "I can't afford to send him to college," Big Fred said. "He absolutely has to have a scholar-ship." Coats seemed to appreciate Big Fred's concern, but Big Fred apparently wasn't sure he had made himself clear. "I watch prac-tice every day, Red, and I see what's going on. I'm not here to tell you how to coach the team or what to do. I'm just asking you not to hurt my son's chances for a scholarship." If Freddie had known his dad was coming to the school to talk to Coats, he would have tried to head it off, preferring to let his play do the talking. That was what Big Fred had always taught him to do.

The thing that had got under Big Fred's skin was Coats's apparent determination to see Bobby Mitchell win the state scoring title, which, in Big Fred's view, was leading to decisions detrimental to Freddie's visibility. After three games in which Freddie ran the ball as well as or better than Bobby, but didn't seem to get as much recognition, because Bobby was doing the scoring, Big Fred let Coats know how he felt. Coats made no secret that he wanted to see Wheat Ridge players among the state's statistical leaders. This explained why he would send Mitchell into games to score short-yardage touchdowns even when the Farmers were so far ahead that the starters were on the sideline. It explained why Mitchell was the field goal and extra point kicker even though he wasn't very good at it. Coats knew every point counted. If the weekly stats showed that Mitchell needed eleven points to retake the scoring lead, he would make sure that Bobby got them in the next game. Big Fred had seen this tactic coming weeks earlier, when the team was learning its new offense during two-a-days. On first-and-goal plays, Mitchell was heavily favored to carry the ball.

"I saw your coach today, Freddie Joe," Big Fred said as soon as Gloria finished saying grace at the supper table. "We had a talk. I told him how important it is for you to get a scholarship." Freddie knew that there was more to it than that, and Big Fred said as much without spelling it out. "Son, I'm telling you something now—when you get your hands on the ball, do something with it. I don't care whether you're running with it or tackling somebody who has it. If you touch the ball, do something with it. Every time."

DURING THE WEEK OF THE LAKEWOOD GAME, THE EN-ergy level in hallways and classrooms at Wheat Ridge High was palpable. Students were so giddy that it seemed as if everybody was on a Halloween candy high. "Beat Lakewood" posters were plastered everywhere, and an announcement over the public-address system invited everyone to an after-school poster party in the cafeteria. The pep rally later in the week promised to be a barnburner.

In previous years, the football team's week leading up to the Lakewood game emphasized defense more than offense. The strategy made some sense, because Lakewood always had a very formidable defense of its own. Scoring points against them was so difficult that any possibility of a Wheat Ridge victory lay in keeping the Tigers off the scoreboard. Mike Schnitker recalled a game in which Lakewood was leading 35–0 when Wheat Ridge finally managed to kick a field goal: "Their fans were so excited about scoring three points [that] the game had to be stopped for about ten minutes."

Coats prepared us for the game as if it were any other game. We had our usual two hard-hitting scrimmages during the week. On Tuesday, the starting offense worked against what was expected to be Lakewood's defensive alignments. On Wednesday, the starting defense worked against what the scouts had determined would be Lakewood's basic offense. Wheat Ridge second-stringers running Lakewood's offense couldn't replicate the skillfulness of the Tigers' outstanding quarterback, Art Stapp, nor of end Scott Monson, but they ran it well enough for the Farmers' defenders to become familiar with it.

But there is no denying that tensions were higher than normal that week. During warm-up exercises on Monday, Coats spotted two men watching from the upper parking lot. One of them appeared to have binoculars. Coats sent a student manager scampering up the embankment to tell them it was a closed practice and to leave. While it was true Coats planned to add a few new wrinkles to the playbook for the Lakewood game—plays he didn't want anyone to see in advance—he had to have known those two men were Big Fred and my father. They had been there, in the same spot, every afternoon for six weeks. I learned later that the two of them watched the student manager approach with great purpose and determination until he recognized them. Then he wasn't sure what to say. He managed to do as he was instructed, and although my father was sure that Coats didn't mind them watching, Big Fred felt otherwise and told the manager they would go. Baffled, my father asked Big Fred what was going on. "I don't know," Big Fred said, "but it gripes my ass."

Once privacy was secured, Coats resumed his full practice regimen. He didn't believe in holding anyone out of contact, even at the risk of injuring key players. "We use the best players," he told a reporter. "Sure they might get hurt, but it's the constant practice that makes them good." On Thursday, the focus was on special teams. Kickoff, punting, and punt-return units practiced coverage and protection, and Mitchell attempted a few extra points and field goals. The remainder of practice was given to reviewing offensive and defensive assignments. Coats called the team together at the end of practice and told us to get a good night's sleep. "Think about the game," he said, "and don't get caught up in all the hysteria." He hoped that teachers had avoided assigning a lot of homework. He must have put up a sign to that effect in the teachers' lounge. Nobody had any homework to do.

After showering and dressing, Freddie and I drove in my VW to the Swiss Bells restaurant at 38th and Wadsworth in the heart of Wheat Ridge. We didn't have Sammy with us for once, and prime rib was the Thursday special. We couldn't go there too often because neither of us could afford it, but we each had the four dollars it would cost for prime rib, a vegetable, salad, rolls, a glass of milk, and dessert.

On any other night, Freddie would have gone straight home from practice. His routine was to have supper with his family, study for three or four hours, stop long enough to watch the ten o'clock sports segment on television, then do homework until he couldn't keep his eyes open. Sammy would try to stay awake long enough to watch sports with Freddie, but usually was asleep by the time Freddie came to bed.

But this wasn't any normal night. This was the night before the Lakewood game. There were only two other diners in the Swiss Bells, a middle-aged couple. We sat where we always did, in the first booth by the door. The chef and owner, Ernie, always smiling, always wearing a starched white double-breasted chef's jacket, brought us water and said, "The usual?" Then, as he did every time we had been there, confirmed with Freddie, "Well done, right?" Chefs always have to let you know it kills them to serve meat well done.

While we waited for our food, I tried to lighten the mood by razzing Freddie about Linda Wheeler. Freddie was not one to kiss and tell. He would talk about current events, schoolwork, music, and sports, but never girls or gossip. He had been dating Linda for about a year, and we had never had a single conversation about her or their relationship. I gave it another try while we waited for our prime rib. Freddie's back was to the couple. I noticed them looking at us several times, so I leaned in, still looking at them, "Freddie," I said, "what do Linda's parents look like? I think they may have found out you guys have been parking. Those people keep looking at you." He didn't bite. He frowned and asked whether I had ever tried to park with my little brother in the back seat.

Ernie delivered our plates, and the first thing Freddie did was to cross himself. The principles and practices of the Catholic Church—such as thanksgiving, nightly prayers, daily rosary, and not eating meat on Friday—were woven into the fabric of Freddie's life. I remember one Friday night later that year, after we had played in a basketball game; Freddie and I were driving in my car, looking to get something to eat. It was about ten thirty or so, and I suggested, "How about some burgers?"

Freddie sort of shook his head and said, "Let's wait until midnight."

"You don't have to wait until midnight anymore Fred," I responded. "The pope lifted the ban." It had been a thousand years since Catholics could eat meat on Friday. Just then I wheeled into the parking lot of Davies' Chuckwagon Diner on West Colfax. I was starving.

"I'm waiting until midnight, Bower," Freddie said, looking at me. "He lifted it to make the church more appealing, but that doesn't make it right." In Freddie's view, rules were rules. A Catholic could abstain and still observe. We drove around until midnight.

But at the Swiss Bells, there was nothing standing between us and our plates of prime rib, and we dug in. Freddie squirted mustard all over his French fries. He was certain that mustard had more nutritional value than catsup. "Just try it for once," he said, handing me the yellow plastic bottle. As the couple was leaving, they paused at our table and wished us "good luck tomorrow night." When they were gone, we talked about how the whole town was wound up about the game. Signs of support were in store windows everywhere. A car dealer had soaped "Go Farmers!" on the windshields of a row of used cars. Freddie called it "mullet fever." When Ernie brought our checks, he stabbed the table with his finger in the same way Big Fred did when he was making a point: "You boys beat that Lakewood bunch."

Later that night when Freddie and Sammy were on their knees saying prayers beside the bed they had to share, Sammy finished and started climbing onto the bed. Freddie grabbed Sammy's waistband and dragged him back to his knees: "You're not done." Sammy protested that he had prayed for everything, including for Wheat Ridge to beat Lakewood. "Pray for dad to be safe at work during the night, and for mother to be happy and healthy," Freddie told him. "And you can't pray for us to win or Lakewood to lose. God doesn't take sides. You can only pray for everyone to play their best and not get hurt."

At the afternoon pep rally the next day in the gymnasium, the student body cheered wildly as each player was introduced. Mitchell blew the doors off the place when he was asked to speak and, unsure what to say, held the microphone to his mouth for a second, then blurted, "We're gonna beat the hell out of Lakewood!" School was let out a little early to give everyone time to go home before going to the stadium. Kickoff was scheduled for eight o'clock. The Jefferson County Sheriff's Department advised that traffic would be heavy.

After the pep rally, Freddie jogged home to their duplex on 32nd Street. He would meet Sammy there, and GiGi would prepare their customary pregame meal of a peanut butter and jelly *and* fried egg sandwich. Then GiGi, P.K., Gloria, and Fred would pile into the Mustang and go to the stadium. Freddie and Sammy would walk back to the school and join the team in the locker room.

The locker room was quieter than it usually was before a game. As players were getting taped and putting on their uniforms, low voices could be heard here and there, but the conversations were short. Everyone seemed to be thinking about all the years of frustration that would either end in the next few hours or continue for yet another year. Players who were finished dressing carried their helmets and cleats to the darkened gym, where they lay on the hardwood floor and meditated or napped before boarding the team bus. Freddie sat in front of his locker with rosary beads in his bandaged hand. No one knew he was hiding a broken bone under the Ace bandage. Playing in pain was part of his game, and he was good at it. During his junior year, he played half a game on a fractured fibula.

Most of the team was in the gym when Coats emerged from his office, clapping his hands and shouting, "Let's go! Let's go! The bus is waiting!" Larry Elliot, one of the student managers, rushed back into the locker room, squeezing past players trying to exit.

"Coach!" he said. "I can't find Sammy. He's not on the bus." Coats threw his hands up and stopped in his tracks.

"Aw hell, man! Where is he? Sammy!" Coats looked around in vain. Freddie was still at his locker. "Where's your brother, Freddie? Biggest game of our lives and we gotta stop and look for a mullet! Sammy!"

Sammy emerged from the training room, lugging the black tape kit in front of him with both hands. "I'm right here, Coach."

Coats clapped earnestly and barked, "Get yer ass on that bus, ya mullet!"

Traffic crawled during the last two miles to the stadium. In the darkened bus, players sat quietly listening to fans screaming encouragement from open car windows. Near the entrance to the stadium, the bus came to a complete halt, unable to proceed farther. Coats got up from his seat and wondered aloud whether the team should get out and walk the rest of the way. He took a long look at the stadium and overflow crowd, then faced the team.

"Listen up, mullets," he began. "Wheat Ridge has waited a long time for this. Lakewood's kicked our butts too many years. Not tonight. They're fired up, though. I went to a meeting at their school today. Every wall is plastered with posters, just like our place." He glanced at the stadium again and winked at Sammy, sitting beside Freddie. "I'd hate to be the guy that scheduled us tonight for Lakewood's homecoming. Come Monday he'll be about as popular as a turd in a punchbowl." Laughter erupted, and Coats flashed his grin. "Let's go have some fun, mullets." The bus started moving again and slowly made it around to the east side, where the locker rooms were located. The players were still laughing as they exited the bus.

Both teams warmed up and then left the field for last-minute instructions. Even in the locker room, the noise of the crowd and the clashing of the bands were deafening. Coats was delivering a pep talk when someone outside pounded on the door. Sammy pushed it open, and two giggling Lakewood cheerleaders handed him a large flat box and then fled.

"What is that?" Coats growled.

Inside the box were pink cupcakes with the Farmers' jersey numbers on them. Sammy started to sample one.

"Throw that damn thing away, Sammy!" Coats barked. "All of 'em. They probably put Ex-Lax in 'em." If people outside the locker room could have heard the ensuing laughter, they might have feared that the Farmers were a little *too* relaxed before taking the field against Lakewood.

FOOTBALL IS A TEAM SPORT. FREDDIE ALWAYS WAS FIRST to say so. No matter how well he played, he would tell you he could have played better, and he would always praise his teammates. He wasn't just saying those things. He believed them. In a game of inches, every single decision, every individual effort, combined to make the difference. On Friday night, October 7, 1966, an overflow crowd of nearly ten thousand people watched the Wheat Ridge Farmers play the Lakewood Tigers—two great teams that brought together, for a few hours, two great communities. But the night belonged to a single player who, no matter what he said afterward, could not have played better.

In front of the roaring crowd, along with a slew of local and statewide reporters, the Wheat Ridge Farmers and the Lakewood

Tigers streamed onto the field. From the get-go, the Tigers seemed to be in control of the ground game, but a series of heads-up defensive plays led to a Tiger fumble in the first quarter, and we took advantage of the possession. After a solid run by Freddie, the Farmers found themselves in scoring position. Our quarterback, Roger Behler, threw an incomplete pass on his next attempt, but then came a crucial connection with Freddie once again. As one reporter wrote, "[Behler's] pass slipped off the fingers of Lakewood defender Ted Dill and into the waiting arms of the ever-present Steinmark on the one [yard line]." A quarterback sneak put the ball in the end zone, and the Farmers were on top of the Tigers.

The Tigers responded with a bruising drive that covered sixty-eight yards in thirteen running plays that shredded the right side of the Wheat Ridge line and ended with a Lakewood touchdown. The Farmers might have been put on their heels by that drive, but we certainly were not beaten. After a dramatic back-and-forth series of drives and stalls, we pushed our way back down the field with a balanced attack. This time, Bobby Mitchell took the ball and punched through the line to put Wheat Ridge up 13–7 at halftime.

The second half of the game was possibly even more physical than the first. Lakewood put together another one of its punishing ground attacks, covering sixty-four yards on rushing plays before driving once again into the end zone to tie the score at 13. Each team threw everything it had at the other. At the end of the third quarter, Lakewood once again took control of the ground game and began another merciless drive toward the Farmer end zone. Near midfield, the Tigers had a third-and-one to keep their drive going into Farmer territory. That was when Wheat Ridge's Gary Fallico came up with what Coach Coats would later call the "key play of the game." Jerry Williams, the Tiger halfback, took a pitchout and swung left, a play that had worked against the Farmers several times already, but this time Fallico flashed through the offensive line and was able to drop Williams in the backfield for a loss of four yards. It was an incredible stop, and it came at a critical moment. The Tigers elected to punt and put Wheat Ridge back on offense.

In the fourth quarter, both teams were beginning to show signs of wear and fatigue. This was the exact moment that we had been training for under Coach Coats. This was the exact moment that Big Fred had preached about. This was the moment that Freddie dreamed of when he did his final series of wind sprints or his last set of reps on the weight bench. This was the moment when Roger Behler faked a handoff to Bobby Mitchell and then planted the ball squarely in Freddie's stomach as Freddie shot toward the right side of the line and burst through an opening.

What came next has become the stuff of Wheat Ridge legend. Freddie raced toward the right sideline, and just when it looked as if he were going to be smothered by at least five defenders, he cut back, running directly into them. Again, it looked like an impossible situation, but somehow he wove through them like a whirling dervish. One after another the Tigers lunged and missed. A series of key blocks by scrambling Farmers helped Freddie keep the run going, and the crowd came to its feet, sensing something remarkable. Freddie cut and juked and kept going, racing all the way back across the field toward the opposite sideline. The roar of the crowd grew louder and louder with every yard he gained. The entire stadium was in a frenzy. Could he do it? Could no one really stop him? The next morning Irv Moss of the *Denver Post* put it like this: "If you've ever swatted at a fly with your hand, you know what the Lakewood High School football team faced when it tried to stop a 77-yard touchdown run by Wheat Ridge's Fred Steinmark that whipped the Tigers."

Dave Dirks came up with the last critical block near the goal line, and Freddie soared into the end zone to put the Farmers up 19–13. It was the final score of the game, and the Wheat Ridge crowd went crazy.

By the next day, the whole state was abuzz with the story of Freddie's run and the upset of the Tigers. "Look, Fans, Look, See Freddie Run!" exclaimed one headline. The article went on to say, "It had been billed as the game of the year and when it was over no one was saying it was anything less. The Wheat Ridge Farmers ended the 24-game Jefferson County League winning streak of Lakewood 19–13."

The nightly television sports shows replayed Freddie's run several times. It seemed as if people just couldn't get enough of it. The *Rocky Mountain News* did a half-page diagram with a black zigzag line marking his course from one side of the field to the other, and all the blocks that Freddie's teammates made along the way. A full week after the game, the *Post*'s Irv Moss wrote an article headlined "Steinmark Feats Still Talk Topic." "Every chance he gets," the article began, "Fred Steinmark brings his teammates into the conversation for praise when discussing Wheat Ridge's 19–13 triumph over Lakewood in Jefferson County League play last weekend. However, there is no denying the 160-pound halfback had a remarkable night against the Tigers."

Lakewood coach Hancock, removed from the glare of the lights, was also featured in the papers, "mentally poring over the plays that spelled defeat. . . . 'We let him get outside once all night,' he said quietly, 'and that did it. Otherwise it would have been an old-fashioned Mexican stand off out there.'" The article continued: "The 'him' Hancock spoke of was Farmer halfback Fred Steinmark, who broke the backs of a rugged Lakewood team with a dazzling 77-yard run from scrimmage for Wheat Ridge's third and deciding touchdown."

The sportswriters couldn't get enough of the young phenom. One article carefully broke down Freddie's running style: "What Steinmark has is not great speed but rather a style of running that gives the impression that his body is going in several different directions at once. Coats says it is something you can't teach a player. It is a natural, instinctive thing."

What none of the reporters knew about, however, was the exchange between Coats and his quarterback, Behler, during a Wheat Ridge time-out just before Freddie's great run. Behler ran to the sideline to consult with the coach. The bands were blaring, and the screaming and shouting of fans was so loud that it was hard for Behler and Coats to hear each other. "What play should we run, Coach?" Behler shouted.

Coats shouted back, "Just give the damn ball to Freddie!"

In addition to the dazzle of Freddie's well-publicized run, his stats on the night were equally impressive: on offense, he contributed 116 of the 140 total yards rushing and caught one pass for 14 yards. On defense, Freddie came up with an incredible 15 tackles, plus an interception. All in all, a remarkable effort, and to Coach Coats's credit, he realized that when push came to shove, Freddie was his most dangerous weapon on the field, and he let Freddie shine.

THAT NIGHT, JUST BEFORE MIDNIGHT, FREDDIE, KENT, GiGi, and GiGi's friend Anne Sanzalone were seated in a booth at Jenny's Pizzeria in Wheat Ridge, a popular place with the Farmer faithful, especially this night. GiGi was so proud of her brother, but couldn't imagine how much pain he must have been in: his face was bruised and swollen, and she thought it looked as if he had black eyes. He also seemed to be nursing a sore hand. Kent's hands, too, were swollen. She kept careful watch on the clock on the wall behind the cash register. At exactly midnight, she motioned to a waitress that they were ready to order. It was finally Saturday. Freddie could eat meat.

Freddie Joe riding high with Big Fred, 1949.

Big Fred, Gloria, Freddie Joe, and GiGi, Easter Sunday 1953.

From kindergarten on, one of the first things people noticed about Freddie was his smile.

P.K., GiGi, and Sammy with "the older brother all kids wish they could have."

Big Fred and Gloria never had to look far to find Sammy.

Future Farmers in the formative stage, coached by Big Fred (standing, back row, far right). Freddie is directly behind Frankie Sanzalone, the boy with the white helmet on his knee. (Bower Yousse is standing on the far left.)

First communion at St. Catherine's in North Denver, 1956. Freddie's priorities were faith, family, school, sports, and everything else. Freddie and Johnnyboy are fourth and fifth from the left in the back row.

ROUGH RIDERS
NORTH SIDE COMMUNITY CENTER-1960

*In Freddie's six years as a Rough
Rider, the team never lost a game.
Freddie is on the far left, front row.
Cousin Gregg is third from the left,
front row.*

*Gloria and Freddie, 1960,
photographed by Big Fred.*

Gloria and Big Fred, 1960, photographed by Freddie, age eleven.

Freddie's school photograph from Manning Junior High, ninth grade, 1964. Freddie was happy to be back in Colorado with his family.

Posing for a family picture at a holiday gathering at Nana Marchitti's, 1963.

Freddie, the Farmers' floor general at point guard, 1967. He liked basketball, but preferred playing football and baseball.

Excellent hitting and superb fielding as shortstop earned Freddie all-metro and all-state honors. In his senior year, the Cincinnati Reds drafted him.

Football, basketball, or baseball—when Freddie wasn't in the game, Sammy was at his side.

In 1966, Freddie's fourth-quarter, seventy-seven-yard touchdown run thrilled sportswriters and Farmers' fans, but left Lakewood and their great coach, Tom Hancock, brokenhearted.

TIGERS DONE IN BY FARMERS

Look, Fans, Look, See Freddy Run!

It had been billed as the game of the year and when it was over no one was saying it was anything less. The Wheat Ridge Farmers ended the 24-game Jefferson County League winning streak of Lakewood 19-13. The last and only time the Tigers had lost a league game was to Wheat Ridge way back in 1962.

It was a game of great team efforts and individual heroics. When the fourth quarter opened the score was knotted 13-13. Wheat Ridge had the ball on their own 22 with a fourth down and one. Coach John (Red) Coats decided to gamble and it paid off with quarterback Roger making it to the 23 on a sneak.

An then it came, the play that still has the spectators buzzing. Fred Steinmark took a hand-off and went on a 77-yard touchdown romp that brought the more than 9,000 fans to their feet with a roaring ovation.

"Beautiful, beautiful," sighed one Wheat Ridge fan. "It had to be one of the best executed plays I have seen in 30 years of watching football," remarked a Lakewood booster. "Hollywood couldn't have produced one to such perfection, just like it was out of a story book," commented still another.

Asked about his star 160-pound back, Coats, with a broad smile, said, "some have got it and some don't. Freddy has got it."

What Steinmark has is not great speed but rather a style of running that gives the allusion that his body is going in several different directions at once. Coats says it is something you can't teach a player. It is a natural, instinctive thing.

Steinmark is gifted with a

but Dirks, who went down blocking out the Lakewood linebacker, had picked himself up moved down the field and was on the spot to deliver his second important block of the play.

WHEAT RIDGE got on the scoreboard first after recovering a fumble on the Lakewood 26 midway through the first quarter. Steinmark, who accounted for 116 yards of the Farmers' 140 total rushing, carried to the 15. Behler fired an incomplete pass and on second down his pass slipped off the fingers of Lakewood defender Ted Dill and into the waiting arms of the ever-present Steinmark on the one. Behler went over right tackle for the TD.

Lakewood came right back with a touchdown drive that covered 68 yards in 13 running plays. Tiger halfback Jerry Williams and fullback Chuck Greaser shredded the right side of the Wheat Ridge line and Greaser bulled in from a yard out. Scott Monson added the extra point and Lakewood took a 7-6 lead.

The Farmers came right back driving to the Lakewood three-yard line but the Tigers dug in and held. After a Lakewood punt, the Farmers moved to the Lakewood 36. Faced with a fourth down and 10 yards to go, Behler passed to Youse on the five. Three running plays later, Mitchell smashed over from the one. He also added the point after touchdown for a 13-7 half-time lead.

Early in the third period, the Tigers ground out 84 yards on the ground and halfback Lynn White hit paydirt from five yards out. And that is where

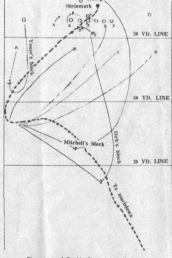

The course of Freddy Steinmark's winning run.

ning of Dennis Ulrich to victory. Ulrich hit Jefferson's fine end, John Ranch, with a scoring pass

touchdown parade with three tallies.

County Budget Figured

Preliminary general budget figures were establi by County Commissioners week, and they represent of $140,000 from original b requests by the county's va department heads.

Many departments, faced an increased work load exp tion, will receive an averag pct. increase over last y funds, although the figures substantially less than asked

Among final figures re mended by Budget Officer I Serr, together with increase quests, are the following:

• Clerk and Recorder, 229 recommended, 17.6 pct. last year and $8000 under request;

• District Court, $246,655 ommended, 12.9 pct. over year but $15,384 less than quested;

• County Court, $154,716 ommended, 12.3 pct. over year's budget and $5000 u the request;

• Sheriff's Dept., $703,663 ommended, 7.7 pct. above year and $3400 under the quest;

• Planning and Zoning, 630 recommended, a 7.7 pct crease but $15,764 under the quest;

• County Library, $168,936 ommended, a 7.7 pct. incr but $24,282 under the reque

• Health Dept. $259,250

Freddie's high school graduation party, 1967. Standing, left to right: *Bob Himes, Mark Carpenter, Bower Yousse, Gene Covello, Tom Wolfe, Rod Barringer, Freddie Steinmark, Dave Dirks, Rick Sanzalone, John Vest, Jim Marsico, Bob Mitchell, and Kent Cluck.* Seated, left to right: *Coaches Larry Vance, Bob Raugh, Red Coats, Joe Newman, Fred Bradley, and Jack Jost.*

Wheat Ridge High principal Don Solem said of Freddie: "To know [him] is to enrich your life—he has the rare combination of human traits that makes everyone who knows him, like him."

Freddie and Linda sharing a moment between classes at Wheat Ridge High, 1967.

Part Two
1967–1969

*Fred—You're an outstanding person
both mentally and physically.
You've received the highest honors
an amateur athlete can receive. They
couldn't have gone to a more deserving
person. Texas is going to be awfully
glad they signed you.*

Note in Freddie's yearbook
from Bower Yousse, 1967

CHAPTER 5

THE SILENT HEART

B Y MONDAY MORNING, THE SCHOOL HALLS had been scrubbed clean, and there was hardly any evidence of the weeklong extravaganza of banners and bake sales, of painted windows and pep rallies, of the pregame build-up that had consumed the entire school just days before. In its wake, something slightly calmer and more enduring filled the halls: pride. The last time that Wheat Ridge High had defeated Lakewood, more than a third of the student body was still in grade school. But now the community had something to smile about, thanks to Freddie and the Wheat Ridge Farmers football team. The pride stretched all the way from the schoolyard to the predominantly Italian sections of North Denver, where they took a special delight in Freddie's all-star play and the honor it brought to the Marchitti clan.

Freddie arrived at school twenty minutes before the first bell, just as on any normal day. He towed his stack of textbooks and the bundle of gym clothes GiGi had laundered for him over the weekend, but even Freddie could feel the special vibe today. High school football players stand a little taller in the hallways on the Monday after a victory, but we felt especially tall after beating Lakewood. Normally, we might fill our idle hallway time by discussing *The Ed Sullivan Show* or Petula Clark's new hit. Freddie might have a new Sammy story for us—for example, how at the dinner table Sammy had broken into a perfect Red Coats impersonation and said, "Aw hell, man!" to the consternation of Big Fred and Gloria.

But on this morning, all anyone wanted to talk about was Freddie's game-winning run. It must have felt good, of course, to make the play that clinched the victory, but the extra attention made Freddie uncomfortable. He smiled and said thanks while emphasizing that it was a team effort. Make no mistake, Freddie loved winning, and he wanted to be in the middle of the action. He wanted to be a game changer and have a hand in determining the outcome, and he wasn't shy about sharing the pride we all felt in having beaten Lakewood. But no matter what heroics he might have performed, he never forgot that in football a victory is the collective product of a multitude of individual performances.

And he knew that the season was still young. We had five regular-season games left on the schedule, but players had already begun to think about the state playoffs now that we had taken down our previously unbeatable rival. Coach Coats tried to keep everyone focused, but the playoff conversations persisted. In fact, Coach couldn't stop himself from participating in the chatter.

One local sportswriter wanted to know how Coats had engendered such a quick turnaround. "Lakewood was known as the hitters and we were the grabbers," Coats explained, meaning that Lakewood had always been the more physical team on the field. "The first few weeks we weren't hitters. We still were grabbers. But you can teach a kid to be a hitter. We kept working at it. When you work at it enough, they'll try to run right through a brick wall." Coats's tone was that of the hard-nosed football coach—the kind of attitude Freddie had always appreciated.

The sportswriter was interested in how Coats had gotten us to make the mental leap as well. After all, we had a losing history against Lakewood. How did we overcome that? Coach Coats must have loved that question, and he used the opportunity to take another jab at Lakewood's Tom Hancock: "Lakewood had never beaten me, and I had no fear of Tom Hancock and what he'd done over there."

It is important to remember that these were different days, and

Coats was the product of an older world of American football. He was not one to "spare the rod," figuratively or even literally in some cases. Rumor had it he once disciplined players with a wooden paddle when he coached in El Paso. In Wheat Ridge, however, he adapted his method of corporal punishment to the environment. Instead of the paddle, we had the Hill. This was the same rampart that Big Fred and my father had been driven off of, and Coats often ordered us to run up and down it until we collapsed. The week after the Lakewood game, Coats needed to remind us we hadn't won anything yet, that the season wasn't over, and that we still had a lot of work to do. So to the Hill we went.

While we raced up the Hill, Coats singled out Mike Rich, an offensive tackle. This was one of the coach's favorite tactics, probably stemming from his days with the Marines, when the "weakest link" in a unit would be singled out in hopes that the whole team would help inspire and reform him, thereby strengthening the unit overall. Rich wasn't a weak link, but he had had a bad practice, and Coats used it as an excuse to penalize all of us. He made us run sprint after sprint and blamed each additional repetition on Mike. Again, then again, then again.

Exhausted, we dragged ourselves to the locker room. Rich heard a few players grumbling his name, blaming him. He stepped aside as his teammates made their way inside. He felt low, unpopular, and he didn't want to go into the tightly packed locker room and face the rest of the team. He sat on the curb outside with his helmet between his legs. In his exhaustion, he considered quitting right there and walking home.

That was when Freddie came walking up from the practice field. Years later, Rich still recalled the conversation he had when Freddie sat down and asked what was going on.

"You know what's going on," Rich told him.

Freddie thought for a moment and then he said, "Mike, today was a tough day. We worked hard. Things happened the way they did, and that's okay. Tomorrow is another day, and you'll see everything's going to be just fine, because you're part of this team."

Then Freddie told him to come on, and together they walked

into the locker room. Rich recalled how he could tell Freddie was speaking from his heart. How Freddie did make him feel like a real part of the team. Rich would later say of that moment, "I've always thought it was a privilege for us to be in the same place and the same time with Freddie. It's hard for people to believe he was the way he was. It was truly his nature."

So many players shared this same thought and emotion about Freddie. Freddie was the silent heart of the team.

WE BREEZED THROUGH THE REST OF THE SCHEDULE AND won the league championship, the first time since 1945. To make the victory even sweeter, it was the first time in eleven years that Tom Hancock and his Lakewood Tigers had not won or shared the title.

In the state quarterfinals, we played the Ranum High Raiders, champions of the Skyline League. We had some concern because Ranum boasted the state's best defense, but these fears soon proved unnecessary.

Ranum received the ball to begin the game, but we forced a quick three-and-out and a punt. We kept two punt returners deep: Roger Behler and Freddie. Ranum's first punt landed in Behler's arms, and on a reverse, he handed the ball off to Freddie, who took it eighty-five yards for a touchdown.

On the next series, we again forced a quick punt. Behler fielded the punt a second time, only this time he faked the handoff to Freddie. Ranum's coverage bit on the fake, and Behler sprinted, untouched, sixty-one yards for our second touchdown. We hadn't yet run a play from scrimmage against the vaunted Ranum defense, and already we led 14–0. The third time that Ranum had to punt, their fans started screaming, "Don't punt! Don't punt!" In the paper the next morning a "jubilant" Coats said, "There is no doubt about it, the two punt returns were the turning point." A week later, we dispatched the state's number one team, the Wasson Thunderbirds of Colorado Springs, on a blustery, chilly day, and then set our sights on the state championship.

Our opponents were the George Washington Patriots of the

Denver Prep League. The contest pitted the suburbs against the city, and the Patriots were favored. We all were excited because the game was moved to Bears Stadium, where the Denver Broncos played their home games.

Practice in the days leading up to the state championship game was surreal. None of us could believe we were there, preparing to take the Wheat Ridge Farmers to a state title game for the first time ever. Even the weather seemed unreal. It was the last week of November, but the weather was spectacularly beautiful, more like early fall. Cool-weather smog that usually blanketed the Denver basin and obscured the purple Rocky Mountains was gone, blown far to the east by chinook winds.

But there was little time to enjoy the scenery. As was Coats's habit, the scrimmaging was as hard hitting as ever, maybe the hardest it had been all season. Between drills, players discussed how remarkable it was to be one of the last two high school teams still playing football in Colorado, and how, after Saturday, many on the team would never play again. Even though Bears Stadium would be teeming with college coaches and scouts, college ball was still a long shot for most of us. For most of the Farmers, this was as big as it would ever get, and we recognized it.

The rest of Wheat Ridge shared in the excitement too. On Holland Street, which ran past the practice field, car horns blared and students shouted from passing windows: "We're number one!" On the opposite side of the school, the members of the marching band blew their lungs out while working on a championship halftime routine.

PEOPLE IN DENVER OFTEN SAY THAT IF YOU DON'T LIKE the weather, come back in five minutes. By game time on Saturday, December 3, the temperature had plummeted to thirty-five degrees, and frosty plumes of breath were being whipped away by the breeze. We lost the coin toss and then kicked off to the Patriots before the largest crowd to ever watch a high school football game in Colorado. The game was a showcase of potential college football talent, and there were numerous star players on both sides of the ball. It was a hard-fought game, but the Farmers emerged victorious, helped by Freddie's two fourth-quarter interceptions. Once more, the fans went crazy. We had just earned Wheat Ridge High School's first-ever state football championship.

The celebrations that followed that victory became something of a blur, but I will never forget one small, strange detail: as the team was celebrating on the bus ride back to Wheat Ridge, we stopped at a red light. Then a man with half a haircut—and the barber's smock still flapping around his neck—burst from the corner barbershop and ran to the side of the bus, shouting, "Thank you, Farmers! You won me five bucks!"

FREDDIE RECEIVED THE *DENVER POST*'S GOLD HELMET Award in mid-December. This recognition is given to the state's top scholar-athlete. It also gave Freddie a sweep of the major awards: all-Jefferson County, all-metropolitan, all-state, and the Gold Helmet. The *Post*'s write-up highlighted Freddie's season statistics: 437 yards on 63 rushing attempts, 298 yards on 18 receptions, and 9 touchdowns against league foes alone. "Certainly," Irv Moss went on to say, "the only thing that could overshadow his capabilities on offense would have been his defensive play." Moss quoted Coach Coats: "[Freddie] made the big play on defense for us time after time. He was the guy that I would have hated most to lose from our whole ball club." The article also retold Freddie's dazzling fourth-quarter run against Lakewood, about which Coats went so far as to say, "That play won the state championship for us. If we hadn't won that ball game, we probably wouldn't have even made the playoffs."

By now, despite all obstacles, Freddie was probably the biggest high school football star in Colorado, but behind his smile as he accepted his awards, he was hiding a deep concern. Despite all the accolades, despite all the impressive statistics, despite all the championship trophies and newspaper write-ups, Freddie had not received a single major Division I scholarship offer. Bobby Mitchell had received numerous offers, but he outweighed Freddie by almost fifty pounds. This reality was slowly dawning on Freddie even as he walked across stages and shook hands in front of flashing cameras. In the whirlwind of the state championship and all the awards, everyone was asking Freddie where he was going to play college ball. There was no reprieve from the question. Nearly everyone assumed that Freddie, like Mitchell, was swamped with offers, but they were wrong, and this hidden truth was beginning to alarm Freddie.

He did receive attention from some smaller colleges, like Dartmouth and Purdue, both as an athlete and as a student (Freddie ranked 25th in our class of 530). Freddie appreciated the interest, but those schools' football programs lacked one critical thing in his view: national-title aspirations. As Freddie's cousin Johnnyboy explained, Freddie's lifelong goals were larger than just college ball. "It wasn't just that he wanted to be on a team that could compete for a national championship," Johnnyboy said. "Freddie wanted to play pro ball after college. He believed that because of his small size, pro scouts would overlook him. He felt he needed to be playing for a major university to get noticed, and of course, Notre Dame is really where he always wanted to play."

Everybody knew that Notre Dame had always been his dream school, just as it was for many Catholic high school football players in America. Freddie was also interested in other major schools, such as Oklahoma and Alabama. But none of them were interested in him, so Freddie took it upon himself to write letters to each program, asking them to consider him for a scholarship offer. It was a desperate move. Even Freddie had to know that an unsolicited letter to a coach was an unlikely route to a college scholarship. Big-time college athletic programs receive thousands and thousands of letters just like his, and the reality is that the United States is a country full of excellent high school football players. On paper, frankly, Freddie probably looked a lot like many other high school running backs and safeties; plus, his size was on the small side.

Freddie also knew that his time and options were quickly running out. If this remarkable season and his shelf of awards weren't enough to earn him some interest, what would be? Besides, what other option did he have—to do nothing at all? He sent the letters.

As the holiday season arrived, preparations began for the annual Steinmark-Marchitti Christmas dinner, which drew over fifty of the extended family members together at Nana's home for a raucous, good-spirited reunion of sorts. Freddie invited Linda to the family feast—a sure sign of his growing affection for her. He was starting to see her as part of the family. Everything was made from scratch, and took days of preparation. Antipasto plates. Fresh bread. Spaghetti, meatballs, and sausages. Short ribs. Ricotta-stuffed ravioli. Meat sauces. Ham, turkey, and all the trimmings. Italian *pizzelle* cookies. Tables were arranged upstairs and downstairs, but seats were never assigned; you sat with whomever you were talking to when the dinner bell rang.

And, of course, Freddie was the topic of discussion that year. Every member of the family had an opinion about where he should play college football. Some suggested Colorado. Some felt that he was too small for the big universities and that a small college with great educational opportunities was the best route. No matter their opinions, though, many of his family members seemed to hold the notion that Freddie's options were practically unlimited. No one knew how bleak his situation really had become, or how difficult it was for him to keep having these cheerful conversations about his future.

CURT REPLIES TO FREDDIE'S LETTERS BEGAN TO ARRIVE. Alabama asked to see films, if he cared to send them, and Purdue invited him to visit on his own, but those were the only encouraging replies. Colorado's major schools stated that he was not big enough to play their kind of football. If the college coaches who had seen him play week in and week out weren't interested, then who would be?

GiGi discovered Notre Dame's reply letter in the mailbox the day it arrived. As she did every day, GiGi ran out to the mailbox when she heard the mailman. She quickly thumbed through the letters and spotted the one from the Irish. She came back into the house, waving it over her head and shouting for Freddie. He opened the envelope without any obvious emotion, read the letter, folded it, and put it back into the envelope without changing his expression.

"What did it say?" GiGi inquired.

"Same thing they all say. I'm too small."

GiGi recalls the day with vivid emotion. "I felt so awful," she says. "He dreamed of playing for Notre Dame his whole life. All he got was a form letter. What I remember most is that he didn't want me to be upset. . . . He never wanted you to worry about him."

As GiGi pressed him for details and began to express her hurt for him, he promised her that everything was okay. That he would be all right. "Don't worry," he said.

But Freddie must have become increasingly worried as those form letters came trickling in. He was a mature young man, but his life had been built on the foundations of hard work and big dreams, and here he was at eighteen years old experiencing what must have felt like an onrushing defeat. It was the fourth quarter, he was losing, and the clock was running out.

But it should be kept in mind that the fourth quarter was where Freddie's hard work paid its greatest dividends. One day at school after Christmas break, Freddie received a message that Coach Coats wanted to see him right away. At the first chance he got, Freddie made his way to the coach's office.

"You wanted to see me, Coach?" Freddie said, standing in Coats's doorway.

"Come in and have a seat, Freddie," Coats responded. "I took it upon myself to send film of the Lakewood game to an old friend, a coach at Texas, Mike Campbell, their defensive coordinator. I told him I had a couple of kids up here I thought he ought to have a look at. He says they like ol' Bobby Mitchell with his size, but the coaches at Texas like what they see of you, too. They think you have some moves. He's sending somebody up here to talk to y'all this weekend, and if they like you, they'll fly you down to Austin for a visit. Now, keep in mind he didn't say anything about a scholarship, so there's no guarantee. But they wouldn't take the time and effort to visit someone who didn't really interest them."

Freddie could hardly believe it. It was like getting the ball in his hands with just seconds left on the clock. The words of Big Fred might have echoed in his head at that moment: "Every time you get your hands on the ball, do something with it." Could he make something out of this opportunity? "Texas," he said. Freddie shook Coats's hand and thanked him, then ran home to tell his parents.

UNIVERSITY OF TEXAS ASSISTANT COACH FRED AKERS and freshman coach Bill Ellington stood by the roadside mailbox and checked the address. This was the right place. They were in Wheat Ridge looking at a blond-brick, one-story duplex on 32nd Avenue. Freddie's house.

"Oh, my goodness," Fred Akers says, recalling that day. "I have to laugh about it." He goes on to add, "Freddie was what we call a 'twenty-footer.' That's how [many feet of] film you have to watch before you know it's a kid you want to go get."

It takes 13.3 seconds to watch twenty feet of film. The coaches at Texas, it seemed, had looked past Freddie's physical size to see the magnitude of his impact on the field.

"We knew [Freddie] was going to be a smaller guy," Akers continued. "Ellington rang the bell, and this young man opened the door, and we looked at him, and past him, and Ellington said, 'Is your brother home?' The young man said yes and yelled over his shoulder, 'Sammy! Someone's here to see you!' That was our introduction to Freddie. We all laughed." Akers gets wistful. "Freddie sure had a great laugh."

FREDDIE VISITED THE UNIVERSITY OF TEXAS ALONG with Bobby Mitchell. They arrived in Austin on Saturday, February 26, 1967. Ted Koy and Mike Sullivan, two Longhorn players, met them at the airport.

"Freddie," Koy recalls, "was very, very polite. And he was confident. Not cocky or arrogant or anything like that, just confident. Comfortable with himself."

Koy took Freddie around campus and gave him a good look at 67,000-seat Memorial Stadium. They had dinner at Hill's Steak

House and went to see *The Good, the Bad and the Ugly* that night. On Sunday, Koy dropped Freddie off for mass at St. Mary's in downtown Austin, and later he took Freddie and Bob to Coach Royal's office. They were just two of a number of high school players visiting that weekend, and so each meeting with Coach Royal was short, but this was Freddie's first look at the man who would help shape his destiny. "The head coach doesn't overwhelm you with personality, not at first," Freddie wrote in his memoir, *I Play to Win*. "He's no glad-hander or joke teller. You are immediately aware of the direct look he gives you and his sincere approach and his close attention to what you are saying. He's not one of these people who looks away when he's talking or listening. You have his undivided attention and he wants yours."

Freddie wasn't sure what exactly to expect from his meeting with Coach Royal, who had a knack for keeping people slightly off balance, a trait that served him well throughout his long, record-shattering career. First of all, the music. As Freddie observed in his own understated way: "There *was* one rather strange thing he did. He put a cassette of country-western music on his office stereo before we began talking."

Once they did begin to talk, the coach never once brought up Freddie's size, much to Freddie's surprise, even though he noticed that Freddie was wearing cowboy boots to give himself an extra inch of height. Finally, even the decor of the office was notable for its understated strangeness. Freddie observed the painting hanging behind Coach Royal's desk: "an oil painting of the toughest, mangiest, skinniest, meanest-looking Longhorn steer." The painting was a gift to Royal from his wife, Edith.

Royal likely told both Freddie and Bob that playing for Texas was a privilege few ever got, and that the university was one of the finest schools in the country, and that every member of the football team had a responsibility to represent the institution on and off the field with his best effort. Royal surely would have discussed academics too, since Texas was the first football program to put an academic adviser on its staff. After their brief meeting, excited and inspired, Freddie left Royal's office with a deep desire to play for the University of Texas (UT). Freddie's decision to become a Longhorn took no more than a few minutes.

Once Freddie was back in Wheat Ridge, a few of the coaches who had previously declined to recruit him reconsidered, based purely on the interest from Texas and Darrell Royal. Attention came from the University of Colorado, the US Naval Academy, and the US Air Force Academy. But Freddie's mind was made up. Texas was the school that had answered his prayers. The Texas coaches were the ones who had evaluated him based on his talent and heart instead of his size. And UT had one of the best football programs in the nation. Freddie and Bob signed their Southwest Conference letters of intent together at a dinner arranged for them at the exclusive Pinehurst Country Club.

Aware of Freddie's interest in playing ball at UT, Linda decided to apply to Texas as well. UT had a renowned Spanish department, the course of study she intended to major in, so Texas offered her vibrant possibilities, too. When she told him that she had been accepted and would attend Texas, Freddie was excited. After all those months of worrying, everything seemed to be working out very well.

Freddie recognized that his mother and father might not be as excited about Linda going to Texas with him as he was, so he looked for the best moment to tell them. Family dinners had always been the time for discussing big plans, so naturally it was at supper one spring evening when Gloria innocently inquired, "How is Linda doing?"

"Linda's been accepted to Texas," Freddie replied.

The table fell absolutely silent. Big Fred and Gloria had mixed emotions about Linda's decision to attend Texas. Big Fred was worried that Freddie might get distracted or lose his focus. Freddie's grades might suffer, or even his playing. He told Freddie that if this happened, there was "going to be an ass-kicking." In the end, he had nothing to worry about—Freddie was an intensely focused young man—but that worry hung over the table, even though Big

Fred and Gloria knew there was little if anything they could do about it. Freddie and Linda were growing up, after all.

In June, Linda went on a weeks-long trip to Mexico to study in a Spanish-immersion program. It was their first significant time apart, and Freddie missed her. Distance may or may not make the heart grow fonder, but it certainly throws certain feelings into stark relief. Freddie and Linda exchanged letters that summer, and one he wrote to her is particularly revealing in a number of ways—not just for his youthful zeal and affection, but also perhaps for the very thing Big Fred had worried about—Freddie becoming distracted:

> I'm so happy—I received four letters from you today. Hang tight—I've been writing you every day, but I get up before the Post Office opens and I get home after it closes. . . . I will never love you less, [always] the same as the day before—only more. . . . When you're home alone—make sure all the doors are locked, don't let anyone know you're home alone, and don't let anyone in the house unless they're the Sito family, comprendez? . . . Study hard and you can teach what you learn to me. It's going to be so great going to our university.
>
> > All my love and my life,
> > God bless you baby,
> > Freddie Joe

In the meantime, Freddie kept himself busy as he counted down the days until he joined the Texas Longhorn football squad for official team activities. He played baseball in a Denver league and worked in the Rickenbaugh Cadillac tire warehouse. The warehouse's manager, Frank Caputo, was a longtime friend of the Steinmarks. Moreover, the Steinmark family had recently begun to build a new home in South Denver in the Cherry Creek school district, on a piece of land given to them by Uncle Al. Big Fred believed that getting the children out of Wheat Ridge would give them a chance to be known as more than just Freddie Steinmark's sister or brother. The new lot was close enough to Freddie's work that he could conveniently get to the building site and help with the construction.

In June, Freddie received some further unexpected good news: the Cincinnati Reds had selected him in that year's baseball draft. Freddie never considered it seriously—he was thrilled with his commitment to UT—but it certainly served as a reminder that Freddie's dreams of playing professional sports were very much alive. Plus, at the very least, it would be something to tell his kids one day.

Finally, the day arrived for Freddie to leave. Everyone in the family had been filled simultaneously with excitement and dread at the thought of this moment. For a long time, most of the family's activities had orbited around Freddie and his athletic schedule, and now he was about to depart, leaving what felt like a giant hole in the closely woven fabric of the family. GiGi and P.K. hadn't been looking forward to it, though they knew it was the natural course of things. No one was sure how young Sammy would take it; he and Freddie had been near constant companions for about as long as Sammy could remember. Big Fred, the most stoic of the bunch, was already in the car in the driveway, waiting to take Freddie to the airport. Everyone else stood at the front door to say good-bye. Freddie wore a white shirt, jeans, and cowboy boots—as Texan an outfit as he owned.

This was not a day Gloria had looked forward to either, but she embraced it as the next step in Freddie's life. The closeness that Gloria and Freddie had shared during their first eighteen years together was more than that between a mother and her firstborn; they had become friends and confidants. Gloria started to well up as she said her final good-byes. "I have all the confidence in the world in you, honey," Gloria told him. "Never forget that. Remember, God gave you everything, just like the other guys, and whoever uses these gifts to the fullest comes out on top. Always. And always make God proud of you. Show those Texas boys what you've got from day one, just like you've always done. You're my champ, and I love you, and I'm going to miss you."

Just then, Sammy appeared. In his arms was a brown grocery sack packed with his neatly folded clothes. He was dressed just like Freddie, right down to the cowboy boots. Sammy cried out, "I'm ready to go, Freddie Joe!"

Gloria hid a smile. "Where do you think you're going?"

"I'm going to Texas with Freddie Joe!" Sammy beamed.

"Oh, honey," Gloria said. "You can't go with Freddie Joe, Sammy. Freddie Joe's going to college."

Tears filled Sammy's eyes. "But I always go with Freddie Joe."

Freddie dropped to a knee and pulled Sammy tight to his chest. "I'll see you in no time, Sammy Scott. You're all going to drive down and see me play, but now you have to be the man of the house and look after things when Dad's at work, okay?"

Sammy sniffed back his tears and nodded. "Freddie Joe," he asked, "Can I be on the sideline with you at Texas?"

"I'll see what I can do," Freddie said, and hugged his brother. "I promise."

When Freddie kissed him and stood, Sammy ran from the room, bawling.

"Go, honey," Gloria said. "Your dad's waiting in the car. I'm sure going to miss you."

As they drove to the airport, Big Fred tried to offer his son some parting wisdom. He told Freddie it was going to be different at Texas, that everyone would be talented, that everyone would be tough. He asked Freddie to make a promise to himself to give 100 percent effort on every play, every drill, every day. He reminded Freddie that all his life he had been a leader, and now he would have to start anew and rise up to become a leader, a leader in actions, not words. At the airport, outside the car, Big Fred hugged and kissed his son good-bye, then watched him walk away in his cowboy boots. Freddie disappeared into the terminal. Wheat Ridge was behind him, Texas ahead of him.

CHAPTER 6

YOU HAVE NO FRIENDS
ON THE FIELD

FREDDIE WOKE ON HIS HARD MATTRESS TO the bare walls and sparse furniture of room 246 in Moore Hill Hall. It was strange. Sammy wasn't sleeping in his bed. He couldn't smell the breakfast that Gloria prepared. No cool Colorado air came through the window. Instead, he awoke to the snores of his high school teammate and new roommate, Bob Mitchell, to a wave of Texas summer heat, and to his own nerves on his first day as a Longhorn. Freddie knew that he was in a new world, and a far larger world than the one that he had grown up in around Wheat Ridge.

For starters, he had become part of a long burnt orange line stretching back to the previous century. The Republic of Texas became the twenty-eighth US state in 1845. As part of the terms of annexation, Congress specified that Texas would retain control of its public lands, the only state in the Union granted such authority. Under this power, Texas established the Permanent University Fund in the state's 1876 constitution, setting aside nearly two million acres, including the forty in Austin that would become the main UT campus, for the benefit of public higher education in the state, including establishment of a "University of the first class." The wisdom of this action is difficult to overstate. Massive unknown mineral reserves were lying under all that land, and when oil was discovered in 1923 on university-owned land, the largest public university endowment began to germinate, today totaling an estimated $20.4 billion.

Construction of UT's Main Building commenced in 1881, with a grand proclamation by Ashbel Smith, president of the board of regents: "Smite the rocks with the rod of knowledge, and fountains of unstinted wealth will gush forth." The University of Texas officially opened its doors for business in September 1883, with twelve faculty members and 221 students.

UT's original colors were gold and white, but two female students introduced the now-famous burnt orange and white by bringing ribbons to a pep rally before a baseball game in 1885. The reason for the color change? The general store's shopkeeper gave them white, his most abundant color because of weddings, and orange, his slowest-selling color, because he had plenty to spare. Burnt orange and white became official in 1900 by a popular vote among alumni, faculty members, and students.

Unofficially called the "Varsity" or the "Steers" for many years, UT athletic teams were not christened the Longhorns until 1913, when J. J. Lutcher Stark popularized the name, embroidering "Longhorns" on the sideline warm-up blankets he donated to the team each season. In years to come, his son H.J. would make his own contribution to the university, establishing the Center for Physical Culture and Sports, which bears his name today.

In 1967, the city of Austin had a population of 223,000 people. In that same year, the school officially changed its name to the University of Texas at Austin. And with a booming, energized city surrounding the university, events of all stripes found huge crowds flooding the malls and greens—concerts, protests, and football games.

Soon after their arrival on campus, Freddie and Bob would have learned how to make the famous "Hook 'Em, Horns" hand signal— extend the index finger and pinky while tucking middle and ring fingers beneath the thumb, in the shape of horns. The story goes that in 1955 a student named Henry Pitts got his friend Harley

Clark Jr., the head cheerleader, to make the sign at a pep rally and declare, "This is the official hand sign of the University of Texas, to be used whenever and wherever Longhorns gather!" Wondrously, the hand sign stuck, and it was firmly in place when Coach Royal arrived on campus two years later.

Freddie was curious about everything, and he learned about UT's proud history. He was always reading something, and he sought to discover what he could about his surroundings. In part, this desire came from early advice given to him by Big Fred. "Don't just watch a game," his father instructed. "Watch a particular player, the same one every play, see how he reacts to different situations." This was his mandate—to be not just an observer but also an active learner—and Freddie applied the lesson to other experiences because it helped him perform in each facet of his life. It created a kind of harmonious relationship between him and his world, the kind of relationship upon which Freddie thrived.

He always enjoyed learning, but he had an incredible memory, too. He had what always seemed to me to be a massive repository of information. He picked up details quickly, stored them away, and was able to access them precisely, sometimes years after the fact. I suspect that these abilities were central to Freddie's success on the football field. He was the kind of player who didn't need to be corrected more than once. Freddie remembered what coaches told him. He noticed opponents' tendencies and filed them away. Use of these skills wasn't limited to the gridiron.

I remember an August night in the summer before our junior year of high school. Freddie, Roger Behler, and I were at Denver's Elitch Gardens amusement park. We were walking around, watching the girls, and feeling big, as only rising high school juniors can feel. As we passed the back entrance to the summer stock theatre, out stepped a man with a cigarette. Freddie stopped us.

"You guys know who that *is*?"

I looked. I had no idea.

"That's Tom Ewell!" Freddie said.

"Who?"

"Come on! He was in *The Seven Year Itch* with Marilyn Monroe!"

This was the summer of 1966. The *Seven Year Itch* had come out in 1955, when we were six years old. I swear, if Trivial Pursuit had been around at the time, Freddie would have been a champion at it.

In the fall of 1967, as Freddie got accustomed to life as a student on one of the largest and most active university campuses in the nation, he couldn't have missed the social and political tensions gripping students and citizens alike. The war was raging in Vietnam, the civil rights movement was in full swing, and social upheaval was sweeping across the country, driven largely by the youth culture as epitomized by hippies. Austin, like many cultural hubs around the country, would have been caught up in the political debates, social revolution, and student activism.

DESPITE TENSIONS IN THE LARGER WORLD, FREDDIE remained focused on what he was in Austin to do: get a degree and play football. He was one of sixty-five Yearlings—what they called the Texas freshman football team in the 1960s. Freshman teams across the conference practiced and played separately from the varsity. Young players were groomed and developed before being promoted to the more advanced squads. At football orientation on his first day on campus, after a quick checkup by the team's doctor, the coaches issued lockers, shoes, helmets, pads, and uniforms to each player. In addition, each freshman received two sets of "must-have" undergarments, T-shirts, and workout sweats, necessary for two-a-day practices in the hellish heat.

The players' conditioning was overseen by the head trainer, Frank Medina, known far and wide for pushing players to their limit and beyond in his own peculiar fashion. Medina was a character, and an intense one at that. He stood just shy of five feet tall and wore an overcoat that obscured his feet. When he walked, he seemed to glide, like some kind of phantom. But players who hated him in the midst of grueling workouts were often grateful for his work after the fact. Earl Campbell would give Medina credit for his Heisman Trophy: "He had more to do with it than anybody."

Freddie had set a personal goal for himself (one he shared with his father) to start every game he played at Texas. Passing by the varsity practice that first morning, he encountered upperclassmen who were much larger and much quicker than Freddie had anticipated. They were grown men. In addition to this, once on the field, Freddie found that his helmet and his shoes didn't fit. He felt uncomfortable in his uniform, which was troubling, since he knew instinctively that these types of equipment miscues limited one's ability to perform, even if only in a minor way. He also knew that as an outsider, one of the very few players recruited from outside Texas, he needed to excel. Freddie wanted nothing to stand in his way of executing, and those first couple of days of workouts included some mishaps and frustration because of the ill-fitting equipment. Freddie's need to prove his worth on the field and the adrenaline of being a new student far from home—the academic rigor, the freedom, the attempts to fit in—made his head spin during those first weeks on campus.

MEANWHILE, BACK IN DENVER, THE STEINMARK FAMILY was also adjusting to a different day-to-day dynamic. Freddie had been the emotional center of the household since Gloria had allowed Big Fred back into the home. Further complicating things was the absence of GiGi, who had remained with family friends, the Sanzalones, in Wheat Ridge so that she could finish high school there. GiGi had long been in charge of many of the household chores. Fred and Gloria's nest wasn't yet empty, but it was definitely quieter, and they suddenly had space in which to be alone with thoughts about their children.

During the first weeks he was away, Freddie tried to write to his dad as often as possible to keep him informed about how things were going in Austin. Big Fred responded with letters of encouragement. He would have preferred to talk with Freddie on the telephone, but long-distance calls were so expensive as to be unaffordable except for emergencies and a couple of short conversations each week, mostly on Sunday nights, when long-distance rates were cheapest. That September, in one of the earliest letters, Big Fred wrote:

Don't worry about the bad day you had, clothes not fitting, helmets and shoes. I'm sure you know enough to get the right fit. . . . Son, just relax on the field, easy does it, don't press and you will be all right. Just give it a 100% and everything will be OK. Study hard & play hard—by the time this letter reaches you, you will have had some contact and I'll bet everything is going better—Don't get it in your mind that anybody is better than you. They have only got two arms & two legs like you, and I'm sure you know what to do with yours. I sure would like to be watching some of those practices. . . . Keep your legs moving. Spin. Hit hard. Fake one way then another and above all don't forget to cut against the grain once in a while when you get them going the way you want—Keep playing—Well, that's all for now, waiting to hear from you.

    Love,
    Dad

Their written communications weren't much different from discussions they used to have at the supper table—the focus was football or whatever sport Freddie was playing at the time, then school, and then everything else. In a letter dated September 26, Big Fred offered Freddie more encouragement and included these words: "Don't forget, you have no friends on the field."

You have no friends on the field. This was another part of Freddie's personal credo. Once he crossed the sideline onto the playing field, it was all about the game. It was about competition. It was about winning. "He played to win," Big Fred later told a newspaper. "I always told him that if you play the game, you play to win. That's what they have scoreboards for. If you're just playing for fun, then turn off the scoreboard." To Freddie, this single-mindedness had to do with respecting the game and the spirit of competition.

"Oh, yes," Freddie's cousin Johnnyboy recalls, "Freddie was extremely competitive. When you were playing against Freddie, he was not your friend. But as soon as the game was over, you were friends again. Things might get pretty heated during the game, but as soon as it was over, it was over. It was like he had a switch he could turn on and off."

I recall something similar from the first time Freddie tackled me. We were boys on the same youth football team, scrimmaging in practice. He tackled me, and it was the hardest I had been hit up to that point in my life. Football players, no matter at what level their careers end, remember the times they were really walloped. We lay on the grass face-to-face after the collision, and I said, "Geez, Freddie!" He looked at me with a perplexed expression and replied, "Geez, what?"

That is the way it is supposed to be on a football field.

In one of Freddie's letters before the first Yearlings' game, he informed his family that he had been moved from running back to safety and return specialist, positions where the Texas coaches thought he was a more natural fit. Coach Akers explained the Longhorn strategy this way: "We recruited athletes as opposed to players. We'd let them find the position their skills were best suited for, whether offense or defense. Freddie loved playing football, and you knew wherever you put him in the mix, he was going to give you everything he had. I knew he could go both ways, because he understood what endurance was, and he prepared for it. You looked for guys like Freddie because that's where you find your leadership."

"COME ON, YOU KIDS," BIG FRED SHOUTED AS THE FAMILY piled into the '65 Ford Mustang after work on Friday and embarked upon the fifteen-hour ride to Austin for Freddie's game versus the Rice Owls. "Get in the car! This bus is leaving, and if you're not on it, you don't go."

Big Fred did all the driving. He remained at the wheel through the night and into the sunrise. One by one, Gloria and the kids would fall asleep. If he got tired, he would pull off the road for a quick nap before resuming the journey. Gloria never worried about their safety. Big Fred could defend them if necessary. The trips in the Mustang to see Freddie play became a family tradition over the next few years. On the outskirts of Austin, Big Fred would find a motel where everyone could shower and, if time permitted, rest a little. Then it was off to the game.

The Steinmarks arrived at the stadium early enough to see Freddie for a few minutes before he went into the locker room to get suited up for kickoff. Sammy ran for his brother, calling out, "Freddie Joe, Freddie Joe! Did you get me a sideline pass?"

"Hi, Sammy Scott! How are you?" Freddie hugged Sammy and then greeted the family.

Big Fred smiled. "Are you ready, son?"

"You bet."

Sammy tugged on his brother's leg asking again, "Did you get me that sideline pass?"

"Well," Freddie said. "I spoke with Coach Ellington, but no answer yet."

Coach Ellington was just then passing by the family. He shook hands with Big Fred and greeted Gloria and the girls.

Freddie reintroduced Sammy, saying, "Coach, remember that thing I talked to you about?"

Sammy later recalled how he locked in on two strings hanging out of Coach Ellington's shirt pocket, hoping it was a sideline pass for him. Cutting right to the chase as only a boy with a one-track mind could do, Sammy asked, "Is that something for me?"

Coach Ellington made a show as if he were surprised by what was in his pocket. Then he pulled the pass out and said, "Well, look at this. It's a sideline pass for you, Sammy."

Sammy shouted with glee. By the time the game started, he was on the sideline, looking as official as possible, a towel thrown over his shoulder, as he gazed out on the field.

With his family in the stands and Sammy by his side, Freddie played a great game, making twelve unassisted tackles and intercepting three passes. After the final whistle, Coach Akers found Sammy and Freddie together. The sideline pass hung proudly from Sammy's belt loop. "Freddie," Akers said, "if you play like that each time your little brother is on the sidelines, well then we might need to have a ticket waiting for him at the Denver airport every Saturday morning."

The freshman season was a short five games, but the family made it to three of them, and those weekend trips provided important moments of interaction for Sammy and his brother. Freddie encouraged him not only to advance his football skills, but to concentrate on school as well. Freddie could show him how he was doing himself, providing an example for his young brother. They kept in touch throughout the semester and between visits, reminding each other to work hard. Sammy, in a letter to Freddie later that school year, proudly displayed his grades for Freddie's consideration:

> How are your grades coming along? . . . This grading period I got as follows: Reading—B, Math—B, Spelling—A . . . Momma isn't feeling to [sic] hot. Everybody else is feeling okay . . . Wheat Ridge beat Lakewood and everybody else . . . God bless the best brother in the whole world.
> Love,
> Sammy

For the remainder of the fall semester, Freddie worked hard both on the field and in the classroom. His performance in the secondary was more than solid, and he was fast becoming a team leader. Alternatively, Bob Mitchell saw little playing time, and his frustration was rising. Mitchell was the high school player with dozens of scholarship offers, yet here he was struggling to even get on the field, whereas Freddie was developing into a key player. As Mitchell continued to flounder, he and Freddie had several long talks about their futures with football. Mitchell's doubts kept growing until they reached critical mass; despite Freddie's encouragement, he was about to quit the team. Mitchell took an important trip to San Antonio to seek advice from his brother, Mark, who was training as an army helicopter pilot at Fort Sam Houston. Mark was about to ship out and join the fighting in Vietnam. Bob couldn't know it at the time, but it would be the last time he ever saw his brother. The last thing Mark told him was: "Don't quit. See this thing through."

Mitchell stuck it out with the Longhorns, eventually finding his niche as an offensive guard. The varsity team struggled in 1967, but the Yearlings were electric over their short season, finishing undefeated for the first time in seven years. In five games, Freddie returned 22 kicks for 371 yards and intercepted 4 passes. Dick Collins, an Austin sportswriter, called him "UT's Defensive Ace." With a successful first football season at Texas in the books, Freddie prepared himself for the next chapter.

BY THE SPRING SEMESTER, FREDDIE WAS FULLY SITUATed at UT. He had settled into a routine of catching an occasional meal with Linda, studying, attending class, and going to mass. Spring also meant baseball season. Freddie had always wanted to play two sports, but most universities had given him the impression that they preferred their athletes to play only one. Texas, however, as he later said, "not only didn't discourage me from playing more than one, but they like you to play two sports." With this understanding, Freddie started spring baseball practice.

Freddie loved baseball. It was so different from football, and spring training on the diamond created a wonderful counterbalance to the hard-hitting energy of fall practices on the gridiron. He knew that college baseball was the purest rendition of the game, the highest level of amateur ball. Most play for their love of the game, and what a beautiful game it is. The game has no time limit, having been conceived never to end in a tie. The outfield theoretically stretches into infinity, and the infield forms a diamond. The four bases are set ninety feet apart, forming a perfect square. The layout of a baseball field demands from players a harmony of speed, instinct, finesse, and particular athletic abilities. The game is layered with competitive strategies that resemble simple moves on the surface, but when plumbed to their depths reveal a complexity beyond that of chess. The game—and its most demanding element, hitting—requires Zen-like hand-eye coordination. These were the elements that had intuitively attracted Freddie to the game since his days as a child, just as they had drawn his father and grandfather before him. These were the elements that impelled Freddie that spring to pick up his glove, put on his cleats, and step onto UT's Clark Field.

The expansive Longhorn tradition in baseball goes back to 1896. The spring of 1968 marked Cliff Gustafson's first year as head coach. Unbelievably, Texas had had just two head coaches in the seventy-two years before Gustafson's tenure. As of 2015, Texas has had only four (including Augie Garrido, the current skipper). Freddie, early in practice, established himself as a player with potential, though the Longhorns were particularly deep and talented at the middle infield positions. By the end of the season, the Longhorns had taken the Southwest Conference championship, gone to the College World Series, and finished with a final record of 23–11. Freddie was a reserve player and pinch runner.

THE BASEBALL PARK WAS A WONDERFUL PLACE TO SPEND the spring season, but in many other ways the spring of 1968 was an especially turbulent time in the world outside campus.

On April 3, in the pews of the Mason Street Temple in Memphis, Tennessee, the audience witnessed—and offered spontaneous responses—as Martin Luther King Jr. delivered a speech with a prophetic message:

> Well, I don't know what will happen now. We've got some difficult days ahead. But it really doesn't matter with me now, because I've been to the mountaintop. And I don't mind. Like anybody, I'd like to live a long life. Longevity has its place. But I'm not concerned about that now. I just want to do God's will. And He's allowed me to go up to the mountain. And I've looked over, and I've seen the Promised Land. I may not get there with you. But I want you to know tonight, that we, as a people, will get to the Promised Land. And so I'm happy tonight. I'm not worried about anything. I'm not fearing any man. Mine eyes have seen the glory of the coming of the Lord.

On the next evening, while King stood on the balcony of his room in the Lorraine Motel, a single bullet ripped through his jaw, severing his jugular vein, two arteries, and a vertebra in his neck. The force of the impact tore off his tie and propelled him against the wall.

The bedrock of the country shook. Everybody felt it, including Freddie and Linda and Bob in Austin.

Two months later, on June 6, another assassination jarred US society. Sirhan Bishara Sirhan, a Palestinian-born self-proclaimed anti-Semite, shot Robert F. Kennedy with a revolver, at point-blank range, in the kitchen of the Ambassador Hotel in Los Angeles. Intending to hit him in the face, he was later quoted as saying, "[But] that son-of-a-bitch turned his head at the last second." Sirhan was instantly brought to the ground by those in the room, including the Los Angeles Rams defensive lineman and Kennedy friend Rosey Grier.

Two days later, an ex-convict named James Earl Ray, using a passport in the name of one of his three aliases, was apprehended at London's Heathrow Airport while attempting to board a plane for Brussels. Ray cried with his head in his hands as officers from Scotland Yard arrested him for killing King. The FBI had discovered that Ray checked into the rooming house opposite the Lorraine Hotel shortly before King's murder, and was seen fleeing the area right after the crime. Ray's fingerprints were found on the rifle he left at the house and in the getaway car.

Two assassinations of influential leaders. And although the two assassins were apprehended, their capture provided little solace for an America still bruised from President John F. Kennedy's assassination in Dealey Plaza less than five years earlier.

WHEN FREDDIE RETURNED TO DENVER THAT SUMMER, there was no denying that he was a slightly different young man. He had just completed a successful year at UT, in athletics and academics. He and Linda had a strong relationship, and Freddie was learning more and more about himself and the world around him. The country might have been a volatile and troubling place in those years, but things were looking bright for Freddie Steinmark. His incredible hard work and dedication were paying off.

That summer, he fell into a familiar routine with family, friends, work, and training. Linda again went abroad to study, and between them a steady stream of letters flowed. Freddie worked at the Rickenbaugh Cadillac tire warehouse once again, spent time with Sammy, and continued to intensify his training and workouts. He knew he had a momentous year coming up, and he had a clear idea of what he would be walking into when he arrived for Longhorn training camp. He spent his summer with his sights fixed on the upcoming fall. He was determined to outdistance the others in Medina's grueling conditioning sessions. Once more, Freddie set a goal of working his way into a starting position that, as far as he was concerned, was his to win.

CHAPTER 7

NOBODY DOES IT BETTER

THE TEXAS HEAT WAS LIKE A LIVING THING. It scorched Freddie's throat and lungs. It blanketed him in a thick sheen of sweat. It challenged him on every coverage drill and wind sprint that he and his teammate Bill Zapalac ran together in an open field in Austin—weeks before regular team practices began. After enjoying the cool, thin air of Denver, Freddie had returned early to the sweltering humidity of Central Texas for exactly this reason: to acclimate himself to Austin's extreme summer heat. He knew that once official football training began in late August, he would be immersed in the grueling campaign of two-a-day practices—and he wanted to gain every advantage he could before then. Freddie described the agony of two-a-days: "The most punishing part of football . . . spending those two weeks practicing twice a day in miserable heat, rubbing blisters on your feet, dragging your bruises back to the dormitory and flopping down on the sack for maybe fifteen minutes' rest before it's time to go to a squad meeting or watch films. Nothing but twenty-four hours of football."

Like everything else Freddie did, he intended to excel in the Longhorns' harsh regimen of practices. Ever the underdog in size and weight, Freddie knew that this was where he could stand out. He could compensate for his small frame with the immensity of his effort and heart. It wouldn't be long before Coach Royal would be standing tall in the withering heat and urging his exhausted team on with a spirit of competitiveness. "I know this is tough," Freddie would recall him saying, "but a hundred miles east of here, the Aggies are going through the same thing. Up at Fayetteville . . . Arkansas is practicing twice a day just like we are and they're just as tired and sore as we are. Our success this fall will depend [on] if we're willing to work harder this particular day than the Aggies are working at College Station or the Razorbacks are working at Fayetteville." Freddie found encouragement in those words. He shared the dreams and aspirations of the Longhorn team, but also was driven by his personal goal: "I worked harder than I ever had before because I wanted Monzingo's job."

As a rising sophomore, Freddie wasn't about to be content in a backup role. His goal was to be a varsity starter, and Scooter Monzingo was the unlucky junior who sat squarely in Freddie's sights. Against long odds, Freddie spent the next weeks demonstrating his laser-like focus, working toward that goal of unseating the upperclassman starting safety. He had already proved himself to be nearly inexhaustible in practices—no matter how grueling— and now he threw himself into the workouts with redoubled effort. If practice started at eight in the morning, then Freddie would be there at seven. Monzingo was larger and more experienced, but Freddie would be faster, smarter, and more versatile. The Texas heat was going to soar regularly to temperatures past 105 degrees, and Freddie would be ready for it, unfazed. As he later wrote, "I *had* to be in shape all of the time because of my size and the extent of my abilities. . . . I could not lose if I tried harder than the other guy. It was like that thin edge the house has in roulette and dice."

Sure enough, when the end-of-summer practices commenced, they proved to be demanding. And sure enough, a fully acclimated Freddie seized his opportunity and excelled at every aspect of his game. His pass coverage was sharp and instinctive. His tackling proved ruthless. His punt returns were gutsy and agile. Coming off a strong freshman season, Freddie was third on the varsity depth chart for safety. By the end of the first full intersquad scrimmage, he had leapfrogged to the top of the roster.

In a moment of great personal triumph, as the 1968 regular season was about to begin, Freddie heard his name called out as starting safety for the world-renowned Texas Longhorns. Freddie had achieved his lifelong dream, with the added distinction of joining Tommy Nobis, a tenacious linebacker on the 1964 team, as the only two sophomores to start for Darrell Royal.

Now that his personal goal had been met, Freddie was in position to focus on the larger, more important goal: helping his team win. The Longhorns under Royal had closed out three lackluster campaigns; in 1965–1967, UT had gone 19–12—not nearly good enough. This was a crucial year for the team to prove itself.

The UT administration, the boosters, and the Texas Exes had intensified their scrutiny of Coach Royal; there were whispers that he should be replaced. The enormous pressures on a head coach are difficult to fully articulate or understand. Alumni demand championships, but those with a deeper understanding of the position recognize that the greatest pressure on a head coach to perform comes not from the alumni, but rather from within the man himself.

WITH EACH PASSING MONTH, 1968 RATCHETED FORWARD with a ruthless intensity. As conflict throughout the world increased, it almost surely became hard for the Longhorn players to focus on the game—and yet perhaps this made college football more important than ever. In the short stretch of weeks between the beginning of Freddie's summer workouts and when he was named starting safety, dramatic events crowded the world stage: Warsaw Pact troops swarmed across the border of Czechoslovakia in an ominous escalation of the Cold War; France detonated its first hydrogen bomb; and police clashed brutally with protestors outside the Democratic National Convention in Chicago. Meanwhile, the bloody Tet Offensive continued in war-torn Vietnam, and in America the Black Panthers and other extremist groups became increasingly militarized and engaged in large, deadly shootouts with police in several cities. It must have felt as if the world was coming apart at the seams outside the white lines and locker rooms of the practice fields and stadiums.

Even on the sheltered grounds of the University of Texas campus, this reality came creeping in as a brand-new university police force patrolled lanes and open areas for the first time in direct response to the horrific shootings just two years prior. The gruesome memories of Charles Whitman's ninety-six-minute killing spree were still fresh. The UT student had gunned down forty-three students and passersby from the top of the University of Texas Tower; thirteen of his victims died. Although similar incidents have become tragically common in recent years, the Tower massacre was the first event of its kind in the United States—a public mass murder—and it garnered worldwide attention. "The cover of *Life* the next week made a big impression on all of us," UT alumnus Shelton Williams told *Texas Monthly* in 2006. "The photo, which was taken from the victim's point of view, was of the Tower, as seen through a window with two gaping bullet holes in it. From that vantage point it looked menacing, even evil—not the triumphant symbol of football victories we were used to."

Freddie, Coach Royal, and the rest of the team did their best to shut out these distractions, but there was no mistaking the pressures that were inevitably building, pressures that came to affect the team in more ways than one. Within this context, many people thought of football as a frivolous distraction. How could people spend so much time, money, and energy on a game while the world was so wracked by political upheaval, violence, and uncertainty?

The response that Freddie, Coach Royal, and many others would later come to understand is that this is *exactly* when the traditions of a time-honored sport become invaluable to a nation. In the face of such widespread fear, the green field of play, with its neat lines and clear rules of engagement, with its all-American boys, mascots, marching bands, and cheerleaders, with its legendary rivalries, its heroes, its victories, its heartbreaks, its truly meritocratic nature, was more than just a setting for a game. It was a uniquely American gathering place, a realm of optimism, a showcase of competitive spirit, an idyllic locale for a display of skill, grit, and determination that people all over the nation could support and find comfort in. The team that boasted remarkable young men like Freddie Steinmark went on to become not just a footnote in football history, but a rich chapter.

Before they could become legends, however, the Longhorns had to start winning. Their 1968 season opener was against the University of Houston, which was ranked eleventh in the nation and boasted some of the best players in the country. In particular, the Cougars had a pair of speedy split ends who were constant scoring threats, along with one of the nation's best running attacks. In other words, Freddie and his defensive teammates had their work cut out for them. The responsibility to execute was acute, as revealed in an *Austin American-Statesman* article written from a series of pregame interviews: "Freddie Steinmark, the rookie safety, said he'd just take things as they come. 'We'll just play it the way the coaches have been telling us. We'll play our regular techniques and just play the keys as usual.' The idea, Steinmark allowed, is not to let anyone get behind you." As Freddie sat with Ed Fowler, the sports reporter, for his first set of interviews as a starting Longhorn, he must have felt a great rush of pride and excitement. He had no way of knowing how fateful these words would become, how they foreshadowed his final on-field moments as a football player just fifteen months later, when he would make the last play of his career.

SEPTEMBER 21, 1968, WAS WARM AND RAINY—PERFECT conditions for what many fans would later call "a clash of champions," referring to the two star halfbacks of the game. Texas Memorial Stadium overflowed with fans and the usual pregame cacophony of marching band anthems, cheering, and jeers. As underdogs, the Houston Cougars had everything to gain from a road victory, and as the fourth-ranked team in the nation, the Longhorns had much to lose if they didn't put this one in the win column.

Finally, it was the moment Freddie had been dreaming of for so many years: he came streaming through the tunnel into Texas Memorial Stadium and onto the field with the rest of the Longhorns to begin his starting career with one of the great teams in college football history. This game, however, did not go exactly according to plan. The two teams pounded each other with ruthless ground attacks, the Cougars famous veer offense versus the Longhorns' brand-new wishbone. Houston halfback Paul Gipson traded runs and touchdowns with UT's Chris Gilbert. Murray Chass of the Associated Press was impressed enough to draw comparisons with the emerging superstar O.J. Simpson of the University of Southern California: "O.J., however, did not overshadow the play of Gilbert and Gipson in what some people called the championship game of the Southwest. Both had a lot to do with the 20–20 tie that resulted from the clash between the nation's Number 4 team, Texas, and the Number 11 team, Houston."

Although ending in a draw, the game could easily have been much worse for the Longhorns if not for some heroic plays by the young safety Freddie Joe Steinmark. Most notably, Freddie came up with a critical stop on the powerhouse Gipson, dropping him in his tracks as he was about to rip off a scoring run. Then, in the final minutes, Freddie swooped in for a beautiful, game-saving interception. There it was again—Freddie's delivery of fourth-quarter heroics.

With game one barely in the books, Freddie was already turning heads. The press corps certainly took notice of the new youngster: "One of the UT's out-of-staters, safety Fred Steinmark, broke in Saturday with a strong debut," wrote Lou Maysel, sports editor of the *Austin American-Statesman*. Maysel also observed, "The two eye-catching defensive plays by Steinmark, who also handled two short punt returns, were a saving tackle on Paul Gipson when he was just about to break for a touchdown in the second period and a pass interception that stopped Houston's last scoring effort." Even the Longhorns' star running back, Chris Gilbert, was asked about the young safety and his fiery play: "Freddie's a good open-field tackler. . . . He's hard to fake out and he keeps his position well."

While the game marked an auspicious beginning for Freddie,

the tie with Houston was a disappointing start to the season for the team. Looking to piece together the combination that would establish real dominance on the field, Coach Royal's newly unveiled offense had hoped for supremacy, but was denied. The new, option-based offense had debuted, yet the highly recruited quarterback "Super Bill" Bradley struggled with it. The rumors about Coach Royal instantly increased—in direct proportion, it seemed, to the level of the team's performance. Another piece of the puzzle had to come together.

One week later, the Longhorns (surprisingly, without the UT marching band, much to the chagrin of their fans) flew four hundred miles above the rolling Hill Country and the High Plains of the Panhandle to Lubbock to take on the Red Raiders of Texas Tech at Jones Stadium. Once again, the game did not go according to plan. Before the day was over, Freddie would experience the sensation of losing a football game while wearing a Texas uniform.

This time, the wishbone offense with Bradley at the helm stuttered and utterly collapsed, leaving the defense to fend off the Red Raider onslaught for long stretches. Unable to score a single point in the first two quarters, the Longhorns were down 21–0 at halftime.

Coach Royal was so frustrated that he was moved to action. Scott Henderson, sitting next to Freddie in the visitors' locker room, recalls that every player was full of anxiety—all sensing that something had to change. Scott remembers feeling a great sense of responsibility as Coach Royal gave his players a speech focusing on the heritage of being a Longhorn, of giving every ounce of effort out on the field. It was the perfect moment for the coach's popular expression: "Now, God does determine size, strength, and speed, but you determine how hard you try."

At the start of the second half, Royal made a bold move. He believed in his new offense, but a critical detail was missing—the chemistry was just not right. Standing on the sideline, Royal reached out and grabbed the feisty backup quarterback James Street by the arm. Street later recalled: "[Coach Royal] looked for a minute as if he were having second thoughts about putting me in. Then he looked me straight in the eye and said, 'Hell, you can't do any worse. Get in there.'" During the second half, under Street's leadership, Texas scored 22 points, but UT lost 31–22.

Although Street sparked the offense into action, the change of quarterback wasn't enough to overcome the scoring deficit. Still, the results were encouraging. Street instinctively played to the new offense's strengths. He was known as a prankster, so the new offense must have been a delight for him with its feints and fakes, with its dueling halfbacks and triple-option threats that flummoxed opposing defenses. No defense knew what Street was going to throw at it next, or how to stop him. No one had ever seen an offense quite like this, and for the first time it began to live up to its potential. Coach Royal had discovered the trump card in the hand he was holding: the joker.

After the game, Freddie, disappointed and dejected, walked off the field and into the locker room. Little could he know that he would never experience that feeling again. Freddie and his teammates were unaware that the Longhorns were about to begin one of the most successful winning streaks in all of football history, a run of thirty straight victories that would include two national championships. Freddie wasn't just playing safety for a top program—he was helping build the foundation for a football dynasty.

There is one word to describe how this all came together so perfectly: wishbone. During the previous summer, Coach Royal had asked his offensive coordinator, Emory Bellard, to devise a new offensive system. There was no mistaking the reason for the directive: if Texas didn't score more points and win more games, Royal and his staff might well be sent packing. What Bellard invented was both generally innovative and specifically tailored to Texas's strength of fielding three strong running backs. Partly inspired by full-house backfields he had seen in his high school coaching days, Bellard created a playbook that would expand beyond Texas and, for a time, become the dominant offensive strategy in college football.

It worked by placing the fullback close to the line, directly behind the quarterback. Two halfbacks lined up a yard behind him (seen from above, the formation looked like an inverted *Y*). The entire playbook was built around a "triple option" running play—depending on isolated defenders' choices, the quarterback, the fullback, or a halfback would end up with the ball.

With the snap, the quarterback stuck the ball in the fullback's belly, as if on a quick dive play. The defensive end, however, was intentionally left unblocked, and the quarterback watched him. If the defensive end crossed the line of scrimmage into the backfield, the quarterback let the fullback take the ball for a quick gain of at least a few yards. If the defensive end crashed toward the fullback, the quarterback pulled the ball and ran down the line of scrimmage. One of the halfbacks went out ahead as a lead blocker, and the other ran parallel with the quarterback. The next free defender, either a linebacker or a defensive back, had to choose to take either the quarterback with the ball or the free halfback. If he chose the quarterback, a quick lateral to the halfback was meant to net a big gain. Everything was geared toward a brief one-player advantage. Ultimately, the concerted running efforts set up the potential for crippling big plays on play-action passes.

Texas, over the 1965–1967 seasons, averaged around 20 points a game. In 1968, with this new offense, the team averaged 34.3 points, two touchdowns better per game. This figure included the opening-game tie and second-game loss, which accounted for Texas's lowest scores of the season. Once James Street became the starting quarterback in game three, versus Oklahoma State, the new offense hit its stride, scoring fewer than 35 points only twice for the rest of the season—gaudy offensive numbers in any era of football.

Bellard and Royal never officially named their new offense. It was the *Houston Chronicle* sportswriter Mickey Herskowitz who, during a postgame press conference, compared the formation to a "wishbone." The name stuck. Everywhere Royal went, people asked him about his revolutionary offense. By all accounts, Royal gave full credit to Bellard for inventing it and Herskowitz for naming it.

The wishbone offense was eventually adopted by Bear Bryant at

Alabama and Barry Switzer at Oklahoma. Seven of the teams that won or shared the national championship from 1969 to 1979 were wishbone teams. Football has always been a sport of innovation; teams are forced to constantly seek slight schematic advantages. Coaches who develop previously unimagined strategies (for example, the forward pass, the shotgun formation, the wishbone) are hailed as geniuses in the sports media. Yet the wishbone is unique in that it took more than a decade for defenses to sufficiently adapt to it. Finally, only great leaps forward in overall size, strength, and athleticism ended the wishbone's heyday.

The genetic fragments of the wishbone can still be found in the spread option offenses popular with college football teams—the formations look different, but the ideas are essentially the same. And a variation on the wishbone, called the "flexbone," has become the standard offensive scheme for schools such as the US Air Force Academy and the US Naval Academy—colleges where Sammy Steinmark would one day coach offensive players using the principles initially laid out by Bellard. As it turned out, the schemes underlying the wishbone have become the soundest strategy available for undersized teams to remain competitive with larger, more physically gifted teams. It is not uncommon, now, to hear a coach at a so-called bigger school lament a game pitting his team against one of the rare ones running the last vestiges of the wishbone. This is the kind of fact, certainly, that underdogs like Freddie Steinmark and Darrell Royal (a "small" player in his time as well) would have been proud of today.

ALL FREDDIE COULD HAVE KNOWN FOR SURE IN THE week following the Texas Tech game, however, was that he needed to get his "A" game ready for Oklahoma State. His team required a win if it was going to salvage the season, and he wasn't about to let all his hard toil in the heat of summer go to waste before the weather even cooled.

Freddie's top performance, combined with the newly clicking offense, did the trick. In front of a roaring home crowd, the Longhorns beat Oklahoma State 31–3. Despite the lopsided final score, it was a clutch, hard-fought win. The game remained close into the fourth quarter, when the Cowboys were just inches from seizing momentum and making it a one-score game. That was when Freddie and his teammates shut the door on their opponents, when the defense made a great stand. As Lou Maysel declared in the *Austin American-Statesman,* "The Texas secondary of Ronnie Ehrig, Fred Steinmark, and Denny Aldridge held down the OSU air game." The Cowboys completed only 12 of 31 pass attempts for 125 yards. Maysel went on to detail the terrific fourth-quarter stop: "Aldridge and Steinmark came up with two picture plays on OSU's best threat of the night, a 72-yard drive that stalled out at the Texas eight at the start of the fourth period when the score was still 17–3. Aldridge shocked end Ted Dearinger and knocked him loose from a short Johnson pass at the five-yard line and Steinmark swept Dearinger's feet out from under him on fourth down. . . . The quick hit limited the pass completion to three yards and it was inches short of a first down."

Football, for this very reason, is known as a game of inches. As with many sports, victory is not won in a single moment or a single effort, but in the compilation of play after play, inch after hard-fought inch. When the result is as lopsided as this one was, it can become easy to overlook the hundreds of crucial things that had to happen throughout the game for it to end up as it did. Freddie never forgot that, however. He was a master of extra effort, fighting for every play, battling for every inch, and that was what set him apart and contributed so much to the Longhorns' historic run of victories.

In their fifth game of the season, the seventeenth-ranked Longhorns hosted the ninth-ranked University of Arkansas in what turned out to be a prelude to the "Game of the Century," which occurred the next year. Freddie's big plays in the secondary helped propel his team to a 39–29 victory over the Razorbacks. And once more, Freddie turned heads on the sidelines and in the press box: "[Quarterback] Montgomery, a slender sophomore from Carrollton (TX), looked unstoppable in the first half until Texas' Fred Steinmark halted an Arkansas drive with an interception at the

Texas 27. It may have been the turning point of the game. Stein-mark ran it back to the Texas 49."

By game seven of the season, the wishbone offense had been honed into a lethal weapon, supported by the strength of the defense. The Longhorns tallied 547 yards of offense against the thirteenth-ranked SMU Mustangs, spurred by an early Steinmark interception that set up their first score of the game. With that win, the University of Texas clawed its way back into the national top ten.

NOVEMBER'S MORNING LIGHT SLOWLY WORKED ITS WAY through the trees and patio windows into the kitchen. Gloria placed a large bowl on the counter next to the sink, poured out a mound of flour, added water and eggs, and put in some olive oil and salt—just as her mother had done every time she made fresh pasta—and began kneading the dough. She heated up the pan to fry the sausage and brought out a large pot that she filled with to-matoes, water, oil, garlic, seasonings, and herbs. Gloria did all this with a love built upon generations.

As Gloria worked the pasta dough through her fingers, she sang softly so as not to wake any of her family. Her mind drifted to thoughts of Freddie in Austin, how he had played so well the day before, what the future might hold for him. She thought about her two daughters and what might be in store for them: college? where? marriage? She thought of young Sammy and his aspira-tions to be a ballplayer like his brother.

Her thoughts then returned to the dough. It was already get-ting late; she needed to cut the strands of spaghetti, complete the sauce, and prep the salad, since it would soon be time to leave for church. Sunday was a day of ritual: mass, followed by an afternoon meal with family and friends, some quiet time afterward, and, fi-nally, an evening phone call from Freddie.

In the late afternoon, the Steinmark family gathered around the dinner table. Joining them were Uncle John, Aunt Betty, and their son, Johnnyboy. Their conversation eventually worked its way to Freddie Joe and the strong year he was having at Texas. Big

Fred smiled. He was eager to speak with his son later that evening. Big Fred wanted to congratulate Freddie on winning the game and talk about his fine performance, particularly his pace-setting interception.

THE NEXT WEEK, FREDDIE HELPED HIS TEAM SECURE A 47–26 win over the Baylor Bears. Ed Fowler of the *Austin Statesman* quoted Coach Royal in a postgame interview: "Royal singled out safety Freddy Steinmark as his top defensive performer. . . . 'He had about nine unassisted tackles,' Royal said, 'and that doesn't speak too well for the front.'" It did speak well of Freddie's efforts, however, and his ability to assist with plays and situations all over the field.

The season wasn't without its embarrassing moments. In the same game in which Freddie was recognized as a defensive standout, he botched a punt return, which led to an entertaining moment that was captured in the media for posterity. Blackie Sherrod of the *Dallas Times Herald*, who would later assist Freddie in penning his memoir *I Play to Win*, wrote: "A comedy of errors gave Baylor its final points. Bear punter Ed Marsh sailed a mighty punt downfield that Fred Steinmark tried to catch over his shoulder on his own 18. He fumbled and a dozen lads booted the ball this way and that until it wound up in the end zone where Derek Davis covered it for a Baylor touchdown. Steinmark had his mitts on the ball three times during the tangle, but could never capture it." Andy Yemma of the *Austin American-Statesman* interviewed Freddie after the game: "'I shouldn't have tried to catch it,' Steinmark admonished himself, 'they teach us not to try to catch them over the shoulder.' Steinmark tried to field the ball at the UT-20, then saw it bounce off his hands and start a Mexican jumping bean bounce routine. The resulting scramble was the wildest since the Democratic convention."

BY THE END OF THE SEASON, AND DESPITE A RARE FLUB, Freddie had made a mark on the UT football program larger than many would have predicted. His Longhorns finished the season as the fifth-ranked team in the nation. Before the team's Cotton Bowl matchup against the Tennessee Volunteers, the national media ran a feature on Freddie. The piece highlighted not only Freddie's contributions, but the admiration he had earned from his head coach as well: "Despite his star status, most colleges were not interested in him because he was so small. But Texas coach Darrell Royal, perhaps recalling that All-American James Saxton weighed only 165 pounds, happily offered a scholarship to this 165-pound back whom he has said 'runs like a knuckleball.'"

When asked about making the switch from offense to defense, Freddie offered a great glimpse into his unfailing dedication to team achievement and his personal competitiveness: "You don't get to handle the ball as much on defense, in fact you can go through a game and not handle it at all. But you're out there competing against a man. There's satisfaction in being able to keep him from going all the way on you."

It was December 1968. Freddie was on top of the world. At almost the exact same time that he stood shining in the limelight of success on the football field, two remarkable things were happening outside the world of cleats, pads, and pigskin. First, US astronauts in Apollo 8 reached the far side of the moon, becoming the first human beings to look upon the entire earth from outer space. And second, in the small universe of Freddie's body, a genetic time bomb went off in the tip of his left femur. Unbeknownst to him, a cluster of cancerous cells began its insidious work.

Meanwhile, Freddie and his team trounced the Volunteers 36–13 in the Cotton Bowl that New Year's Day. Ending the 1968 season on a high note, the Longhorns were poised for a historic run at the national title in the year to come.

CHAPTER 8

WORLDS COLLIDE

A T TIMES, WORLDS COLLIDE SLOWLY. WHEN hippies, activists, and other pioneers of the 1960s counterculture first appeared around the University of Texas campus, they were considered something of a sideshow—curious in their appearance, their manners, and their missions. The dominant culture still consisted of conservative, clean-cut, working-class folks who labored hard Monday through Friday and took their families to church on Sundays. Even the Austin nightlife was rooted in old-school country and honky-tonk traditions.

By the winter of 1969, however, this collision of outlooks was creating serious tension in the local fabric, a fact not lost on Freddie and his teammates—especially teammates such as Bob Mitchell, whose brother Mark was flying helicopters for the US Army in Vietnam. Antiwar activists took a hard, and often personal, line against members of the military.

Tensions in Austin were rising along with the body counts in Southeast Asia. The previous year was by far the bloodiest for US forces, with almost 17,000 American soldiers killed in a conflict that had no clear political goals and no end in sight. Freddie, Bobby, and the rest of the Longhorn football players largely tried to block out the distractions as they focused on sports, studies, and their college lives, but it was getting harder to do. Protests roiled the campus, marijuana smoke permeated dorm parties, and conflicts became more and more intense as city officials, university directors, and police began to crack down on activist groups, "radical" publications, drug use, and even local businesses that catered to the left-wing set. It became commonly known throughout Austin that the number one moving violation was driving with long hair. Hippies were pulled over by police, searched, and arrested at an alarming rate as part of the aggressive response to their activities. The gradual evolution of these two worlds slowly colliding allowed Freddie to navigate these tensions with a balanced perspective.

Other times, however, worlds collide violently. These are the moments that no one can sidestep, no matter how quick they are in pass coverage. For example, Freddie had no idea, as he walked down the hall toward his dormitory room on the evening of January 17, that tragedy was waiting behind his closed door. By now, he had walked that hall hundreds of times, a pattern that had grown as routine as warm-ups before practice. Who knows where Freddie's mind might have been as he made his way to his room— thoughts of his studies? An upcoming test? A disagreement with Linda? Or perhaps of the baseball season that he was looking forward to in the spring. Whatever he was thinking about, when he finally arrived, pushed his door open, and saw Bobby's face, Freddie was immediately jolted back into the present moment. Here was a friend reeling with anguish—Bob had just learned that his brother, Mark, had been shot down and killed in Vietnam.

The realization and grief were impossible to process in that instant, but the closeness of the two young men from Wheat Ridge was never stronger. Upon hearing of Mark's death, Freddie dropped to his knees and began praying. He made the sign of the cross and whispered, "Hail Mary, full of grace . . . pray for us sinners now and at the hour of our death, Amen." Afterward, Freddie and Bob talked into the night (and for weeks and months ahead) as Freddie did his best to console his friend. There wasn't much he could do to ease the pain of such a loss, but Freddie offered what he considered to be his greatest strength: his faith. Bob wasn't especially religious, but he was moved by Freddie's gesture and comforted by his friend's support. As the Longhorns' athletic trainer,

Spanky Stephens, recalls, "You know, the personality of Freddie was, like, magical. People would just be drawn to him when he'd start talking. We all admired his spirit, his spiritual life, and his faith in God." Bobby himself would recall that "Freddie was a great comfort to me."

Freddie led by humble example, not by preaching or offering judgment, and in so doing was able to sincerely offer empathy and compassion. He had met Mark and could appreciate why Bob looked up to his older brother with so much admiration. Mark was a good-looking, funny guy, and Bob's biggest fan. The terrible loss and pain that Bob felt touched Freddie deeply: how does one replace an older brother?

With Mark's passing, the war hit home for Freddie and Bob in a completely new way, filling them with gutfuls of mixed emotions. The Mitchell family was no stranger to the call of duty—Bob's father had fought at the Battle of the Bulge—but even so, it was hard to support the confusion of efforts that seemed to plague the Vietnam War. "I was upset with the way our government was playing the war," Bobby would later recall. "It was the old 'Fight it to win or get out,' and it was this political attacking and pulling back. You're either in it or you're not."

Unfortunately, Freddie did not live to see the end of the war; yet he and Bob saw an end to that long winter when, in March 1969, spring finally arrived, bringing with it another of Freddie's favorite pursuits—baseball. He was a changed young man by the time he stepped onto the diamond that season—and he would be challenged mightily once again before the year was over—but for now he could cherish playing America's pastime.

There were several Longhorn footballers on the university's baseball team, including quarterback James Street, a starting pitcher, and tight end Randy Peschel—an impressive .333 slugger. Freddie, however, had a tougher time finding his niche. Despite his strong play as an infielder in high school (resulting in his being drafted by the Cincinnati Reds, the offer he turned down), the team was already stacked with infielders—Freddie was thus designated a role player, filling in whenever necessary. This was a comfortable situation for him, as confirmed in that year's baseball media guide: "Appeared briefly with the Longhorns in '68 prior to football spring training . . . fine attitude and hustle make him a contender."

But in Freddie's sophomore year, when he had been a starting safety and leader on the football team, there were new pressures on him. As Ed Fowler pointed out in the *Austin American-Statesman*, "Like all sovereigns, King Football has its recalcitrant subjects. Street might fall into that category, but he swings enough weight to pull it off." Freddie, on the other hand, was a more loyal subject of the "king" of Texas sports. As Fowler went on to say, "Another gridder who likes to take his springtime pleasure on the diamond is safety/infielder Fred Steinmark. He has worked out with the baseball team this season but, not of Street's stature in the horsehide league, has opted to report for football spring practice."

Despite Fowler's tongue-in-cheek reporting, Freddie had a unique situation to deal with and more pressure than others to return to the football field sooner rather than later—he was the only returning starter from the defensive secondary. Coach Royal and the team needed Freddie to solidify that position group in the off-season. The other starters had graduated, and without some player leadership on the spring practice fields, it would be difficult to work out, train, and insert the rising underclassmen. It wasn't just the coaching staff that recognized the challenge. Lou Maysel observed in the *Austin American-Statesman*: "The Longhorns have one gnawing need, some help in the defensive secondary to go with safety Fred Steinmark."

Freddie knew that his fortunes were more closely tied to the football program than to anything else. He had the instincts and commitment to be an excellent team member, even when that required sacrifice and making challenging decisions. So he agreed to stop playing baseball, be redshirted for the remainder of the season, and return to the football field, where his contributions would be invaluable in rebuilding a defensive unit, solidifying his own position, and preparing for a national-title run in the fall.

Baseball, however, still occupied a place in Freddie's dreams, as he would later write: "I had hopes of playing either professional football or baseball." Thus, ever mindful of accomplishing one of those goals, he worked to keep his options open. Freddie continued to trigger some interest from several big league clubs, and the Office of the Commissioner of Major League Baseball sent him a letter in the spring of 1969: "Dear Mr. Steinmark . . . I am asking your cooperation in keeping this office advised of your status as a college baseball player. Will you please complete the enclosed questionnaire? . . . . If you are a student in a four-year college which plays baseball, and your birthdate falls between July 22, 1948, and July 20, 1949, your name will be selectable at the Free Agent Selection Meeting, June 4–5, 1970." Content with knowing that his baseball options were still open, that he could be drafted after his junior year, Freddie completed the questionnaire and focused on football.

WITH FREDDIE TAKING THE LEAD IN THE SECONDARY, the new players began to find their roles and show promise. Still, it was premature to make any significant predictions for the group, as Ed Fowler pointed out in the *Austin American-Statesman*: "Defensive backfield boss Fred Akers allowed that he likes the hustle of all his charges, but won't be able to seriously assay their ability until Saturday's first scrimmage. 'Of course Steinmark's ahead of everybody else at his position,' he said of his only 1968 starter returning."

By the end of spring drills, however, it was clear that Freddie was leading a talented squad. It was one thing to perform well in exercises and activities, but when it came to scrimmages and game simulations, the young secondary was beginning to soar. The local media wrote of the action on the field during the Longhorns' final drill week: "Defensive halfback Danny Lester went high to pick off a bomb Phillips intended for Speyrer and safety Fred Steinmark nailed a flat pass and returned nine and stepped in front of Speyrer to nab a bomb and returned 38 yards, both at Phillips' expense." They had speed, smarts, football instincts, and the ability to lay big hits and make big plays. Freddie and this defensive secondary were going to be a force to be reckoned with.

Freddie was at the top of his game and growing into a great leader on the field, yet he still displayed his trademark humility. When Ed Fowler, who had razzed Freddie for his lack of baseball prowess, interviewed the young standout about the revamped secondary, Freddie took a familiar tack:

> For Fred Steinmark, the Texas safety, it's a new ball game. "We've had to start over from the beginning," the sophomore Colorado product mused after Wednesday's practice. "I think we're coming along. We've had a couple real good scrimmages."
>
> But perhaps it's modesty that moves Steinmark to say the secondary has had to start all over. He is the one stabilizing influence, the only 1968 starter returning next fall. . . . So Steinmark is the old veteran of the three-deep now.

WITH SPRING DRILLS SUCCESSFULLY WRAPPED UP AND classes coming to an end, Freddie looked forward to spending a summer in Colorado, where he could relax, see his family and friends, and keep up with his off-season workouts and training. Back home, Freddie again went to work in the tire department of Rickenbaugh Cadillac. Freddie fell into the easy routine of hustling tires, working out, and playing summer baseball.

When the preseason football publications began to roll off the presses that summer, the Longhorns, and Freddie himself, earned page time and attention. *Texas Football*, the cherished publication of the state, declared the Longhorns the preseason favorite to become national champion—a prediction that proved accurate. The *Dallas Times Herald*'s sports editors predicted that safety Fred Steinmark would earn a spot on the 1969 All–Southwest Conference first team. Freddie had everything going for him, and he must have been thrilled to see these enthusiastic predictions in the sports news media. His future was bright. His family was supportive. Life was looking good. In fact, life was looking *great*.

In the midst of the preseason hype, Freddie had no way of realizing that the malignancy growing in the tip of his femur for the past six months was about to make its presence known. All Freddie knew was that he was enjoying his off-season and preparing for what he thought would be one of the greatest years of his young career.

On one clear July night while playing semi-pro baseball, he attempted to stretch a single into a double. The throw was a good one, a low laser beam, the ball and Freddie both converging on the same location. He pushed hard and slid into second, an instant before the ball struck the shortstop's glove with a pop. Freddie was safe, but with his leg extended, he felt a pop of his own—a spasm of pain in his left leg, just above the knee.

Freddie was no stranger to pain on the field, so he stood up and shook it off, thinking it was nothing more than a slight muscle pull. He had no way of knowing that this was the beginning of a long slide, that this pain would become a constant companion. Worlds collided slowly: Freddie's magnificent young life with the universe of rapidly multiplying cancer cells.

It wasn't long before the people who knew Freddie noticed that something wasn't quite right. First, Frank Caputo saw Freddie limping at work. Freddie's father commented on the limp during one of Freddie's workouts. And Linda asked about his limp when he visited her. Each time someone said something about it, Freddie just shrugged it off. "I wrenched my knee," was all he said, believing it to be true. A lingering charley horse, that was all.

In the waning days of summer, Freddie's teammate and good friend Scott Henderson visited Denver. They planned to work out together before returning to UT early so that Freddie could once again acclimate himself to the grinding heat before two-a-days began. With Scott's arrival, Gloria made fresh pasta, and the expanded family shared several meals together. There were conversations with Big Fred concerning football strategy and Freddie's and Scott's goals for the coming season. Sammy tagged along to their workouts when he could, and GiGi and P.K. enjoyed becoming friends with a dynamic upperclassman like Scott.

Two notable things happened while the good friends were together—one lighthearted and the other more serious. First, Freddie took Scott on a grand tour of the Denver area, including "all the places that had Steinmark lore connected" with them. At one high school stadium, Freddie included a long and exhaustive description of his performance in a game there, including how he had "scored five touchdowns and had three others nullified by penalties and made twenty unassisted tackles on defense." Scott listened patiently, but later found great amusement in the grandiosity of the presentation. It became a running joke of theirs. "[Scott] never let me forget that tour lecture," Freddie would remember. "He repeated it many times in front of my teammates."

Years later, people still remember how Freddie and Scott joked with each other. As the trainer Spanky Stephens recalls, "Freddie had this little mischievous part to him, and Scott had this wicked sense of humor. . . . It was a great friendship. When you'd see them together, they were always laughing and one-upping each other."

It wasn't all fun and games, however. Soon, Scott noticed the limp in Freddie's step as well. After leaving Denver, they stopped off at Scott's home in Dallas for a few days of conditioning before continuing on to Austin. The two Longhorn starters were working out together on a field at a school close to Scott's home when they ran across a few of the high school football players prepping for their upcoming season. They all decided to run some pass drills together: Freddie and Scott set up a basic defense, and the high school boys tried to run pass plays on them. Freddie was still adjusting to the 105-degree heat, but even that didn't explain the ease with which the younger boys seemed to slip past him. At first Scott thought that Freddie was going easy on the boys, letting them score some simple connections. But soon he realized that Freddie really was going all-out and that the speedster was simply getting beaten on the routes. "In retrospect," Freddie later recalled, "Scott said he noticed something that day, that those high school receivers with their simple maneuvers were having very little trouble escaping me. I wasn't aware of it."

And why would he be? This was the summer of 1969. Freddie was full of hope. His star was rising. His name was in the papers. He was preparing to play for one of the greatest teams in college history. Here, entering the hundredth season of college football, the Longhorns had a chance to do something special, and Freddie Joe Steinmark wasn't going to let some charley horse ruin the opportunity.

PART THREE
1969–1970

*Athletes are supposed to play
with pain.*

FREDDIE STEINMARK

CHAPTER 9

RUNNING HIS OWN SHIP

THE TEXAS LONGHORNS ENTERED THE SEA-
son amid high expectations. They began the year ranked
second in the country, behind Ohio State and just ahead
of perennial rival Arkansas. Still, many wondered whether the
vaunted wishbone offense could be as effective in its second season, now that the novelty had worn off. As Darrell Royal put it,
"We're going to find that people have gone over in the corner and
thought about it," meaning that he expected defenses to have or-
chestrated new countermeasures. With his characteristic sense of
humor, Royal reflected, "We didn't know what we were doing [last
year], so there's no way they could have." Of course, all the best
coaches show such signs of prudence—they believe in their teams,
but being the foremost experts, they also see the holes and know
the limits.

The expectations were there for Freddie Steinmark as well. A
seasoned veteran looking to build upon his solid 1968 campaign,
he had garnered impressive preseason accolades over the summer, and as the semester started, publications placed him on all-
American watch lists. Freddie's measured approach to the season,
however, reflected his coach's. "I've got a lot of work to do to get
ready," Freddie told the *Austin American-Statesman*. "There are a
lot of good ball players in the secondary. . . . I don't really feel better
about my situation than this time last year. There are a couple guys

pushing me for my position. Seems like I've got to go out and make the team every year."

A starting position needs to be earned, and one must never rest on past laurels. It is essential to remember the "you have no friends on the field" philosophy that was instilled in young Freddie Steinmark by his father. Those considerations, coupled with the fact that he was an undersized guy, acutely aware of how he had had to prove himself throughout his career, can help explain why Freddie believed he could never falter, and why the growing pain in his leg was something to keep to himself for as long as possible.

As it turned out, the 1969 Longhorns improved upon their previous season's success. In retrospect, it becomes difficult to overstate just how good this team was. That year, in seven of their ten regular-season games, the Longhorns led by at least three touchdowns at halftime—in a game where a twenty-one-point difference at the end of a contest can generally be regarded as a blowout.

The Texas defense was stifling, and there wouldn't be a better Longhorn offense on paper for thirty-six years. In 1969, the offense averaged 472.1 yards a game, and the defense allowed less than half that many. The Longhorns scored, on average, 41 points a game while only giving up 10. Simply put, the 1969 Longhorns were dominant in nearly every facet of the game.

After a strong set of practices in August and September, the first nine weeks of the season saw the Longhorns win handily, with the exception of a close win during week four against major rival Oklahoma. The ability to scratch and claw and win tough games often doesn't get nurtured in teams so frequently invincible, but true championship-caliber teams always find a way to win. Texas fell behind by fourteen points in the first quarter versus the Sooners, but the Longhorns ultimately came back and won the game 27–17. Freddie contributed an interception.

Aside from a big play or two like that one, though, Freddie's individual 1969 performance didn't seem to mirror the team's evolution. Whereas his 1968 statistics were more than solid—40 tackles,

5 interceptions, and 252 all-purpose yards—his 1969 output was diminished: only 12 total tackles, 2 interceptions, and 53 return yards. At first glance, his drop in stats would seem to confirm the extent to which Freddie's leg had begun to hamper him. Of course, stats alone cannot tell the whole story. Indeed, one sign of a truly good defense is that the safety—the last line of defense—doesn't have to make many tackles.

We are able, in hindsight, to understand the significance of the "pulled muscle" that Freddie felt in that summer baseball game, and of Scott Henderson's observations of Freddie's foot speed on that high school field in Dallas. Freddie, as a lifelong athlete, was familiar with aches and pains. If something hurt, he didn't think twice about it unless it physically kept him from being able to play. Soreness and stiffness were nothing to fret over. Nevertheless, Freddie indicates in *I Play to Win* that he began to be aware of a consistent pain during two-a-days.

Though Freddie was tight-lipped about it, others naturally noticed when Freddie arrived early at the practice field to take himself through extra calisthenics in order to warm up his leg. The coaches observed Freddie pull up slightly on certain plays, and Coach Akers brought it to Freddie's attention after their opening game with California. "I told him I had a pulled leg muscle," Freddie writes, "and I didn't want to aggravate it. He let me run my own ship after that." Although Akers later said that the 1969 season was the first time he had seen Freddie practice at other than full speed, he knew that Freddie would continue to give maximum effort come game day.

NEARLY TWO MONTHS EARLIER, ON AUGUST 1, FATHER Fred Bomar had begun his first day in service to the people of Austin as the pastor of St. Peter the Apostle Catholic Church, located six or so miles southeast of the UT campus. It was a tough day for the young priest.

For the previous eight years, Bomar had been the assistant pastor of St. Mary's Catholic Church in Temple, Texas. Dedicated to his parish, he had built a home for himself in a community that he loved. But his life was disrupted abruptly when the Austin diocese assigned him to St. Peter's, a post he initially viewed as a mistreatment by the church and the breach of a promise made by Bishop Louis Joseph Reicher. So frustrated was he with the decision that Bomar found it "hard to see the tiny parish as anything except the site of my final days as a Roman Catholic Priest." At times, however, there can be a certain divine providence to the obligations, duties, and path of a priest.

Fred Bomar grew up in Central Texas south of Austin, and upon graduating from high school, felt a call to the service of God. The Diocese of Austin (127 parishes in twenty-five counties) directed young Bomar to enroll in St. Mary's Seminary in Galveston for the seven years of study required to become a priest.

The history of the Catholic Church in Texas goes back to the Spanish conquest. In 1519, Hernán Cortés and his army conquered the Aztec Empire of central Mexico, and Pope Clement VII erected the Diocese of Mexico in 1530. Missionaries were sent to the frontiers of New Spain, and 130 years later, in 1659, the first churches were established in Tejas, Spanish Texas. In 1841, the Diocese of Galveston was established, with St. Mary's Cathedral becoming home to the first bishop in the Republic of Texas, which had gained independence from Mexico just five years earlier. After Texas joined the United States in 1845, the Diocese of Galveston was placed under the Archdiocese and Ecclesiastical Province of New Orleans.

Fred Bomar joined this long history when he was ordained a priest on March 28, 1960. As a new priest, he could trace his apostolic ancestry through Bishop Reicher, back to Bishop Christopher Edward Byrne (who had ordained a young Father Reicher), then back to Bishop John Joseph Glennon, and so forth in a line back to the first pope, Peter the Apostle, who was the namesake of Bomar's new parish. Peter, according to Catholic tradition, had been ordained by Jesus through the sacrament of the orders that Jesus gave to the twelve apostles during the Last Supper.

One of the final questions asked of Bomar during his ordination was this: "Are you resolved to consecrate your life to God for the salvation of his people?" The traditional response is "I am." And so holding this promise in mind, Bomar fulfilled his duty and began his pastoral service at St. Peter's. The saving grace for Bomar was a friendship that he had kindled several years earlier while in Temple. Bomar had become a good friend of the Temple High School football coach, Jay Fikes, who by chance was a friend of Coach Royal. When Royal visited Temple to recruit players and promote UT football among local civic clubs, Bomar would host dinners and cookouts to provide a venue to encourage supporters. Upon hearing of Bomar's arrival in Austin, Royal immediately drew him into the Texas football community, asking him to attend team functions and visit practices—in a way, making the priest an unofficial chaplain of the team. With this assistance from Royal, Bomar's outlook drastically improved.

One custom that Coach Royal and Father Bomar established was a Thursday-night cookout at the rectory of St. Peter's. The coach would bring ten football players—often, Catholics like Street and Henderson—over for a meal and socializing. At one of these Thursday-night dinners in the early fall of 1969, Bomar met Freddie. Around the dinner table at the rectory, the players would talk of their undefeated season, Saturday's upcoming game, and the dream of a national championship.

After meeting Bomar, Freddie often attended mass at St. Peter's. Forged in a deep connection with the venerable and sacred rituals of the Catholic Church, Freddie and Bomar established a relationship of respect and trust. This relationship would soon provide needed solace to Freddie and offer Father Bomar a sense of meaningful contribution.

As the season progressed, the level of pain that Freddie experienced fluctuated daily. In the last several weeks of the season, Freddie paid frequent visits to the training room and the whirlpool. Spanky Stephens recalls that Freddie's leg "would hurt, then it would feel good, then hurt." It was a perplexing injury to all involved.

In week six, the Longhorns crushed SMU, 45–14, but on a

touchdown pass completed in the middle of the field, Freddie was not even close to the receiver. Big Fred, who had traveled to attend the game, discussed this play with his son afterward. "Looks to me," Big Fred said, "that you've slowed up about a half step. You weren't meeting plays quick as you usually do." This stung Freddie a bit, but he finally admitted to his father that he was having a "little trouble" with his leg, probably just a calcium deposit. Freddie writes, "I could just feel Dad's memory clicking back to that limp I had in the summer" after the painful slide into second base. Big Fred continued to press his son, thinking perhaps of his own youthful struggles with injuries and the difficulties in recovering from them. He eventually made Freddie promise that he would have his leg seen by a doctor.

Of course, Freddie intended to wait until after the season. Scott Henderson recalls frequent conversations in which Freddie invoked Mickey Mantle as an inspiration. Mantle, who had long been one of Freddie's athletic heroes, was famous for playing with excruciating pain in his legs. If Mantle could do it, then, Freddie thought, he could too. "Sometimes," Freddie said, "the spirit is the same, even if the physical talent is on a smaller scale." And so although Freddie's stats weren't what he thought they should be, the victories were, and Henderson recalls Freddie's play that season as "awesome," in light of everything that was revealed in December.

Freddie's backup, Rick Nabors, saw significant playing time in 1969 (fourteen tackles and five interceptions in six games), but this was due in part to the coaches' practice of taking the starters out when games were well in hand. And Freddie started every regular-season game. He did what he had to do—meaning that he played deeper, benefiting from the exceptionally stout defensive front line—but his skill, his intelligence, his instincts, his savvy, and his experience kept him on the field.

Moreover, the Longhorn football culture established by Coach Royal had no room for players who let pain hold them back. In this, Freddie found his home. Preseason workouts were engineered to cull the weak from the ranks, and for all the technical innovation that went into the Longhorn playbook, players were trained to out-tough the other team, to outfight them. Freddie believed that fatigue and pain, to a certain extent, were merely to be ignored. Winners carried on as if those things didn't exist.

Freddie was a scholar of this particular kind of winner. One of his favorite anecdotes while he was at Texas involved what Vince Lombardi had said before the 1967 Super Bowl. The championship game had been played in Green Bay amid subzero temperatures, and several players had frostbitten toes. When the Super Bowl media asked Lombardi about the frostbite victims a couple of weeks later, Lombardi replied, "Frostbite victims? Packers don't get frostbite. Packer *opponents* get frostbite."

In Freddie's mind, winners carried themselves in this Lombardi-like fashion. The physical world bent to your will, and when it didn't, you ignored the conditions. "Athletes are supposed to play with pain," writes Freddie. "They're expected to perform despite pain. This is an unwritten code for winners. Most of us learn this at an early age and no coach has to tell us. The childhood logic is simple: if you admit pain to someone, you may be forbidden to play." This was Freddie's creed, and he put it into action. In the eyes of Darrell Royal, Fred Akers, and the other coaches, it was enough to keep him on the field. Still, the belief didn't make certain realities disappear.

THE LONGHORNS CAME OFF THEIR ANNIHILATION OF TCU (69–7) with two games left in the regular season. Texas still sat firmly at second place in the national polls, for Ohio State remained unbeaten as well.

On Saturday, November 22, Ohio State played Michigan. The Longhorns had the day off, since they were to play Texas A&M on Thanksgiving Day, the following Thursday. Freddie worked out in the morning and then joined several teammates in Bill Zapalac and Scott Palmer's dorm room to watch the day's games. Unfortunately, the regional broadcast showed an inconsequential game between Missouri and Kansas. Still, the announcers periodically broke in with updates on the Ohio State contest. Freddie writes, "When the first-quarter score was announced, 7–6 in favor of

Michigan, a sort of silent electric shock ran through the room. Not a word was said, but we all looked quickly at each other, and you may be sure all the pulse rates jumped."

Freddie and his teammates sat in silent tension, watching a game they didn't particularly care about but hanging on every word, just waiting to hear the latest update about the game they did care about. Now and again, the tension bubbled over and someone would shout out encouragement to Michigan, and the rest of the room would tell him to shut up for fear of a jinx. "But," Freddie writes, "when the final score was announced, the walls came tumbling down."

"Michigan Wolverines, 24 . . . Ohio State Buckeyes, 12." The players ran up and down the corridors of Jester Hall, whooping and hollering, for they understood what the Michigan victory meant. Ohio State would tumble from the throne and Texas would ascend. The Longhorns' destiny now rested firmly in their hands. If they could take care of business at A&M on Thanksgiving, the Longhorns could be fairly certain their last game of the season, against Arkansas at Razorback Stadium in Fayetteville, would determine the national champion.

NOVEMBER 27, 1969, WAS A COLD DAY IN COLLEGE STA-tion, Texas, and Freddie's leg was stiffer than usual. When head trainer Frank Medina suggested it might be better for Freddie to sit the game out, Freddie rebuffed him: "Oh, no," he said, "I'm gonna play."

The Longhorns crushed the Aggies from the get-go. On the game's opening drive, Jim Bertelsen broke through the Aggie line and sprinted sixty-three yards for a touchdown. Freddie, despite the anchor of his injured leg, seemed en route to having his best game of the year. He was all over the field in the first quarter, breaking up passes and making four tackles, which was his season high for a single game.

In the second quarter, Freddie was going man-to-man against Aggie tailback Larry Stegent on an off-tackle run. Stegent was having a typically stellar season. By the time his career ended at

A&M, Stegent had been selected all-SWC three times and became an eventual first-round draft pick. His name still populates the Aggie record books.

Stegent went low in his collision with Freddie, his helmet squarely drilling the sore spot in Freddie's thigh. Freddie went down, bellowing in the most intense pain he had ever felt. As numbness overtook him from toe to hip, Freddie believed his season was over: *My leg is broken.* The discomfort he had dealt with all year had finally gotten the better of him, and he came off the field.

On the sideline, feeling eventually pulsed back into his leg, and Freddie returned to the game, coming out only after the Longhorns took a 42–0 lead in the third quarter. After the season, upon discovering the cancerous tumor in Freddie's left thigh, doctors told him they were astounded that this particular collision had not irreparably broken his femur.

CHAPTER 10

LIKE PARACHUTING
INTO RUSSIA

THE SKY CLEARED ABOVE THE UNIVERSITY OF Texas Tower, but the air over the south mall was thick with collegiate anxiety. Final exams approached, and campus spirit ratcheted up for the weekend's impending football game between the Longhorns and the Arkansas Razorbacks, the first- and second-ranked teams in the nation. There was something else in the air as well, a dissonant rattle. Austin's atmosphere in the preceding days had become a disorienting mix of "Hook 'em, Horns" enthusiasm and distress over the quagmire in Vietnam. The United States had been increasing its troop numbers in Southeast Asia every year since 1961, and by December's end in 1969, 40,024 American service people had perished—a figure that is difficult to imagine in twenty-first-century America.

For the United States to continue its perceived mission, the military needed more able-bodied men. At 8:00 CST on the evening of December 1, CBS preempted the regularly scheduled *Mayberry R.F.D.* in order to provide breaking live coverage. The newsman Roger Mudd turned toward the camera and began the broadcast from the noisy government headquarters, speaking in hushed tones: "Tonight, for the first time in twenty-seven years, the United States has again started a draft lottery."

Numbered slips of paper, one for each day of the year including February 29, were placed in individual plastic capsules and gathered in a large glass fishbowl. The order in which the capsules were drawn would determine the order, by birth date, in which young men would be called for physical examination and conscription into military service as needed. Representative Alexander Pirnie (R-NY) drew the first capsule and revealed number 258. Those who were born on September 14 had "won" the lottery.

In the lobby of Jester Hall, Scott Henderson and several of his teammates gathered around the television set. Five days shy of the most important game of their lives, they were about to learn whether they might expect to die in Southeast Asia within the next couple years. In Fayetteville, Arkansas, their opponents likewise awaited their fates.

Rumor had it that President Nixon would attend the matchup, which the networks were already hyping as the "Game of the Century." It seemed ironic that on this night Nixon could order some of these boys to pay what might be the last full measure of devotion, and then watch them play football on Saturday.

FREDDIE STEINMARK DIDN'T STAY WITH HIS TEAMMATES to watch the lottery. Instead, he hurried through Jester Hall's main doors. Freddie hated to be late, especially when a friend was waiting for him, and he had plans to meet Linda for the basketball team's season opener versus Ole Miss.

When Freddie walked UT's campus, he always acknowledged others with a quick smile or slight nod, exhibiting his cheerful nature, offering no inkling of a negative thought. Yet as he headed toward Gregory Gym, there had to have been much on his mind. A man's birth date would either protect him or draw him into a confusing war. Some of his teammates and their families were going to receive good news in the midst of others receiving the worst. Many had siblings in the draft pool. And some of them, such as Bobby Mitchell, had already lost brothers.

Moreover, the pressure mounted in anticipation of the Arkansas game. Freddie had played in eighteen straight victories, going back to last season, and a potential national title was within reach. Last year, Texas had triumphed over Arkansas, 39–29, in an Austin barnburner. But the dangerous tandem of quarterback Bill Montgomery and split end Chuck Dicus had returned—and improved. Freddie knew that a unique challenge awaited him.

As he made his way across campus, eager for the temporary diversion of the basketball game, Freddie wasn't able to stretch his stride much—the persistent pain lingered in his left thigh. With pain came doubt. He had told himself and others that it was just a calcium deposit or a bone bruise, but it had grown worse. His limp, ever more severe, resisted concealment.

Freddie walked Linda home after the game, kissed her goodbye, and then returned to his dorm, his concerns undiminished. As he did almost every night, Freddie lifted his rosary from his desk drawer and knelt next to his bed. He bowed his head, crossed himself, and began in a whisper, "I believe in God, the Father Almighty, Creator of heaven and earth."

The rosary is an ancient prayer, commonly understood as an involved meditation, something that requires sustained effort, practice, and even endurance. It is easy to see why the rosary appealed to Freddie as it did. Things mattered more when he put effort into them, and so the rosary became a concentrated outpouring of his faith, often connected to the effort he was prepared to give on the field.

The rosary beads—five "decades" of prayer beads along a rope or string—are used to symbolize the repetition of the Hail Mary, fifty times over, as a devotional to the mother of Jesus, each repetition symbolizing a single rose and ultimately creating a bouquet of fifty roses that the devotee gives to the Immaculate Heart of the Virgin. "Rosary," the word itself, is derived from the Latin *rosarium*, "a crown or garland of roses." Each decade of prayer serves to crystallize one of the mysteries—episodes in Jesus's life as defined by the Catholic Church. This fundamental practice was standardized by Pope Pius V in 1569, and we can imagine Freddie participating in this enduring tradition, contemplating the suffering present in the mysteries, and drawing strength from them.

The exact origin of the rosary as Freddie knew it is shrouded in mystery. Rooted in the Judeo-Christian tradition of reciting the 150 psalms, the practice reaches back to monasteries located from the Middle East to Ireland, and its power lies in tales of the Virgin and her manifestations to those in need. These are stories that Freddie was familiar with. And so the practice of the rosary is the evolutionary sum of the faiths and devotions of multitudes, as timeless and as deep as the precepts underlying the world of athletic competition itself. When looked at this way, it becomes easier to imagine the fortifying effect such a deep well of faith had on Freddie. It would have been not unlike the inspiration he drew from his father as an athlete, and all the others who had come before him.

ATTENTION FROM THE NATIONAL PRESS WAS RELENT-less. Reporters from all around the country came to Austin to spend a couple of days on campus. They roamed the coaches' offices, the dorms, the student union.

"The first question always was," Freddie writes in *I Play to Win*, "'How do you feel about putting it all on the line, on the last day of the season? How is the pressure?' The answers were usually the same. 'This is everybody's fondest dream,' said [star split end Cotton] Speyrer. 'I figured we would be playing for the conference championship in this last game, but never for the national championship. This is really something.'"

Freddie's week was given to little else than preparing for the game, and because of his leg, he spent his days resting: "So that was my exciting routine before the biggest game of our lives. . . . I would eat breakfast and stay in bed all morning, get up and eat lunch, and go back to bed until it was time to walk the few hundred yards to the training room for my whirlpool session and workout."

In the empty, quiet training room, Frank Medina set up the whirlpool, likely with no suspicion of how badly Freddie's leg hurt. "I didn't tell Mr. Medina the whole truth," Freddie writes, "because I wanted nothing to endanger my playing against Arkansas. People, lots of them, go through their entire careers without a chance to play in a game like this."

Once his leg had warmed, Freddie got dressed for practice—"I wore full pads every afternoon." He never allowed himself to miss the chance to play, yet was careful not to aggravate whatever was wrong. In his words, "I had already determined I was going to find out exactly what [the injury] was, after the season was completed. Of course, every now and then, when my leg loosened up, I would fudge a little on my private resolution. I'd say to myself, well, the season actually doesn't conclude until the bowl game. I'll wait until January 2nd."

The Steinmark's house on South Kingston Street in southeast Denver resounded with the *ring!* of the telephone. GiGi ran to it.

"Collect call from Freddie Steinmark. Will you accept the charges?"

"Yes . . . yes!" GiGi was overcome with worry over Freddie and his leg. Everyone in the family had been discussing the injury and how he must be feeling about playing in the Arkansas game. That past week, GiGi had noticed her mother worrying about Freddie Joe.

"Freddie?"

"Gloria Gene! You keeping up with your studies?"

"Yes, Freddie." GiGi was glad to hear her brother's voice, but didn't have long to speak with him before P.K. grabbed the receiver.

"Freddie Joe! You need to win on Saturday! I made a bet at school," she explained. She had fifteen dollars riding on a Texas victory, and she couldn't afford to lose. Freddie laughed, promising to do his best.

Since it was an expensive long-distance call, Big Fred let P.K., GiGi, and Sammy speak with Freddie for just a few minutes. Then it was time for Big Fred to speak with his son. He had been considering that whole week what was at stake in Saturday's game, and he asked Freddie what special plan Coach Akers and Coach Campbell had to counter the Arkansas passing attack. He cautioned Freddie to cheat his position deep in order to give himself some cushion.

Big Fred and Freddie Joe discussed the speed of Chuck Dicus, the challenge he would present in man-to-man coverage. Freddie told his dad that practice earlier that day had been miserable. Coach Royal had said it was the worst day they had had since the second week of the season. Freddie later wrote, "I know I had a bad practice because Coach Campbell told me about it, frequently and quite loudly. I think it was the worst he ever fussed at me."

Gloria remembers her husband specifically asking Freddie Joe about his injured leg. Freddie's collision during the Texas A&M game had triggered a great pain in Freddie's thigh—Big Fred pressed Freddie to see the doctor. Freddie promised he would, after the season.

Yet Freddie confided in his father: "I'm not able to go full speed and it bothers me some, but I plan to get it checked."

"I trust your judgment," Big Fred told his son. "But you make sure you get it checked. We love you, son." He told him how proud he was, what an accomplishment it was to be playing for the national championship.

As always, Gloria spoke with Freddie last. She told him how much she missed him. She would pray for him during the game. Freddie ended every phone call in the same way: "I love you, Mother."

As Wednesday's practice ended, UT fans and students entered the stadium for what would be the largest pep rally in university history. Scott Henderson recalls the event as surreal. The Longhorn Band, the bands of nine local high schools, the UT cheerleaders, the hog-calling contests, and more than twenty-five thousand Longhorn fans created an utter cacophony.

The players, dressed in coats and ties, paraded into the stadium, perched on the back seats of convertibles from the local Ford dealer. It was like a parade following an ancient Roman triumph, but it wasn't lost on either the coaches or the players that they hadn't won anything yet.

James Street addressed the crowd: "This is the greatest thing

I've ever seen." He continued, "This is the most important game of my life. All those past victories are meaningless, just building up to this game. I wish we could take you with us."

Enthusiastic telegrams were read, one coming from Apollo 12 astronaut and UT alum Alan Bean, still in quarantine after returning nine days earlier from NASA's second lunar landing. "YOU CAN BET YOUR MOON DUST," the astronaut's telegram read, "I'LL BE WATCHING ON TELEVISION AND PULLING FOR YOU."

Arkansas had its pep rallies as well—throughout the entire state. In Little Rock, more than 180 miles from the University of Arkansas campus, five thousand people turned out for some hog calling with the Razorback cheerleaders—no band, no team. On the Fayetteville campus that Friday night, they held a full-blown pep rally for an overflowing crowd in the university's Greek theatre. Freddie writes in *I Play to Win*: "The night before a Razorback home game, Dante's *Inferno* becomes an also-ran. You can bury your head beneath the pillows but you will still hear those W-O-O-O-P-I-I-G-G S-O-O-O-E-E whoops all through the night."

THE LONGHORNS BOARDED A BUS ON CAMPUS SHORTLY before noon on Friday. They would drive to the airport and fly to Arkansas. Freddie was one of the last ones to take his seat, walking slowly, his leg aching but his mind focused.

As Freddie would later write, "If you've never invaded the state of Arkansas to play their sainted Razorbacks, you don't know what real horror is. Coach Campbell, our resident philosopher, once described it: 'Playing in Fayetteville is like parachuting into Russia.'"

I like to think that as the plane lifted off from the runway in Austin, anticipation eased some of the pain in Freddie's leg. The fields of Texas fell away beneath the plane, and the Ozark valleys of Arkansas loomed. Nobody on the plane imagined that this would be Freddie's last time to travel with the team as a player. That this would be his last time to suit up in burnt orange. That this would be the last football game Freddie ever played.

CHAPTER 11

THE GAME OF
THE CENTURY

F REDDIE STOOD IN THE BACK OF THE HUDDLE, shaking out his leg and tapping his left toe against the turf. The previous play had been damaging for the Longhorns. On third down, Chuck Dicus had run a twenty-yard crossing pattern, twisted at exactly the right moment, and caught the pass from Arkansas quarterback Bill Montgomery. Freddie's ailing leg wouldn't cooperate, and he arrived late—much too late.

The sea of Razorback red roared. The stadium shook. Cowbells clanged. The university marching bands, each perched behind their team's bench, worked to overcome the other. They bobbed to the rhythms, jabbed their instruments into the air, and shot out close-fire notes. The low ceiling of grey clouds amplified every cymbal crash, every rat-a-tat drumbeat, every lung-bursting note, every shout in the stands, every grunt on the field.

Texas linebacker Scott Henderson, breathing heavily, looked to the sideline for Coach Campbell's signal. Henderson would later remember Campbell as a defensive "genius," a man often capable of predicting the offense's next play. With the flashed signs, Henderson pivoted to the huddle and leaned in. "80 regular!" he screamed. "80 regular! Ready—break!" The Longhorn defense clapped in unison and spread out.

Arkansas, leading 14–8, had a first down on the Texas thirty-eight-yard line. If the Razorbacks scored, the game would probably be out of reach.

Freddie cheated backward a few steps to compensate for the lack of mobility caused by his painful leg. He nodded to Danny Lester on his right and then to Tom Campbell on his left. They silently acknowledged the coverage scheme—each was responsible for a deep third of the field. Though this "cover 3" spread zone had proved stout all season, it seemed vulnerable to the Arkansas offense. So far, Montgomery had completed twelve passes, seven of them to Dicus.

The scoreboard clock showed 12:27 left in the game. If Texas could stop Arkansas now, there was enough time for the Longhorns to score again. Freddie crouched with his weight on his toes, catlike, ready to pounce. Dicus set slot right, and flanker John Rees split to the left. Freddie knew they were coming his way. He splayed his fingers and fixed his eyes on Dicus.

AIR FORCE ONE HAD TOUCHED DOWN EARLIER IN THE day at Fort Smith, sixty miles south of Fayetteville. The game, referred to by the media as the "Big Shootout"—Coach Royal's description—was set to begin at high noon in the style of a Gary Cooper–like showdown.

President Richard Nixon, a well-studied college football fan, appeared uncharacteristically excited as he stepped from his plane and addressed the crowd gathered on the tarmac: "All that I know is that we're going to see, today, in this hundredth anniversary of football, one of the great football games of all time." Marine One lifted off for Fayetteville shortly after eleven thirty. Among those accompanying Nixon were Congressmen George H. W. Bush of Texas and John Paul Hammerschmidt of Arkansas. Four Chinook helicopters, one of them carrying members of the press, embarked for the stadium.

The lumbering Chinooks had a tough time in the thick cloud cover and cold, drizzling rain, and were forced to run the contours of the Ozarks. Marine One slowed its arrival to allow the press helicopters to land before the president.

Shortly before noon, Bud Wilkinson, one of the announcers for ABC Sports, called Nixon's aide Tom Meurer and offered to delay the start of the game until the president arrived. The university bands continued to play, and the fans worked themselves into a frenzy. By twelve twenty, the stadium was a sea of noise. Wilkinson again called Meurer, who told the announcer he had no further news about Nixon's arrival and to go ahead and start the game.

The Reverend Billy Graham walked onto the field to deliver the pregame prayer, his mellifluous voice quieting the crowd: "We pray that every one of us will rededicate ourselves, not only to God, but to the principles that made this country great. And we pray that it be Thy will that we might have peace in our time. Amen."

The first Chinook landed just after the Razorbacks won the coin toss. Arkansas deferred to the second half, and Texas received. The ball traveled through the end zone for a touchback, and the high-powered Longhorn offense charged onto the field.

A football sideline is a chaotic place. Like an auto race, the game unfolds with a velocity that can truly be appreciated only up close. Decisions have to be made with conviction and without hesitation in an environment where one frequently cannot hear the person standing next to him. Players may scream or panic, or may hunch and vomit from the stress. Often, the team that maintains grace under pressure has the advantage. And now, just outside Razorback Stadium, helicopters were setting down, compounding the chaos.

As Texas approached the line for their second play from scrimmage, Marine One appeared in the sky, its thumping rotors momentarily distracting the crowd as it landed just beyond the end zone bleachers. "It was an unreal atmosphere for everybody," recalls Scott Henderson. "I had no idea what was going on."

As Nixon disembarked, the Arkansas line exploded into the backfield, and Longhorn halfback Ted Koy fumbled. The crowd erupted with approval when Razorback Bobby Field fell on the ball for a turnover. Hearing the excitement, Nixon turned quizzically to Meurer, who replied, "Well, sir, I think they're just cheering for you." Nixon beamed and strode into the stadium, waving to the crowd. When he realized the fans were not in fact cheering for him, he glared at Meurer and then followed the Secret Service agents to his seat.

Arkansas, with the benefit of a short field, scored first. Montgomery's initial two attempts fell incomplete as he rushed his throws under pressure from Henderson. But on his third attempt, Montgomery connected with Rees for twenty yards on a deep out to the sideline. This reception is still controversial. Watching the broadcast today, it is impossible to tell whether Rees dragged his toe inbounds before landing out of bounds. Arkansas scored two plays later. 7–0.

Freddie was on the field; yet on the television screen, he hardly seems to be present during these first few plays because of the depth at which he was lining up in the formation. This trend continued through three brutal quarters of football. Henderson recalls similar moments from that season's previous film sessions. "A time or two," he says, "we would watch the film and he wouldn't even be in the frame." Freddie's slowed action during his junior season, specifically in the Arkansas game, was in stark contrast to his "spectacular" sophomore season, when, Henderson recalls, Freddie was "all over the field."

THE ATMOSPHERE SURROUNDING THE GAME FELT AS strange and chaotic as the times—enthralling, jubilant, angry, confused, reactionary. In retrospect, the game seemed to exist in a surreal tug-of-war between quainter times and modernity.

It was the culminating game of the first century of college football, and the last championship game in which no African American players took the field—both rosters included black players, but as freshmen they weren't eligible for the varsity squad. President Nixon attended the game and sat in the stands amid the crowd—something unimaginable for any president today. Billy Graham's pregame invocation was likewise uncontroversial. Graham was a close friend of Arkansas head coach Frank Broyles, which later prompted many Texas players to remark that for the first three quarters of the game, it seemed as if God was a Razorback that day.

Likewise, the game-day atmosphere seemed to reflect both the nation's hope and despair in equal measure. Symbols of progress and hate abounded. During the first quarter, a group of student antiwar activists constructed a peace sign on the hill overlooking the corner of the end zone. The white circle of the cloth sign, tacked to the slope, spanned fifty feet in diameter. The students filled the interior space with two-foot-high black crosses pounded into the hillside—representing the rising Vietnam War death toll. They held banners reading "My Lai" and "Give Peace a Chance" in full view of Nixon's seat. During halftime, however, fans marched out of their seats, stomped the peace sign into the ground, and demolished the crosses, destroying a peaceful protest. Later, one of the protesters found that his American flag had been torn to shreds.

Confederate flags, on the other hand, waved throughout the stadium. Several student members of Black Americans for Democracy, including Arkansas freshman football player Hiram McBeth, planned to storm the field should the Razorback band play "Dixie" after Arkansas's first touchdown, as was the school's seventy-five-year-old custom. The organization had taken the stage at the Thursday pep rally in order to block the band from playing the song, and on the eve of the game, an African American student named Darrell Brown had been wounded in a drive-by shooting in front of the Black Americans for Democracy campus building. But upon the first Arkansas score, in a refreshing display of unity, the band launched into the Arkansas fight song instead of "Dixie." To the surprise and relief of many, the University of Arkansas student senate had voted against playing the old Confederate anthem and hallmark of nineteenth-century blackface minstrels.

THE VISITORS' LOCKER ROOM AT HALFTIME WAS CRAMPED and sweltering, the ceiling so low one could reach up and press a palm against it. Freddie sat in front of his locker where, before the game, he had prayed the rosary, as he did before every game. His boyhood dream of playing in a national championship was now half over, but was not going as well as he had imagined—Freddie and the Longhorns had played poorly. It was a miracle that the score was only 7–0.

Scott Henderson recalls a "businesslike" atmosphere in the locker room during halftime. Royal told the team, "We're better than what we're playing and we'll go out there and get this thing straight." As the defense gathered with Coach Campbell to review their assignments and adjustments, all knew what they were up against. Henderson said later: "I had a great respect for Montgomery. He was a very good college quarterback, that's for sure." The previous year, they had faced Montgomery in Austin. It had been difficult, but completely different. Here, in their own environment, Arkansas and Montgomery, Henderson recalls, "played out of their minds."

Texas's struggles continued through the third quarter. Dicus added a touchdown reception, then Arkansas shut out the Longhorn offense for the final nine minutes of the quarter. Freddie, in *I Play to Win*, summarized the team morale at this moment: "The Razorbacks were playing with headlong abandon. There was no hesitancy on their part. And before we could get untracked, we had lost four fumbles and two interceptions and it was 0–14 at the end of three quarters. National champions, you say? We were almost like the boxer who was so far behind he'd have to knock out the other guy to get a draw."

THE FIRST PUNCH TEXAS LANDED CAME EARLY IN THE fourth quarter in the form of an improbable scramble by quarterback James Street. It is widely regarded as one of the most famous plays in college football history.

Street dropped back to pass, but his receivers were smothered under a blanket of Arkansas coverage. Street shuffled to his left, slipped the grasp of one Arkansas defender, and then stepped forward into a collapsing pocket. Tucking the ball under his arm tightly, he darted straight ahead, broke a tackle ten yards downfield, and miraculously squeezed between two Razorbacks. Street then was off on a dash from the left hash mark to the right, then to the sideline, with a final Razorback defender to beat to the end zone—finishing with a forty-two-yard touchdown run. The TV camera followed Street, number 16, as he slowed and caught himself against the chain-link fence behind the end zone amid the raincoat-clad security men. Arkansas 14, Texas 6.

Before the game, Royal had informed Street and the rest of the team that the coaching staff had stayed up late the previous night considering just such a contingency. If the Longhorns were behind and scored a late touchdown, they would attempt a two-point conversion rather than settle for the extra point. The boldness of this move cannot be overstated, since this kind of decision is all but extinct in college football. With the advent of overtime, coaches always choose to play for the tie in regulation. And even back then, more than four decades ago, coaches still frequently opted for the potential tie. They would play it safe and then leave it up to the voters to decide the standings. But not Royal. He made the call: counter 49.

Chris Schenkel, announcing the game for ABC Sports to millions watching it on television, set the stage: "And they are going for two."

Street took the snap and reversed out from center. The Arkansas defenders shuffled sideways, playing cat and mouse with Street and Koy on the option. Street stutter-stepped, faked a pitch, and dived across the goal line into a mob of red jerseys, which met him just a fraction of a second too late. Arkansas 14, Texas 8, with 14:47 left to play.

After the kickoff sailed through the end zone, Arkansas started its next possession on its own twenty-yard line and once again marched effectively down the field. On the fifth play of the drive, Dicus cradled the ball for a catch at the Texas thirty-eight.

FREDDIE'S THIGH THROBBED IN THE COLD, DAMP AIR. HE focused on Dicus and cheated his position another step. The crowd, sensing an imminent Arkansas touchdown, let it all out. Their excitement filled the stadium and overflowed it. On the snap, Freddie backpedaled and kept his eyes on Dicus. Montgomery rolled right. When Freddie saw that Montgomery was looking for Rees, not Dicus, he sprinted toward the left sideline. Montgomery's pass was perfect, hitting Rees right on the numbers. Tom Campbell wrangled Rees before Freddie could get there, and then Freddie went sprawling, hit hard and knocked off his feet by a block from Dicus. The ball was now on the Texas twenty-four-yard line.

Arkansas hustled to the line for the next play. Montgomery, over center, surveyed the field. He looked at Freddie then backed away, making a *T* with his hands. Time-out.

Freddie watched the Razorback bench as he caught his breath. Later, he would speculate that Arkansas had noticed his limp and, during the time-out, conceived a play that would come right at him.

Henderson got the defensive signal from Coach Campbell, turned to the huddle, and looked Freddie in the eyes as he made the call: "80 special, rover blitz! 80 special, rover blitz! Ready, break!" *Clap!*

Lining up, Freddie nodded to Campbell and then to Lester. No one had to clarify their obligations when the blitz was on. With fewer Texas players dropping back into coverage, they each had man-to-man responsibility.

Dicus lined up again in the right slot. He was Freddie's man all the way. With the snap, Dicus fired off the line. Freddie backpedaled. Dicus juked outside, then broke to Freddie's inside and raced up the field.

Freddie's leg was lifeless. He couldn't accelerate. Even if he could play the angle right and reach Dicus, he wouldn't be able to stay with him. Freddie knew that if Dicus caught the pass, the game would be out of reach. Arkansas would be national champions. He closed on Dicus and lunged for him.

BIG FRED STARED AT THE CONSOLE TELEVISION IN HIS living room in Aurora. He had been pacing the floor throughout the contest. He would later recall that watching this game against Arkansas was the first time he had seen Freddie play on television, a notion that is difficult to imagine in today's world of weekly college football broadcasts. He recollected how it felt abnormal for him to study Freddie's every move on the TV screen. Intimately knowledgeable about his son's ability on the gridiron, Big Fred muttered about the extent to which Freddie was cheating his position, and noted that Freddie was often out of view.

When the Arkansas quarterback signaled for a time-out, Big Fred froze. "Geez, Montgomery saw something. Damn." The cameraman zoomed in on Montgomery and Coach Broyles talking on the sideline.

GiGi, Sammy, and P.K., sitting on the carpet, were fixated on the screen, and pointed out Freddie each time they saw him. Gloria, in bed with strep throat, strained to decipher the broadcast announcers' voices from Big Fred's comments and the oohs and ahs of her children.

After his discussion with Broyles, Montgomery returned to his teammates on the field. Arkansas broke the huddle and set up, spread wide left, Dicus in the slot. Texas showed blitz and man-to-man on the receivers.

Big Fred put a hand to his head. "Freddie's on Dicus." Montgomery took the snap and dropped back. Freddie adjusted his footing—one step, then two—as Dicus fired off the line, broke to the inside, and ran upfield.

Defensive back is a uniquely challenging position. Success is determined by one's ability to maintain a virtually nonexistent spatial relationship with a receiver while still reacting to his movements with lightning-fast speed. Freddie possessed a natural defensive back's intuition and understood what Dicus intended, but his leg had become an anchor, holding him to the turf as Dicus shouldered past. Freddie had become physically incapable of turning and running with Dicus.

Montgomery, seeing his desired matchup, let loose. The football arced toward the end zone, reached its zenith, and spiraled down toward the outstretched hands of Dicus. The crowd was on its feet and the crescendo was deafening. This was it. No way Dicus would miss this.

"Lofting one to Dicus!" Schenkel shouted into his microphone.

In the span of a breath, Freddie decided what to do. Not even. A half breath. He knew the consequences if he failed. Instinct, desperation, intelligence—all these things factored into his decision to lunge at Dicus and grab his jersey with both hands.

"No, no," Big Fred groaned. "Freddie's a half step slow. Something is really wrong with that leg." He watched as Freddie seized Dicus by his jersey. Yellow penalty flags flew. Big Fred knew his son had saved the game, for now, in the only way he could have.

"A marker is down in the secondary," Schenkel announced. "It's holding." Big Fred later recalled how he had felt the weight of his son's frustration. Sammy would add that it was at this moment that he realized Freddie had finally reached his threshold of playing with pain.

Hearing her husband's concern, Gloria dragged herself out of bed and struggled down the hallway into the living room. "Glo," Big Fred said, seeing her, "Freddie's leg is really bothering him. The coaches are taking him out."

The family watched as their number 28 walked into the top of the frame, his hands on his hips. Freddie glanced at the spot of his foul and then jogged out of view toward the sideline. Gloria still recalls the heartbreak of this moment. It was the first time that Freddie was pulled from a game.

The referee paced off the penalty, which gave Arkansas first and goal from the nine-yard line. The Razorbacks resumed the attack, with Montgomery rolling right. The Texas front penetrated and sacked him.

On the next play, Montgomery rolled left. With another great rush, Texas hit him as he threw, and the ball skipped incomplete along the turf.

On third and goal, Montgomery again sprinted out to the left. Dicus ran a corner route, creating some separation between himself and cornerback Danny Lester. Montgomery released the ball, but it was slightly behind Dicus.

"There is the interception by Lester . . . preventing the field goal!" announced Bud Wilkinson. Wilkinson could have been revealing some allegiance to the Longhorns, having been Darrell Royal's coach when Royal was a defensive back and part-time quarterback for the Oklahoma Sooners.

The elation in the Steinmark living room following Lester's interception was short-lived because a steady drive down the field ended with another turnover when a lateral on an option was bobbled. Arkansas recovered at its own forty-two. Texas fans fell silent. The Arkansas fans could barely contain themselves. Just less than eight minutes were left on the game clock.

Texas made an impressive stand, stopping three plays and forcing Arkansas to punt. Sure-handed punt returner Cotton Speyrer moved under the ball and gathered it in safely at the Texas thirty-six-yard line. The clock was down to 6:10. Big Fred shook his head in dismay. The Texas offense had been stymied all day; he later confessed that he doubted that they could score.

The Longhorns began a series of plays using their powerful wishbone running attack, which had been successful all season. The first play was a handoff to Koy; the next two were "grind 'em out" runs by Steve Worster, but to no avail—they advanced the ball only seven yards.

The clock showed 4:47 left in the game. Facing fourth-and-three at the Texas forty-three-yard line, Street called time-out and trotted over to Coach Royal.

Big Fred looked at Gloria and tried to muster an encouraging smile. He was nervous. The game, the season, the potential championship—it all came down to the next play. If Arkansas stopped Texas, it was over. The Razorbacks would simply run out the clock. If Texas could gain just three yards, they would still be alive.

ABC didn't go to a commercial break during the time-out. The producers focused the camera on Street at the sideline, getting instructions from Coach Royal, with Coach Campbell at Royal's elbow.

In *I Play to Win*, Freddie quoted Coach Royal's postgame explanation of his decision for the next play: "We went for an unorthodox play, one that broke the pattern. I couldn't be concerned with what people thought about it. We had our backs to the wall. Every now and then, in a situation like that, you don't use logic or reason. You just play a hunch."

Coach Royal looked at Street: "They'll be expecting our option. I think we'll just run 53 veer pass to the tight end." Coach Campbell took a step back. "My God!" said Campbell, realizing that Coach Royal had just called a play that the Longhorns had only attempted four times all season—and it hadn't worked once. It was a long pass, and surprisingly, it didn't even get thrown to their best receiver, Cotton Speyrer. Speyrer didn't even run a pass pattern on the play, but faked a block as if it was a running play. The receiver who would get the pass was Randy Peschel, a senior who had become a tight end only after other players had been injured, a player who had caught only twelve passes all season.

Coach Royal had observed that Arkansas predictably used the same defensive strategy on important third-down situations. Also, he noticed that Arkansas cornerback Jerry Moore had been neglecting Peschel on nearly every play, coming up to the line of scrimmage instead. During halftime, Coach Royal had asked Peschel about it, and he agreed that Moore had been leaving him uncovered in order to prevent a huge running play.

Street was amazed by the coach's call, having not heard any of the reasons for choosing that play. He ran toward the huddle and then paused. Thinking that he may have misunderstood, he turned back to Coach Royal. "Are you sure it's a 53 veer pass?" he asked.

"Hell, yes, I'm sure!" snapped Royal.

Street returned to the huddle, later saying that he knew he needed to sell this play to the guys. Looking straight at Cotton Speyrer, Street said, "Peschel, don't look at me. You aren't gonna believe this, but I think it's gonna work." Street paused. "Right 53 veer pass—and that means you're the only receiver, Peschel, and you're going deep. Okay? Right 53 veer pass. Ready, break!" *Clap.*

A national television audience of more than fifty million viewers watched as Chris Schenkel announced, "A most crucial fourth down play."

Street, under center, started the count. Forrest Wiegand snapped him the ball. Street stepped left and faked a handoff to Worster, freezing the Arkansas defense as it tried to stop the run. Then he dropped back and planted his feet to throw, squaring his shoulders. Peschel momentarily made a blocking action at the line, then broke off and streaked down the left sideline. With a precision he had rarely demonstrated, Street cocked and threw way downfield, leading Peschel and forcing him to run harder to catch up with the ball.

With two Arkansas defenders collapsing on him, Peschel watched the ball sail over their outstretched, crossed arms and land *in his own hands* at the thirteen-yard line.

"And Peschel catches the ball!" Schenkel shouted.

Arkansas was in shock. Texas snapped the ball before Arkansas could get set at the line of scrimmage. Street faked to Worster going up the middle and handed off to Koy, who exploded through the left side, breaking tackles and driving hard down to the two-yard line. As Texas's strong offensive line powered forward on the next play, halfback Jim Bertelsen rammed over the goal line for the touchdown, tying the game 14–14.

With the help of a great hold by Donnie Wigginton on a high snap, Happy Feller punched a pressured extra point through the uprights, giving Texas the lead, 15–14, for the first time all day. There was still 3:58 on the clock.

Cheers filled the Steinmark living room as Feller's extra point sailed through the uprights. The joy waned, though, as the Arkansas offense once again began moving efficiently down the field. The Razorbacks needed to get just close enough for a field goal.

On second and three from the Texas thirty-nine-yard line, Montgomery looked for Rees, who was running an out pattern. A reception would put them within field-goal range. Texas cornerback Tom Campbell was close on Rees, matching him stride for stride. Just as Rees turned to the sideline, so did Campbell, who stepped in front of the Arkansas receiver and made the interception. Razorback fans were stunned and deflated. The Texas bench exploded in loud cheering. The Colorado living room exploded as well.

The only task left for Texas was to run out the clock. Chris Schenkel and Bud Wilkinson used the final seconds of the game to make their way to the Texas locker room. Because Arkansas had been leading until the last minutes of the game, the ABC camera crew had already set up in the Razorback locker room and now had to scramble. President Nixon and his entourage left the stands and followed the path of the victors.

Gloria made her way back to the bedroom, worried about Freddie.

REACHING THE PINNACLE IN ANY ENDEAVOR IS A DIFFI-cult experience to describe. To be a member of a national championship sports team encompasses a jumble of emotions often beyond words. It is a dream that many young people know but few ever realize. Those who experience the dream as reality say it is something that stays with you forever. Freddie realized this, and in *I Play to Win* he tried to explain his emotions surrounding the events after the game:

> If you've ever been in a victorious locker room after a championship game, multiply it about ten times and that was ours in that crowded, low-ceilinged, concrete blockhouse in Fayetteville. This was pretty much a Longhorn squad affair. Usually some alumni and former players and some relatives will sneak in, but [Nixon's] secret service men pretty well put a crimp in that practice. It was a wild scene. . . . In the middle of all the celebration, I remember looking at Worster, the big fullback, and shouting close to his ear, "Hey, how come you're crying?"
>
> "I dunno," he yelled back. "How about yourself?"

Coach Royal was so full of emotion that he actually gave Randy Peschel a kiss on the cheek, on national television, amid the din of cheers and excitement.

As President Nixon, with two Secret Service men and some White House staff, made his way through the locker room, the Longhorn team quieted down. Nixon stood on the elevated grandstand and congratulated the team, shaking hands with James Street and Coach Royal, calling the contest "one of the great games of all time, without question." Nixon then turned to Royal and placed his right hand on the coach's shoulder, "How do you feel?"

Coach Royal looked down for a second and then back up at the president: "I've got to be the happiest guy in America tonight."

President Nixon then handed Coach Royal the national championship plaque. "I want all of you to know that we did make up the plaque in advance and it doesn't say what team, and I'm taking it back to Washington and putting in Texas!"

Amidst the elation of the moment, Freddie was still reminded of his injury, of the nagging pain: "Frank Medina somehow waded through the morass of soggy jerseys and discarded tape and asked me how my knee felt. I told him it was fine and, truly, in those exhilarating moments, nobody could feel any pain. But when the hilarity died down to a gentle roar and we could make some move toward getting undressed and taking showers, I was again conscious of pain and stiffness in my left leg."

THE LONGHORNS—NUMBER ONE IN THE COUNTRY, NATIONAL champions—flew into Austin that night, and from the windows of their Braniff 727, they could see the UT Tower, bathed in the victorious illumination of orange lights. Yet this commemoration was different from previous ones—the lighting had been arranged so that the middle window of each floor was illuminated to create a bright "1" on all four sides. Freddie later wrote, "It had never looked so beautiful or meant so much."

Their plane circled Austin several times as authorities cleared the runways of over fourteen thousand people who had climbed the airport fences to greet the team when it landed. As the 727 taxied to the terminal, crowds of people swarmed the plane, forcing the captain to cut the engines when they were still a quarter mile from the gate. A tractor towed the aircraft farther, to about a hundred yards from the gate, and gave up to the masses surrounding the Longhorns' plane. Freddie wrote in *I Play to Win*:

Coach Royal said it was the nearest thing to V-J Day. People were going wild—students, parents, alumni, townspeople. A few players tried to deplane, but people were packed so closely at the foot of the steps, grabbing and calling for them, that the guys scrambled back up the steps to the plane. The Arkansas defense was never like this!

. . . There was some sort of corridor formed but still it was a roaring jungle of pushing and shoving and hugs and backslaps. Several times I was lifted completely off my feet and just swept along helplessly. . . .

By this time my leg was so stiff and sore I could barely walk, but somehow I got through the crowd.

There was a large party thrown that night for the Longhorn players at the Terrace Motel in Austin—no coaches allowed. Freddie and Linda went with Scott Henderson and Scott Palmer and their dates in Henderson's GTO. It was one of the greatest nights of Freddie's life, so he decided to celebrate:

There was a big buffet and some go-go dancers and I took the first drink of alcohol in my college life. I drank a beer. Several beers, in fact. First time I ever broke training, high school or college, in season or out, but this was a special night. I even tried a cigar, but that was a little too much. There was a jukebox going full blast and Linda and I danced many times, sore wheel and all.

Linda had to be back in her dormitory by 2 A.M. As Henderson, Palmer and I walked down some steps to the parking area, the pain hit my leg again, a real jolter. I grabbed it with my hands instinctively like I could choke the pain out of it, and then I turned to Scott Henderson, "How come all that beer doesn't make my leg quit hurting?" I was half kidding, but he didn't say anything.

CHAPTER 12

THE GAME CHANGER

O N SUNDAY, DECEMBER 7, FREDDIE WOKE up, a national champion. He, his teammates, and his coaches were the champions of college football. Generations pass without a school approaching—much less attaining—such a feat. And now there was just one more game to play: the Cotton Bowl. That was going to be something. He tried to savor the magnitude of the accomplishment, but found himself distracted. Plus, his leg throbbed. He had to acknowledge the fact that with the national championship game now behind him, he had reached his breaking point with the pain. As he writes in *I Play to Win*: "Sunday was a bad day. It wasn't exactly a time of rest, because it had become obvious to me that the time had come for definitive action on my leg. I realized now that I couldn't wait until after the Cotton Bowl game against Notre Dame. Enough was enough."

Since he couldn't see a doctor until Monday, Freddie spent most of his day worrying about what was wrong, what procedure he would have to go through, how long it would take him to recuperate, and whether he would be full speed in time for the Cotton Bowl.

There was still much to thank God for that day, so Freddie went with Linda to five o'clock mass at the Catholic Student Center. He told her that he was going to see a doctor on Monday morning.

Freddie writes, "She was relieved and I guess I was too, in a way. I was just hoping it was something that could be cleared up before the Notre Dame game. Heck, maybe just a week's rest would do it."

In Freddie's mind, maybe he could find a way to be ready to play by New Year's Day and fulfill another dream of his: to play against the Fighting Irish. It seemed like a miracle, really, that he might have this opportunity, since Notre Dame had not been to a bowl game since 1925, when Knute Rockne was their coach and the famous Four Horsemen ran in the backfield.

On Monday, Freddie awoke early and squeezed his leg to find increased pain. It was time to act. Freddie cut his morning class and went to the stadium to see Frank Medina. When Freddie arrived in the training room, the first thing he said was, "My knee is hurting." Medina sensed the urgency in Freddie's normally stalwart voice. He called Dr. Joe Reneau, the team physician, and made arrangements for Freddie to see him right away. Dr. Reneau's office was the first stop on what would turn out to be a long medical journey.

Freddie hustled back to the dorm and borrowed Linda's car to make the drive four miles across town to Reneau's office. Reneau briefly examined Freddie's left leg, mostly focusing on the knee, where Freddie said he felt the most pain. "[I] had x-rays taken of my knee," Freddie writes. "As an afterthought, a shot of my thigh was also taken."

After the X-rays were developed, Reneau stepped into the exam room and told Freddie he was going to send the scans over to Dr. Jerry Julian in the Student Health Center. Something was amiss, Freddie knew; Dr. Julian was the university's orthopedic surgeon. Formerly the team doctor, he now devoted himself full-time to surgery. Freddie wanted to attack this new unknown head-on, as if fielding a punt. "I'll take the pictures," he told Dr. Reneau. "I'm going right by there." He picked up the brown envelope and made the drive back to campus. Of course, Freddie wanted to see the X-rays for himself. He wanted to take in the information unvarnished and formulate a typically well thought-out response and plan.

Before he reached the health center, he pulled Linda's car over and took out the films, placing each against the driver's window so that the sunlight illuminated them. The images were of poor quality. Freddie, not sure what he was looking for, inspected every inch of his bones on the film. Inexperienced as he was, he could still see "something wasn't right." On his femur, just above the knee, was a bump, a curve in the bone. Freddie stared at the pictures for a long while and then started the engine and drove on to the Student Health Center.

That night in Gregory Gym, Texas was playing the University of Mississippi basketball team. At halftime, the football team would be introduced to the student body as national champs. Before the game, Freddie met Linda for dinner in the dorm cafeteria. She asked how the appointment with the doctor went. Freddie told her that "they took a bunch of x-rays and stuff," and indicated that they would do more tests. This attempt to satisfy her curiosity worked for the moment.

At the gym, Freddie and Linda sat in the stands with the rest of the football team and their dates. Freddie had trouble focusing. He knew that Reneau would attend the game as the Athletic Department doctor, so he watched the entrance, hoping to spot Reneau as he entered. By now, Reneau would have discussed the X-rays with Julian.

Eventually, Freddie caught a glimpse of Reneau entering the gym and then turning into a passageway underneath the stands. "Got to go get the verdict," Freddie uttered to Linda. He hopped up before explaining and trotted after Reneau. He found the doctor speaking with Medina beneath the bleachers. Freddie approached and spoke right up: "How's my knee?"

Reneau paused slightly and told him his knee was "fine."

"What about that curvature in the bone?" Freddie asked. "It looked to me like the bone was curved above my knee."

"Yes," Reneau responded carefully. "That is the concern. We can't be certain yet, Freddie, but you may have a bone tumor. I want you to see Dr. Julian in the morning."

Bone tumor. Upon hearing these words, Freddie was stunned. He had always thought of his lingering injury as something manageable, part of the daily athletic grind. Freddie later wrote of this moment, of being confronted with Reneau's words: "It was like a physical collision with something in the dark. A truck just rammed me in the stomach. It wasn't cold that night; I was wearing blue jeans and a shirt, but in a matter of seconds, I was soaking wet. I got this horrible taste in my mouth. A bone chip, yes. A strained knee, even that good old calcium deposit, okay. But a bone tumor?"

In a fog, Freddie made his way back to his seat and Linda. He sat down, numb. It took him a while to register Linda's question. Finally, he said, "They think I have a tumor in my leg."

They sat in silence for a long time, the basketball game around them taking place in a different universe.

"They don't know for sure," Linda offered. "You yourself said they were going to make some more tests, didn't you? That shows they don't know. It could be anything."

Freddie reached down and squeezed his left thigh. "I can feel it in there." Struggling for some confirmation, Freddie took Linda's hand and placed it on his left thigh. "Here, put your hand right there. Feel that?"

Linda squeezed Freddie's leg. "I can't feel a thing."

"Don't give me that. How can you help but feel that?"

Linda, taken aback, replied again, "Honest, I can't feel anything."

"I can. I can sure feel it," Freddie protested, as he continued to squeeze his thigh right above the knee, grasping for verification.

At halftime, the football players were called to the court. James Street, as the squad's gregarious leader, introduced each of the players, one by one, often with a bit of humor and sarcasm. Unaware of the possibly serious problem with Freddie's left leg, Street announced him as "Fast Freddie Steinmark." Freddie made his way to center court. "I tried not to limp," Freddie later wrote, "but I flunked."

Freddie asked Linda to leave with him soon after halftime. His mind was too clouded to stay. She tried to raise his spirits. Together they attempted to rationalize some other explanation, anything other than a tumor. Freddie kissed Linda and left her at the entrance to her wing of Jester Hall.

Restless, his mind racing, Freddie walked a few blocks to the Catholic chapel on campus. Inside the church it was dark and silent, and at some level, within the walls and ancient customs of his Catholic faith, there was comfort. Freddie went down to the first pew, where he liked to sit, and started to pray: "Hail Mary, full of grace, the Lord is with thee." Freddie's eyes welled up. What was this possible bone tumor? Could it be fixed easily? When would he know for sure? Freddie prayed, grasping for comfort.

Freddie left the chapel and walked to the fountain in front of the Tower. He sat on one of the stone benches and, from the shadows, watched other students pass by, laughing and chatting. Freddie felt alone, as if elemental forces were closing in. He kept trying to pray. When you face the deeper questions of mortality, Freddie later wrote, "when that time comes, you go back to grass roots."

Freddie walked the two short blocks to his dorm. Bob was away, and Freddie closed the door. Alone. Freddie called home. His father answered, and Freddie asked him to stay quiet so that his mother would not hear. Big Fred was rocked into near silence as Freddie explained. Freddie said he would know more after his morning appointment with Dr. Julian. Freddie hung up and lay in bed, staring into space.

A world away, Big Fred paced around the house. He couldn't keep such a secret, and soon Gloria and the entire family paced with him.

Borrowing Linda's car again, Freddie arrived at Dr. Julian's office before seven a.m. on Tuesday. Questions flared in his mind, but he waited for the doctor's examination. The first thing Dr. Julian did was to take a set of higher-quality X-rays.

The cleaner and clearer images confirmed Julian's fears. He showed Freddie the new X-rays, pointing out the area of concern: it was the spot just above the knee in the femur, where the curvature had been visible in the first set of X-rays. Julian then said they needed to fly Freddie immediately to M. D. Anderson Hospital in

Houston. "They're better equipped to handle situations like this," the doctor said. "They're foremost in this field."

Houston? Immediately? Freddie was shaken. He had never heard of M. D. Anderson, but as he wrote in his memoir, "I later learned, of course, that it's one of the leading cancer hospitals in the world."

Dr. Julian called Dr. Reneau, who in turn informed Coach Royal and the university administration of the situation. A private plane was promptly arranged to take Freddie to Houston. It was determined that Dr. Charles LeMaistre and Stan Burnham would fly with Freddie. LeMaistre, a vice chancellor of the UT System (the collection of all University of Texas campuses), was a medical doctor, and thus the best person from the university to assess the situation. Burnham was a former coach with a doctorate in physical education.

Meanwhile, word reached Medina, who assigned the assistant trainer, Spanky Stephens, the task of picking Freddie up and bringing him to the airport. When Freddie entered the dorm, his head spinning, Spanky met him and told him to "grab a shaving kit," not thinking he would need much else for what he assumed would be a quick trip.

The only other thing Freddie did was to call home. His father, home from the night shift, answered the telephone. When Freddie told him what was happening, Big Fred replied that he and Gloria would meet him in Houston. After they hung up, Big Fred arranged for the uncles and aunts to stay with the kids. Cousin Janet, who worked for the airlines, rushed a set of tickets, and by three that afternoon Big Fred and Gloria were on their way.

Hurriedly, Spanky drove with Freddie past the administration building to pick up LeMaistre and Burnham, and they all headed straight to the airport. Soon thereafter, the six-seat twin-engine plane was wheels up, en route to Houston.

The plane climbed into the bright morning sky. Freddie's mind was in overdrive. He turned to the vice chancellor. "Dr. LeMaistre," Freddie ventured, "will you tell me what's wrong with my leg?"

"Freddie," Dr. LeMaistre said, "it'd be best if we wait for the doctors to do their tests." He knew, in his profession, that these things took time to properly diagnose.

"No," Freddie replied. "I'd like to know now."

Resigned to Freddie's resolve, LeMaistre picked up the envelope of X-rays and pulled out the clearest film in the set. He then placed the picture against the oval airplane window. LeMaistre pointed and said, "Freddie, here's the tumor." LeMaistre recognized the mass as a relatively newly identified type of cancer, Ewing's sarcoma. "It's torn the bone up in here and it's going to be a question as to whether or not it can be removed without removing your leg."

There is no telling how Freddie felt upon hearing this so directly, on top of the speculation of the previous day. But the emotion must have been immense. He must have looked out that aircraft window and felt anchorless and adrift. Utterly lost. But as Dr. LeMaistre later recalled in his own writing, "When I told him on the plane that I thought he might lose the leg, he didn't let himself break down." LeMaistre continued, explaining how Freddie gathered himself and asked, "Do you think that I can get through all of this and then get back to the Cotton Bowl?"

BACK ON CAMPUS, SPANKY STEPHENS RETURNED TO THE mail room of the dorm just before noon, and by chance bumped into Linda. She had not heard a word from Freddie that morning and was worried after their evening at the basketball game.

"Have you seen Freddie?" Linda asked.

"Oh, yeah," Spanky said. "I just drove him to the airport. They're taking him to Houston."

Linda almost fainted. "*What?*"

"Don't worry," Spanky assured her, "He'll probably be back this afternoon."

DR. BOB MORETON, ASSISTANT DIRECTOR OF M. D. Anderson, met Freddie and LeMaistre at the airport. Moreton checked Freddie into a two-bedroom apartment on the fourteenth floor of the Anderson Mayfair, the accommodations for families of patients, adjacent to the hospital. Then he sent Freddie across the street for preliminary tests.

With Freddie successfully handed off to the Houston doctors, LeMaistre left to catch a flight to New York, his new mission being to brief Coach Royal at the championship presentation ceremonies. (LeMaistre, after his tenure as vice chancellor and then chancellor of the University of Texas System, became president of M. D. Anderson for eighteen years.)

In New York, LeMaistre gave Royal all of the details of Freddie's condition. The university made arrangements for another plane, and at sunrise the next morning, Royal departed for Houston, his mind awash with overpowering emotion and concern for the young man whom he had grown so close to in two and a half years.

In the early evening, Freddie greeted his parents at the door of the apartment. As Big Fred and Gloria settled into their adjacent bedroom, the three were relatively quiet, simply sitting together and praying, their minds racing with possibilities. To comfort his mother, Freddie said, "Mother, if God wants my leg, we'll just have to give it to him."

ON WEDNESDAY, FREDDIE CROSSED THE STREET AND ENtered the hospital early; the doctors and staff at M. D. Anderson were already in high gear. Dr. Dick Martin, the chief surgeon, met Freddie and outlined the strategy for diagnosis by biopsy, and then possible surgery. Immediately thereafter, the battery of tests started. First, they marked Freddie's body with dotted lines to provide a guide as the technicians imaged every inch of his torso. The doctors were looking for evidence of tumors or suspicious growths in any other quadrant of his body. They tested the layers of his bones. They took more blood. Freddie had been a national champion for only four days.

Coach Royal arrived at the hospital in the afternoon. He wasted no time in polite small talk. He gathered the doctors into the private conference room on the seventh floor, a large boardroom with a corporate oval table and plush chairs. Dr. Martin showed the coach the X-rays, explaining that no definitive statement could be made until after the biopsy. But Martin followed up by saying he had never seen an X-ray like Freddie's turn out to not be cancer.

Coach Royal looked around the room and asked, "Has Freddie been told?"

"Not, yet," Dr. Martin replied. "We wanted you to be here."

Royal then followed the doctors to Freddie's room. As Freddie, the coach, and the other doctors listened, Dr. Martin outlined and explained the realities of the situation as well as the possibilities. Of this moment, Freddie later wrote, "Coach Royal stood by the wall, in the background. I noticed he was pale and he had those red spots on his cheekbones, the way he looks before a big game."

So far, the tests had been inconclusive. Martin elaborated: "Maybe [it's] a blood clot or osteomyelitis or something like that. Or it might be a benign tumor." Unsurprisingly, the benign tumor was Freddie's "favorite possibility": "If it were benign, they could drain it and there was a chance I could play in the Cotton Bowl game. But that I knew, was a long shot."

"If the tumor were malignant," Freddie continues in *I Play to Win*, "something they call osteogenic sarcoma, then they would amputate immediately." The protocol was that Martin would take some tissue from the indicated bone and quickly check it in the lab adjacent to the operating room. If the tumor was malignant, the surgical team would, in Freddie's words, "go right ahead and take off my leg, at the hip, while I was still under the anesthetic."

The notions racing across Freddie's mind at this moment must have been bewildering. Freddie writes, "While Dr. Martin was talking, I was staring him in the eyes. I was listening to all the possibilities, all right, but I also was trying to look *behind* his eyes, to see what he *really* thought."

After finishing their explanation, the doctors left the room, but Coach Royal stayed behind. He was visibly upset. Freddie, at this moment of crisis, very naturally conducted himself just as he had at practice and while performing on the field. Commitment, passion, directness, faith, and heart were his guideposts. And so, just as Coach Royal began to speak, Freddie looked him straight in the eyes and politely interrupted. "Coach, he [Dr. Martin] didn't tell me everything, did he?" Royal didn't immediately answer, so Freddie continued, "Now tell me what he told *you*."

After a long moment, Coach Royal began. "Well, we've obviously been given some choices, none of which is too good. The fact that we're here at M. D. Anderson proves that. But the doctor didn't say this was a final diagnosis. He didn't say exactly what it is. There's always a chance it could be something minor. We've been behind before. We didn't give up then and I'm not going to give up now."

Freddie, sensing the real score, replied, "Right now, I'd settle for just losing a leg and nothing else." Already, Freddie had almost accepted the fact that his leg would be amputated. For him, the larger concern was whether amputation would be enough. As always, he wanted to see the big picture.

After Coach Royal left, Dr. Martin ushered Big Fred and Gloria into the room. Freddie laid out the situation clearly and straightforwardly. Gloria and Big Fred started to cry. Knowing the Steinmarks, I suspect that Freddie did his best to appear brave; Gloria recognized her duty as a mother to stand post in the watchtower and bear witness to her son's suffering; and Big Fred was probably feeling great remorse about his transgression, because maybe this was how it was coming due, and his son would pay the price.

As the chaotic afternoon progressed, Linda and Scott Henderson drove in from Austin. Freddie appreciated the friendship he had with Scott. A friendship forged in the fire of defensive teammates, tasked as brothers in arms to stop all opponents. A friendship forged in common academic goals and a common Catholic faith. A friendship Freddie would come to rely on over the next year to a far greater extent than he might have ever imagined. Freddie, in *I Play to Win*, describes Scott in this way:

> Now I got to tell you about Henderson. He's a linebacker and a great one, but you would never pick him out of a crowd as such.... He probably was the most intelligent guy on the squad ... elected to the Friars, which is the oldest academic society on campus. He was chosen on the All-American Academic team

all three of his varsity seasons. . . . I've heard coaches say Scott played his position as well as anybody every played it at Texas, and that means something when you think about some of the Texas linebackers of the past, like Tommy Nobis and Johnny Treadwell. . . . That was my buddy Henderson.

That night, with his family and friends gathered in the Mayfair apartment, Freddie was officially admitted into the hospital and room 416-East.

THURSDAY MORNING WAS THE FIRST TIME THAT FREDDIE had ever awoken in a hospital bed. The telephone rang; it was Father Bomar.

"What are you doing in a hospital?' Bomar asked, trying to lighten a very difficult situation.

After some humorous banter, Freddie said it straight out: "Father, this thing does not look good at all." Bomar asked whether Freddie would like him to come to Houston. "Please, if you would, Father, I'd appreciate it." As soon as they hung up, Bomar prepared to make the drive that afternoon.

For Freddie, the day began relatively quietly. Most of the tests were complete, and the surgery had been set for six thirty the next morning. The Steinmark family attempted to collectively catch its breath. Around noon, Coach Akers, who was recruiting some high school prospects in Houston, came to see Freddie. Akers, as Freddie's position coach, knew him as well as anyone on the staff. Freddie and Akers talked for a good while. Akers had a new recruiting presentation, a multimedia slide show with a sound track extolling the virtue and power of the University of Texas and its football program, that he showed on the hospital room wall. As they finished their conversation, Akers stood up and walked over to the bed to shake Freddie's hand good-bye. As Akers extended his arm, Freddie moved to hop up out of the bed to stand and shake the coach's hand. Akers told him, "Freddie, no, don't get up."

Freddie grinned. "Let me do it now. I may not get any more chances."

Back in Austin, Coach Royal set Thursday afternoon as the first day of practice to prepare for the Cotton Bowl, to be preceded by a mandatory team meeting at the stadium. With speculation about Freddie spreading like wildfire, and with the real possibility that the surgeons might amputate Freddie's leg, he needed to inform the team before they heard it somewhere else.

Royal must have been sick with worry. One minute he was in New York accepting the national championship trophy, and the next he was in Houston in a hospital room with a player, the heart of his team, suddenly facing what seemed to be cancer. And he had to get the players ready and focused to play Notre Dame in the Cotton Bowl, to win, to validate their standing as national champions.

Addressing the players, Royal began slowly. The moment remains a blur to many of them. "I was just numb," Rick Nabors recollects. According to Ted Koy, everybody was in shock. They were hearing about their teammate, their team's heart, facing the ultimate. And out of this collective shock, the memory remains hazy to almost everybody who was present. But what does cut through the haze are the facts that Royal was typically steadfast and typically inspiring.

Koy recalls: "[Royal] didn't sugarcoat anything. He was very much to the point. He told us Freddie had a tumor that was probably cancerous. On one hand we had a lot of work to do to get ready for Notre Dame—a lot of physical and mental work. On the other hand, knowing about Freddie, you just felt so helpless. But Coach Royal steered us through it."

Pulling together behind the coach's words, the team recognized that the best way to carry on, keeping Freddie in mind, was to do exactly what Freddie would want them to: prepare, like always, to win.

"I WAS WORRIED MOSTLY ABOUT MY MOTHER," FREDDIE writes in *I Play to Win*. "She is a strong, strong woman and she had her family there to lean on, but this was getting to her pretty bad. We always had a special attachment, me being the oldest child and all."

Around dinnertime Freddie was moved to a new room, 415-West, which was to be his home for the next couple of weeks. Big Fred, Gloria, Nana Marchitti, the extended family, and Linda were there, and Scott Henderson had returned with Bob Mitchell. A little later Father Bomar arrived. Sometime after dinner, a nurse came in to usher everybody out, saying she had to give Freddie a sleeping pill because he needed to get his rest. Freddie kissed Linda good night and then embraced his dad and hugged and kissed his mother.

As everyone filed out, Freddie asked Bomar to stay, and they talked for a while. Bomar offered to hear Freddie's confession, a sacramental rite providing the final and essential absolution of sins in case the worst should happen while Freddie was under the knife. Freddie, however had already confessed to a hospital-affiliated priest, and this gave Bomar some comfort. Next, Freddie requested Bomar say the rosary with him, which they did. Freddie then asked Bomar to "help take care of" Gloria the next day. Bomar recognized that the family might have some "hard decisions" to make, and he would of course help however he could. Then Freddie asked this: "Would *you* let me know when I wake up what really happened? If I've lost this leg or not?" Freddie paused. "I don't want my parents to have to do that." Finally, Bomar began to say his favorite prayer, the Memorare, and Freddie surprised him by joining him:

> Remember, O most gracious Virgin Mary,
> That never was it known that anyone who fled to thy protection,
> Implored thy help, or sought thy intercession was left unaided.
> Inspired with this confidence, I fly unto thee, O virgin of virgins, my Mother.
> To thee I come, before thee I stand, sinful and sorrowful
> O Mother of the Word Incarnate, despise not my petitions,
> But, in thy mercy, hear and answer them. Amen.

"As a kid," Freddie explains in *I Play to Win*, "I had a holy card with this prayer that I carried in my pocket and I read it every night before I went to bed. I said it so much I memorized it, and I said it all during high school and college."

The two souls then sat in silence for a while. After a moment, Freddie began reciting the rosary again, softly starting, "I believe in God, the Father Almighty, creator of heaven and earth." Fr. Bomar remained quiet for a while, listening, then just as he started to leave, Freddie slowly drifted to sleep.

LATER, FREDDIE VAGUELY REMEMBERED WAKING UP early on that Friday as the nurses attended to his preparations for surgery. At six thirty, family and friends gathered in Freddie's room for support. After a few short whispers, Freddie was wheeled down to the operating room, and everybody else retired to the conference room on the seventh floor, adjacent to Dr. Moreton's office.

Around nine, Moreton opened his office door and said, "Father Bomar, you have a telephone call." Bomar walked across the room and into the next office.

In fact, there was no call. The biopsy had proved the tumor to be malignant, Moreton informed Bomar. The amputation was already underway; they would take Freddie's leg at the hip.

Remaining stoic, Bomar returned to the conference room, and Moreton asked Big Fred and Gloria to come into his office.

Moments later, those in the conference room heard Gloria scream, a deep and anguished sound, indicative of the eternal bond between a mother and her son.

AROUND MIDDAY, FREDDIE BEGAN TO REGAIN CON-sciousness, drifting in and out of the twilight state: "I remember trying to reach down with my hand to feel if I still had my leg but I couldn't manage it before I went under again."

Shortly thereafter, the doctors ushered Bomar into the intensive care unit, to Freddie's bedside. Freddie continued to have fleeting moments of alertness.

Bomar details the scene in his own memoirs: "He was just coming out of his anesthesia and waking up, and I told him that things went well. He looked me right in the eye and asked what happened. He always looked you dead in the eyes when he talked to you, and I knew that he wanted the truth. He just asked: 'Did I lose my leg?' And I said yes."

Freddie had known this was a possible, even probable, outcome, but events had moved so swiftly that he must have been disoriented, peering through the haze of anesthesia and trying to grasp his new reality. Soon it would occur to him that he was now face-to-face with the greatest challenge of his life.

Freddie (28) was the first sophomore to start for Darrell Royal since the great all-American Tommy Nobis in 1963.

Oklahoma Heisman Trophy winner Steve Owens on a collision course with Freddie (28) in 1969.

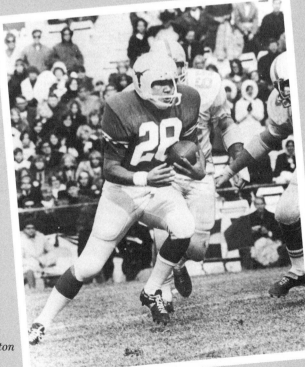

"When you get your hands on the ball, do something with it," Big Fred advised. Here Freddie returns a punt in the 1969 Cotton Bowl win against Tennessee.

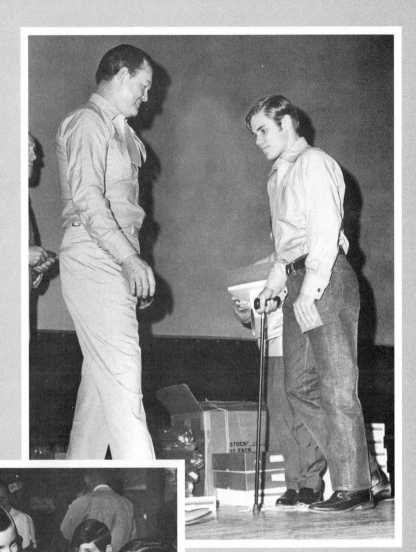

Freddie made many great plays on the football field, but none were cheered more than his triumphant walk across the lettermen's banquet stage to receive his letter jacket from Coach Royal.

A young fan at the lettermen's banquet in 1970 gets an assist with trying on a letter jacket.

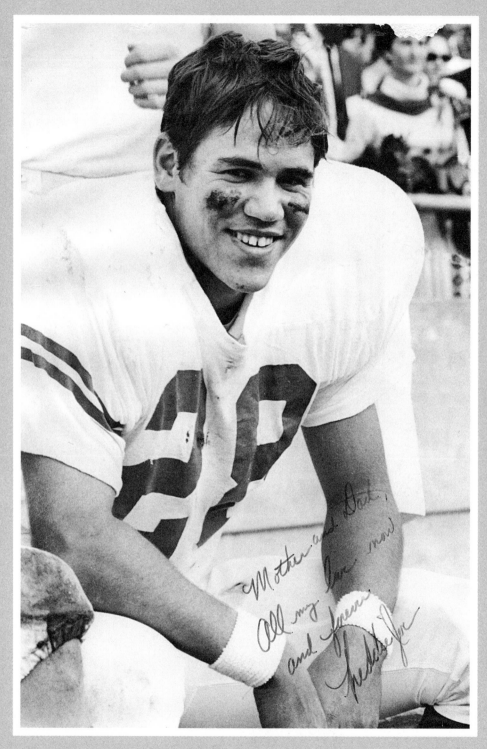

"Mother and Dad, All my love now and forever."

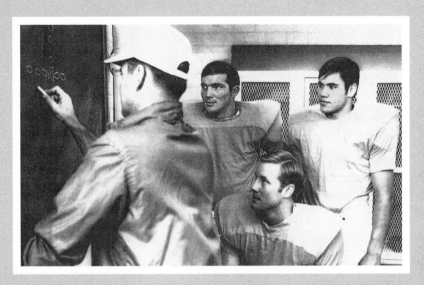

Defensive backs coach Fred Akers having a "skull session" with Denny Aldridge, Ron Ehrig, and Freddie.

The Texas victory over Notre Dame in the 1970 Cotton Bowl made it unanimous—the Longhorns were No. 1.

Celebrating the 1970 Cotton Bowl victory over Notre Dame. Left to right: Scotty Palmer, Bobby Wuensch, Freddie, Scott Henderson, and Bill Atessis.

Steve Worster, Paul Robichau, Freddie, and Jay Cormier at Robichau's wedding in 1970.

BRIAN PICCOLO   CHICAGO BEARS

Brian Piccolo of the Chicago Bears wrote in a touching letter to Freddie, "Our lives are in God's hands now."

"I didn't replace Freddie [at safety]," Rick Nabors said.
"Nobody could. I only stepped in for him."

Congratulating Cotton Speyrer after his key pass reception, which kept Texas's game-winning drive alive in the 1970 Cotton Bowl. Trainer Frank Medina looks on.

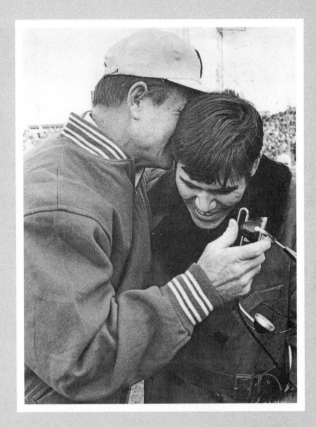

"We got 'em, Freddie, we got 'em!" Coach Royal shouted when victory over Notre Dame was assured.

Flanked by Sammy and Father Bomar, Freddie stood with his crutches and cheered on his teammates in the Cotton Bowl victory over Notre Dame.

Freddie was proud of his first car, a blue Pontiac Grand Prix (pictured here), but really moved into the fast lane with his 1971 burnt-orange T-top Corvette with Texas license plate UT-28.

Soon after his amputation, Freddie moved into Father Bomar's rectory. They developed a close bond, and Bomar often accompanied Freddie to speaking engagements.

President Nixon was a big fan of college football, and an even bigger fan of Freddie Steinmark. Accompanied by Coach Royal, Freddie traveled to the White House to present the president with a football signed by all the members of the 1969 national champion Texas Longhorns.

Discussions with doctors such as Dr. Healey, seen here, were guided by Freddie's demand for the unvarnished truth. Sammy, who always wanted to be just like Freddie, head to toe, looks on.

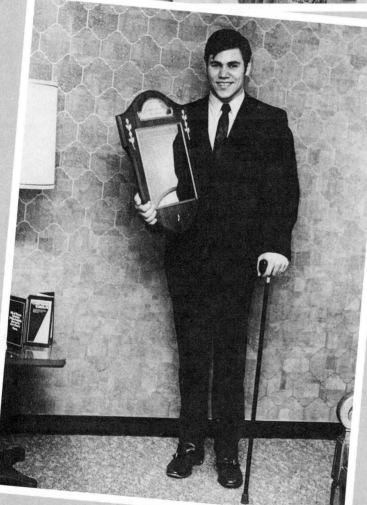

The Philadelphia Sports Writers Association honored Freddie with their Most Courageous Athlete Award. Previous winners included Joe DiMaggio, Ben Hogan, and Freddie's personal hero, Mickey Mantle.

TOP: *Freddie's image is shown at every game on the Freddie Steinmark Memorial Scoreboard's Jumbotron, unveiled in 1972. BOTTOM: It's a tradition for Longhorn players about to take the field to tap "Hook 'em Horns" on an image of Freddie at the base of the Memorial Scoreboard.*

PART FOUR
1970–1971

Christmas has its miracles,
and its sorrows.

GLORIA STEINMARK

CHAPTER 13

NO TIME TO LOSE

A T NOON ON THAT FRIDAY, THE PUBLIC RE-
lations office at M. D. Anderson Hospital issued a press
release:

A surgical biopsy and a pathological examination of tissue
was performed on Mr. Freddie Steinmark. The tumor of the left
femur, or thighbone, was found to be malignant. It was necessary to remove the left leg at the hip. Anderson physicians reported that Mr. Steinmark's condition is satisfactory. He will
remain in the recovery room for the next twenty-four hours.

This type of malignant tumor is termed a bone sarcoma,
meaning that it originates within the bone itself. It gives no evidence of its presence until it either grows outside the shaft of the
bone, forming a bulge, or causes pain from pressure.

When either of these symptoms occurs, an X-ray examination is called for to see the precise cause. In this case, pain was
the only complaint and it was not severe enough to interfere
with activity.

An X-ray was ordered which revealed a change in the bone,
requiring a biopsy. This type of tumor is not the result of injury
and has no connection with the patient's having played football.

In fact, when Dr. Martin consulted with the Steinmarks after the operation, he explained that the musculature of Freddie's strong leg had in essence held his skeleton together, and that upon opening his leg, doctors discovered very little bone left. It was really a wonder that Freddie had been walking, much less playing football.

In Austin, the national champion Longhorns prepared to play the Fighting Irish of Notre Dame in the Cotton Bowl—without their starting safety, Freddie Steinmark. It was unusual—Freddie had started every game in the past two seasons—but the players were determined and proven winners. They went about their business as best they could. Freddie, though, remained on everybody's mind.

Players and coaches who were part of the 1969 Texas Longhorns often use the word "family" to describe how close-knit the team was and how well the players knew and understood one another. Ted Koy, when asked during Cotton Bowl workouts about Freddie and his amputation, told the Associated Press, "He'll react to it like a champion. There's no doubt in my mind that he will." Coach Royal added: "He's got a tubful of guts. [When I recruited Freddie] I suspicioned he had 150 pounds of heart. My suspicions were correct."

This belief in Freddie extended well beyond the team. The University of Texas, during the week of Freddie's surgery, set up a trust for donations to help with Freddie's medical bills and other needs. Gifts of all kinds, from every corner of the country, arrived in room 415-W. Freddie received an untold number of letters, telegrams, and cards from strangers who were moved by his story. Even perennial rivals of the Longhorns reached out to Freddie, demonstrating how mutual respect and sportsmanship ultimately underpin the drama of the college ball field. Texas A&M sent him a telegram with 1,400 signatures on it. The message read: "We're all behind you and hope you get well quick." Rice University sent a note: "To an outstanding athlete and great person. We want you to know in this trying time for you that all of us are on the same side of the scrimmage line." Arkansas, Texas Tech, Penn State, and many others also sent messages for Freddie.

Freddie, lying in his hospital bed, was overwhelmed by the outpouring of support. "No one ever got the psychological therapy I got," he writes in *I Play to Win*, "in those days and weeks that followed. It's a wonder the US Postal Service didn't declare me off limits." Indeed, his room became so overstuffed with flowers, and their pungent aromas, that he could hardly breathe. With his approval, the hospital staff distributed the floral arrangements around the cancer ward, brightening the rooms of the other patients, whose stories hadn't attracted national interest.

In fact, President Nixon himself telephoned Freddie and his family on the Sunday after the surgery. Nixon remembered Freddie from the Big Shootout in Arkansas, and Bud Wilkinson, who was an informal Nixon adviser as well as one of the announcers for the game, told the president of Freddie's ordeal. President Nixon called Freddie's hospital room, where Gloria answered the phone and spoke with the president before handing the phone to Freddie.

Gloria, for her part, remembers that she and the president spoke, but she can't recall what was said. Everything at the time, just two days after her son's surgery, blended into a fog. The same goes for Freddie. "Honestly," he writes, "I don't remember much of what was said; I was excited, of course, and they were still giving me sedation. The president said something about, 'We all admire your courage and we want you to hurry and get well.' He talked some about the Cotton Bowl game coming up with Notre Dame . . . and then he wished me luck." But the president's gesture left an indelible mark on Freddie. "That was the greatest honor I've ever had in my life," he told the AP. "Imagine, him calling me."

Word of Freddie's amputation had traveled to another celebrity as well. This time, Freddie answered the phone. "Hello, Freddie. This is Bob Hope." Freddie talked briefly with the entertainer, and, knowing his mother was a huge fan, quickly handed the phone to Gloria.

Although Freddie was understandably exhausted, his parents, too, were worn thin and sleepless. Big Fred stayed each night in the hospital, catching what few winks he could on the couch in the reception area outside Freddie's room. Freddie was well aware of the stress on his parents, and on the others who cared for him, and he did what he could to ease their burdens. When his beloved cousin Johnnyboy called him soon after the operation, Freddie heard the concern in his voice as he worked toward asking Freddie about the leg. Finally, Freddie told him, "Well, Johnnyboy, I've lost a few pounds and I'm not as fast as I used to be," and they laughed.

Freddie worried for Gloria more than anyone. On December 16, just four days after the amputation, Freddie's rehab began. The hospital staff needed to put him in a wheelchair and get him to the fourth floor. Freddie, sitting for the first time outside his bed (where a bedsheet covered his lower half), was worried about the effect that his appearance minus one major limb would have on his mother as he rolled out of the hospital room. He wheeled in front of the mirror so that he could see what he looked like, mentally preparing himself for all possible reactions.

He looked at himself. He looked strange, but it didn't bother him too much. "The main thing I worried about . . . is how others would react when they saw me. It didn't shock *me*, but I was afraid it might shock other people, and I would feel bad about that. Nobody wants to be pitied, or I certainly didn't. I wasn't helpless, not by a long shot." He wheeled from the mirror to the windowsill and grabbed a potted plant. He placed the small shrub on the seat of the wheelchair, in place of his left leg, and now, instead of looking strange, he just looked funny—"Anything for a laugh."

Members of the media, who were in a frenzy over the Freddie Steinmark story, were denied access to the hospital. "He is a fine boy—really inspirational," an M.D. Anderson spokesperson, Dr. R. Lee Clark, president of the hospital, told reporters. "[Freddie] has demonstrated great fortitude and marked determination to return as swiftly as possible to his life at the university." With not much else to go on initially, spare remarks like these and details like Richard Nixon's phone call were reported over and over in the national publications.

A couple of days after Freddie's rehab started, though, there was a rather harmless encounter with a reporter that started a firestorm. Big Fred and Father Bomar were having dinner in the hospital cafeteria when a reporter from the *Houston Post* stopped by to say hello. The man's name was Jack Agness, and he and Bomar were old friends. After chitchatting awhile, the priest and Big Fred were set to return to Freddie's room, and they invited Agness along. All in all, it was a quick, friendly visit. But a small article in the next morning's edition of the *Post* quoted Freddie saying how grateful he was to the hospital staff and everybody else in the country who had reached out to help him.

"It sure produced some steam around the hospital," Freddie writes. The hospital administration had purposefully put a lid on all media interaction with their patients, but they hadn't foreseen a reporter getting in through friendly back channels. Moreover, other members of the media were furious over Agness's scoop. The whole incident ultimately resulted in a security guard sitting outside room 415-W.

The security guard was still sitting there when Freddie's siblings arrived just a few days before Christmas. It was the first time any of them had flown. Upon arriving at M. D. Anderson, young Sammy leapt from the car and sprinted away from his family. "Sammy!" Big Fred shouted. But Sammy didn't listen, and he dashed through the hospital doors. He was going to see his brother, and that was that. For weeks, Sammy had agonized at home, praying and thinking of his big brother, so far away and in so much pain.

Sammy streaked down the fluorescent-lit hallway, found the stairs, and ran up them. He burst onto the fourth floor, bounced on his feet as he scanned room numbers, and took off in the direction of 415. The security guard, seeing him coming, stood up and gestured for him to stop. But young Sammy would not be denied. He juked and spun and slammed through the door into the room. Freddie, startled, looked up from the bed just in time to catch his little brother as he catapulted into the bed with him, crying out, "Freddie, I'm here!"

Freddie hugged his brother. Sammy shook in his arms, breathing hard from his mad dash. Big Fred arrived soon after, storming into the room. But Freddie stopped his father with a raised hand and said, "It's okay, Dad. It's okay," and whatever scolding Big Fred had been about to deliver just evaporated.

When the immediate emotion ebbed, Sammy asked his brother, "Does it hurt?"

"Not too bad," Freddie replied.

Sammy blinked against his tears. "Can I see?"

"Are you sure? You want to really see?"

Sammy nodded.

"Okay," Freddie said. He pulled back the sheet and let Sammy have a glimpse of the stump of his left leg.

A moment ticked by. "Freddie," Sammy said, "we gotta get you outta here before they take something else!"

Freddie looked at his father, and they all burst into laughter.

ON DECEMBER 23, DR. HEALEY, WHO WAS IN CHARGE OF the rehab regimen, decided to take Freddie to the Astrodome. The enclosed, air-conditioned stadium, only four years old, was known as the "Eighth Wonder of the World." It would be neat for Freddie to see it, and he would have ample opportunity to practice walking up and down stairs and ramps on his crutches.

Freddie, Linda, and his siblings first went to the Houston Zoo and then on to the Astrodome with the hospital crew. Reporters followed them there, and an impromptu press conference was set up. There are photographs of Freddie with his eyes downcast, a small, embarrassed smile on his face, and the Astrodome scoreboard (in 1969, a $2 million state-of-the-art piece of equipment) flashing: "The Astrodome salutes Freddie Steinmark—the No. 1 team's No. 1 guy!"

"This," Freddie told reporters as he nodded toward the scoreboard, "typifies the way people down here have treated me. People all across the nation have been the same. That's the reason I'm cheerful. I don't look at this operation as a defeat in any way. I have to go forward, and I will. The doctors here have given me a lot of hope. [But at the same time] they've never pulled any punches with me, and I'm grateful for that."

Freddie indicated that he would be back in classes after Christmas break and that, while he had been studying engineering, he now planned to go to law school after graduation. Then Freddie continued and, in his own words, *"really* popped off": "I will be in the Cotton Bowl on New Year's Day when my team runs onto the field. I will be in Austin on January 12th for our football banquet, and I'll walk across the stage on my new leg to get my letter."

The reporters scribbled like mad, but Dr. Healey was stunned. He quickly reminded everyone that while these were fantastic aspirations, Freddie hadn't even been fitted for a prosthesis yet and that these kinds of things, particularly a prosthetic leg, typically took months to master.

But Freddie didn't care. Freddie had his goals, and now they were on record.

FREDDIE WAS TO BE DISCHARGED FROM HIS HOSPITAL room on Christmas Eve so that he could join the Steinmark clan (the usual suspects had all arrived in Houston for the holiday) in the Anderson Mayfair apartment for one of Gloria's famous Christmas feasts.

Before he left, though, Freddie commissioned his sisters and his brother to round up some gifts for the children on the cancer ward. Freddie had fifty bucks to his name, and he gave the money to GiGi. Then GiGi, P.K., and Sammy ran down to the department store, returned with small presents, wrapped, and then distributed them to the children in the hospital. Freddie, though, remained in his room waiting for them. He didn't want to tag along. "I'm not that tough," he writes in *I Play to Win*.

At the Mayfair Anderson apartment, Freddie received an unexpected surprise. One of his regular night nurses—with whom he had talked about his childhood in Wheat Ridge and Duke, his father's beloved K-9 partner—brought him a puppy for Christmas. "Bravo" was a purebred, AKC German Shepherd. Bravo and Freddie took to one another at once. Happily holding Bravo on the couch, Freddie asked P.K. to scratch his foot. She jumped to the task and then recoiled just as quickly when he said, "No, the other one," and began to laugh. He'd lost a leg, but his sense of humor and his big brother's penchant for teasing were fully intact.

On Christmas Day, the Steinmarks had a turkey with all the fixings as well as pasta, as Italian families do on the big holidays. Freddie ate his fill and then some.

"I needed the stuffing more than the turkey did," he writes. Without his leg, Freddie weighed only 128 pounds.

CHAPTER 14

THE GREATEST DAY

O N NEW YEAR'S DAY 1970, FREDDIE CLAM-
bered aboard a private Cessna Air King provided by
the University of Texas and flew to Dallas to join his
Longhorn teammates. Freddie's family and Linda traveled separately in Dallas automobile dealer and UT alumnus Finley Ewing's
private DC-10. Ewing piloted the plane and brought along his wife,
Gail, to help the family feel more at ease during the flight. Freddie had defied the odds in making this trip, turning his doctors'
heads with his sheer pluck. "The doctors told Coach Royal I was
progressing, physically and psychologically, much faster than they
had anticipated," Freddie said. With the evidence before them, the
doctors had no choice but to grant Freddie's wishes and release
him for the Cotton Bowl.

Once on the ground, Freddie and his entire entourage got into
a limousine and drove straight to the stadium. In one way, Freddie was finally on familiar turf after weeks in hospital corridors
and rehab facilities. He had been to the Cotton Bowl several times
before. This was where, exactly one year earlier, he had helped defeat the Tennessee Volunteers in a great game, showcased by an
interception and three long punt returns, among other highlights.
Freddie knew this stadium. He knew the scent of the concrete and
the temperamental nature of the playing field: how it could go
from being a perfect, well-groomed playing surface to a slippery,

muddy mess, or even freezing into a solid block of ice in winter months. He knew the buildup to a nationally televised bowl game. He knew the quiet tension of the pregame locker room as well as the electric thrill of charging onto this field in front of tens of thousands of screaming fans. He knew what it was like to defy people's expectations. So in one sense, as he pulled up to the crowded stadium and gazed upon those high, fortresslike walls, he was home. He was with his team and in his element.

On the other hand, Freddie's world had changed so dramatically in the last three weeks that he might as well have been stepping onto the moon with Neil Armstrong. For starters, he was arriving via a limousine, along with a private entourage of oncologists and Father Bomar as his personal "bodyguard." Normally, Freddie would have arrived by charter bus and would be going through his pregame routine and meditations in the midst of his fellow teammates. Second, he was still adjusting to his new relationship with gravity: he weighed less, his center of balance had shifted, and he was still learning to use the aluminum crutches.

And for the first time in his life, Freddie worried that maybe he had made the wrong decision in pushing to get here. "There was this nagging feeling of apprehension when I stepped over the doorsill into the locker room entrance corridor," he later confessed. As much as Freddie wanted to be part of this moment with his team, he also sensed that a distance had already sprung up between him and the intimate circle of players. "In some ways, I felt a little on the outside," he explained, "because I didn't know what special drills Nabors and Tom Campbell and Danny Lester had gone through in the last three weeks." These were the guys that Freddie was normally so in tune with that he considered them all to have "a sort of private ESP," yet now he found himself off the wavelength. After the remarkable and terrifying journey of the last three weeks, Freddie was in a different atmosphere. Father Bomar sensed much the same thing, as he recalled in his memoir: "But this was a big, big thing we were doing. This was the National Championship . . . and we were bringing along a player who'd had major surgery just a few weeks before. I cannot tell you how electric the atmosphere was and how nervous we all were. . . . None of his teammates had seen him since before the operation and the loss of his leg, and there was a chance of psychological shock on both sides."

Even the locker room seemed strange to Freddie: "Everything was real quiet. It was weird. . . . I had never realized what a silence there is in a locker room before a game," he reported. And while he might not have been quite as concerned as Bomar about "psychological shock," he was worried that his presence might be a distraction as the team prepared for the game. "I was happy they dedicated the game to me," he said, "but I didn't want me to put any extra pressure on them. I didn't want them to go out feeling like they had to win the game for me."

But then, as he stood there unnoticed at the doorway of the locker room, amid his own uncertainty, Ted Koy, one of the star halfbacks, looked up and saw Freddie. Whether or not he sensed how vulnerable Freddie felt at the moment, his reaction was perfect: totally normal. "He came over and we said the usual things," Freddie remembered. "Then Eddie Phillips . . . then Scott Henderson. Then, I guess almost everybody came by where I was propped up on my crutches. . . . They didn't treat me exactly like I had just gone to the corner drugstore for ice cream, but not like I had just come back from the moon, either."

And just like that, Freddie was back on solid earth. This was his locker room again and this was his team. And far from being a distraction, Freddie's presence was cherished more than he could know. Ted Koy later recalled, "That was one of the most inspirational moments I had in college football. Not a word was said, but you could feel the emotion stream around the room. Freddie's mere presence inspired us. You could sense a little charge go through the room."

Years later, Coach Royal would also speak proudly of his team at this particular moment:

I don't think any of us trusted ourselves and our own emotions. When Freddie came in, we didn't want to treat him *exactly* like he was still on two legs. We didn't want to act real happy, like nothing at all had happened. But nobody ran up and made a big fuss. And yet, we hadn't even discussed it openly. We had not warned the players how to act or what to say. They just worked it out themselves. Sometimes they can be real mature about something like this. They have a knack for doing the correct thing, more so than some of us older folks.

Freddie stayed out of the way until the Longhorns left to warm up on the field, and then he sat in front of his locker, labeled "Steinmark—28" and prepped exactly as if he were a typical injured player. He even appeared in the program as if he were an active roster member. Father Bomar was with him, and so was Sammy. The equipment manager, Billy Schott, had placed a pair of cleats in Freddie's locker, just as he did for all the other players, but before Freddie's arrival, someone had removed the left shoe. Sammy stood in front of Freddie's locker and couldn't help wondering out loud, "Why did they only put one cleat out for you?" before remembering exactly why. Freddie sat at his locker, his mind swirling. Then he took off his street shoe and laced up the one cleat, his arm over Sammy's shoulder for support.

The team came back in shortly, and then it was time to focus. Game time was fast approaching, and Freddie had always loved this moment of intense concentration. "In those final moments right before kickoff, that's when the team withdraws within itself, coiling like a watch spring or a rattlesnake preparing to strike," he describes in *I Play to Win*. "I wasn't in uniform, but I felt it."

Finally, Coach Royal stood and delivered his final words to the team. He didn't have to tell them that they were the only undefeated team that was going to take the field that day. He didn't have to tell them that they were ranked number one in the nation. He didn't have to tell them that they had the most to lose in this matchup. Everyone in the locker room felt both the strength and the weight of that winning streak, and they knew they had a serious challenge to their legacy waiting just outside those doors. "If you're a longtime winner, you know every opponent is going to come at you in a suicide charge," Freddie later remarked. Fully aware of these pressures, the Longhorns streamed through the doors and down the tunnel toward the field with a quiet focus and an air of grim determination.

When Freddie followed the team down the tunnel and out into the open air of the stadium, he might have felt something like the old camaraderie, something like the familiar thrill he had known as a Longhorn player, but already he was being transformed into something else, whether he realized it or not. In the locker room, he was still "Fast Freddie" Steinmark, safety for the Texas Longhorns, but by the time he emerged from the tunnel on his crutches, Sammy by his side, into that bright clear day, he was becoming Freddie Joe Steinmark, national hero. Freddie described the physical scene vividly in *I Play to Win*: "When you come out of that tunnel into the Cotton Bowl arena itself, it's like somebody just opened a soundproof door to a big, bright earsplitting jungle . . . rows of stadium seats seem to stretch way off into the distance like my home Colorado mountains, and all the music and the yelling beat down on you until you can actually, physically feel the sound vibrations."

What Freddie didn't realize was that the crowd was cheering for *him* as he emerged onto the field. One by one, people recognized him, and the response built throughout the stadium. In that moment, he still saw himself as a small part of a big team. The rest of the world, however, was looking at a young man growing into a legend before their eyes. To a certain degree, Father Bomar recognized and understood this dynamic. As Freddie's future traveling companion, he would often witness this incredible outpouring of support and encouragement from around the country. Bomar realized that Freddie was being lifted by events larger than any of them. As he later recalled:

> You have to also understand that it was a really hard time for the nation. It was near Christmas and the Vietnam War was going on, the Civil Rights issue was very strong, etc., and the country

was in a funk. . . . Freddie's situation was something that Americans could take strength and comfort from. He did not want any attention at all, but I explained to him he didn't have that choice anymore. The story was bigger than he was, and the letters started arriving to prove it. It was like a tidal wave of emotion, and he got thousands of them.

Indeed, some twelve thousand letters arrived for Freddie in just the first two months after his leg was amputated. He received phone calls and telegrams of support as well, from people and organizations across the nation. The appeal of his story and his personality was universal. "Your courage has inspired athletes everywhere," wrote Coach Joe Cipriano and the University of Nebraska basketball players. "In great crises we see great courage, and your bravery is an inspiration to our servicemen and our nation," wrote Brigadier General James Cross, a commander at Bergstrom Air Force Base. Even during the buildup to the Cotton Bowl game, the University of Notre Dame sent words of encouragement to Freddie: "The entire athletic department, staff, coaches and players send warmest regards to you and are remembering you in our prayers and masses."

In other words, as Father Bomar privately recognized, and as the *Fort Worth Star Telegram* publicly declared: "He has become a national sports figure."

Surely, part of the appeal of Freddie's story was the very nature of the disease that he was battling. Here was a handsome young hero fighting cancer, one of the most terrifying illnesses known to man. Cancer has always been a ruthless killer, often striking without warning, but in the early days of diagnosis and treatment, the prognosis was generally dire, since there were far fewer treatment options. In *Making Cancer History: Disease and Discovery at the University of Texas M. D. Anderson Cancer Center*, James Olson describes Freddie's surgeon, Dr. Richard Martin, as one of the most skilled practitioners of his time, but he was still painfully limited by the current state of knowledge in oncology and by the available tools: "In twenty years as a surgeon, Martin had severed a tangled mountain of malignant arms, legs, shoulders, breasts, hips, hands, and feet, a burden that weighed heavily on him . . . but only fools risked lives to save limbs."

Further, Olson describes how cancer has been part of the human condition from the very beginning: "Maybe a supernova somewhere in the galaxy a billion years ago bathed the earth in neutrinos, radiating all living tissues and wreaking havoc with genes and chromosomes. Fossil remains demonstrate that cancer afflicted dinosaurs. . . . Whether the earliest humans ever suffered from Ewing's sarcoma [the specific type of cancer that struck Freddie] will remain a mystery, but when the first *Homo sapiens* trekked out of East Africa, other varieties of the disease surely accompanied them."

Cancer is an insidious affliction. It results from mutations in the genes that regulate cellular proliferation. Such mutations may have a genetic origin or may be triggered by environmental sources such as asbestos or nuclear radiation. In addition, cancer tricks the body into thinking that a mutated cell is healthy and that there is no need to attack it. As a result, in the absence of treatment, cancerous cells multiply without limit, causing failure in the organ of origin and eventually spreading throughout the body. Cancer overcomes the body's immune protection by establishing a perimeter, or "great wall," that prevents antigen-presenting cells (which bind to pathogens and allow immune system cells such as T cells to recognize and destroy them) from identifying cancerous cells as harmful. Worse, cancer directly suppresses and even attacks killer T cells, which allows cancerous cells to run riot.

Cancer strikes a primordial fear. Freddie was a victim in a timeless war of genetics and pain. Even Freddie's teammates felt the weight of it. "That kind of thing brings you down to earth real quick," Bob McKay, senior offensive tackle, told David Flores of the *San Antonio Express-News* years later. Flores went on to write:

The swift, brutal turn of events in Steinmark's life stunned his teammates and generated an outpouring of sympathy from people all over the country. . . . Instead of being totally consumed with thoughts of Notre Dame . . . the Longhorns spent a lot of time thinking about Steinmark.

"It made you understand that national championships weren't the most important things going," then-Texas Coach Darrell Royal said this week, reflecting on the effect Steinmark's amputation had on the Longhorns. "Freddie really was an all-out competitor."

So it was no wonder that people around the world responded so viscerally to the image of this handsome young athlete standing on the sideline, balancing on one leg with the help of brand-new crutches. After all, if anyone could fight back and win, it might just be this remarkable kid from Wheat Ridge, Colorado. Was there anyone better to represent the hopes of the nation?

Freddie was overwhelmed by the response and as surprised as anyone. Over the weeks, in between rehab sessions, Freddie signed and mailed more than four thousand thank-you letters to people who "sent flowers to his hospital room or sent money to the trust fund set up by school officials for his personal use." For thousands of others, he had to rely on the media to help him deliver his thanks. The United Press International gladly assisted: "Steinmark said he wanted to thank everybody for the letters and gifts he received. He said he got among other things, a gold crucifix from a man who said it had been in the family for 100 years, a gold medallion from a Princeton University man, autographed footballs from this year's Notre Dame and Alabama teams and [piles] of mail."

"This is the reason I'm in such a cheerful mood today," Freddie was reported saying. The UPI also reported, "Steinmark's voice came the closest to breaking when he talked about his Texas teammates and about the Cotton Bowl." It was natural that Notre Dame had loomed large in Freddie's imagination from an early age, as it did for many devout Catholics who were dedicated football players. When he realized that he would never play *for* Notre Dame, he then dreamed playing *against* Notre Dame, to one day take the field against that storied program. "I won't get a chance to play, but

I'm still happy my teammates will play," he said. "Even when I was a little kid, I always dreamed about playing Notre Dame one day."

As Freddie crutched his way to the Longhorn sideline amid the roar of the crowd—many of them chanting, "Freddie! Freddie!"—he stood in a world that he never could have imagined. Pausing for a moment, Sammy at his side, Freddie looked up at the crowd and smiled. On the sideline, in unspoken acknowledgment, one by one many of his teammates came up to him and tapped him on the shoulder. Freddie was no longer just a boy from Wheat Ridge, Colorado. He was no longer a "factory worker" or an "obscure safety," as he had often referred to himself. For tens of thousands of Americans, he was now a hero. As James Olson recorded in *Making Cancer History*, "Freddie was determined to watch from the sideline. Wearing a new suit, he hobbled on crutches, the right [*sic*] leg of his pants carefully pinned up. . . . In the press box, broadcasters noted Freddie's presence, and as fans with portable radios listened in, an ovation pulsed through the Cotton Bowl."

Audiences watching the CBS television broadcast were shown pregame images of a smiling Freddie standing on new crutches and graciously granting interviews from the sideline minutes before kickoff. He couldn't know it yet, but this was the beginning of a new world, one where he was transformed into a sports icon, a passionate advocate for cancer research, a nationally recognized humanitarian, and an international symbol of courage and leadership.

But while standing on the sideline of the 1970 Cotton Bowl, Freddie Joe Steinmark had only one thing on his mind: beating Notre Dame.

Texas was riding the longest winning streak in the nation, but Notre Dame was a fearsome team of great talent and size. In addition to boasting future NFL Hall of Famer Joe Theismann at quarterback, their linemen seemed like giants compared with their Longhorn counterparts. Irish defensive tackle Mike McCoy stood six five and weighed 274 pounds. His Longhorn opponent, right guard Mike Dean, was six inches shorter and seventy-four pounds lighter. To make matters worse, days of rain had left the field in terrible condition. The turf had been transformed into a slick, muddy mess that had the potential to hamper the Longhorns' wishbone offense. Sportscasters and writers everywhere were speculating that Coach Royal would have to alter his game plan. In response, however, Royal uttered his now-famous phrase "We're gonna dance with the one who brung us."

Finally, kickoff arrived, and the game began with a surge of momentum for the Irish. Theismann quickly went to work, picking apart the Longhorn secondary, which was playing without Freddie for the first time in two years. The Irish settled for a field goal on an early possession, and then Theismann connected with Tom Gatewood for a fifty-four-yard touchdown pass, and Notre Dame jumped out to a 10–0 lead. Freddie's gut must have been in knots as he watched the Irish receivers do their worst to the Longhorn secondary: all season long, no receiver had gotten behind the Longhorn secondary so easily to complete a scoring play like that.

In the second quarter, however, the wishbone went to work with a long drive down the center of the field. It was clear that the game was going to be a hard-fought, nasty slugfest. The Notre Dame players, according to the Longhorns on the field that day, employed scorched-earth tactics when it came to winning the psychological aspect of the game: cursing like sailors, delivering constant verbal harassment, and administering a cheap shot or two at the bottom of on-field pileups and scrums. The Longhorns were generally a fairly well-mannered group, but they were spirited too, and they began to give as good as they got. In one instance, the badly outsized Longhorn right guard, Mike Dean, knocked his gargantuan opponent, 274-pound Mike McCoy, backward and flat to the ground. Longhorn tackle Bobby Wuensch came over to rub it in, bolster his teammate, and make sure that McCoy knew he was going to get a hell of a game today: "Listen to me, you son of a bitch," he yelled. "This little boy right here is going to kick your fat ass all day long!" During that long second-quarter drive, Dean continued to play well against McCoy, and Texas grounded and pounded its way to the two-yard line, where Jim Bertelsen finally punched the ball into the end zone with a bruising cannonball of a run. At halftime, the score was 10–7, the Irish on top.

When the two sides came back out for the second half, it was more of the same: Theismann throwing for what would turn out to be a record day for him, and Texas grinding it out on the ground. Freddie was brimming with confidence when he realized that the Longhorn wishbone could drive on Notre Dame so effectively. "Everybody had tried to throw the ball against Notre Dame because of their big defense," Freddie said, "but we went 74 yards for our first touchdown in nine plays, and just two of them were passes. I felt then that we would win."

At the end of the third quarter, the Longhorns mounted another impressive drive, one that many still consider an example of the wishbone at its finest. The Longhorns strung together eighteen plays without a single pass attempt, driving seventy-seven yards, eating up eight minutes of the clock, and capping it off with a two-yard plunge by Ted Koy, who took the pitch after a perfect series of feints by quarterback James Street. Texas took its first lead of the game early in the fourth quarter at 14–10.

The Fighting Irish weren't done yet, however, and Theismann led his team back down the field for another scoring drive. With just over six minutes left in the game, the Longhorns needed to mount one more comeback. As Coach Royal had said they would, they "danced with the one who brung 'em." As the wishbone offense again came rumbling to life, the Longhorns began a slow, bruising drive down the field. The Fighting Irish put up a valiant effort, forcing the Longhorns into challenging third- and fourth-down conversions, but each time Texas managed to force their way past the first-down marker and keep the drive alive. It was a drive eerily similar to the one they had mounted just weeks before against Arkansas in the Big Shootout. Finally, with just over two minutes to play, the Irish held again, and the Longhorns found themselves facing a critical fourth down. Texas called a time-out, and Street came trotting over to confer with Coach Royal. Royal had proved himself to be a steely gambler when everything was on the line. In Fayetteville, with his back against the wall, he had called for that unpredictable pass play, and this time was no different. Freddie, hovering nearby, heard him make the call: "Left 89 out."

It was a pass play, but it was also designed to create space for the quarterback to run if he saw an opening in the defense. When Street dropped back, however, there was no opening. As he scrambled to his left, an Irish defender was charging him, so Street fired the ball downfield toward the left sideline. The pass was low and behind his receiver, Cotton Speyrer. It looked so impossible to catch that many of the Notre Dame players (and coaches) immediately assumed it was an incomplete pass. But then the stadium exploded in a cheer. Speyrer had somehow managed to pivot and dive back toward the ball, catching it just inches from the ground, hauling it in, and getting the first down. Three plays later, Billy Dale burst into the end zone to put the Longhorns in the lead once again, 21–17.

Freddie and the rest of the Longhorns were ecstatic, but measured in their response. They knew that even with less than two minutes on the clock, Theismann was still dangerous. Sure enough, he drove hard and fast into scoring position on several long pass plays. The Longhorns held their breath as he dropped back and wound up for another throw. Just one of his sharpshooter passes would put the Irish back on top. But then the sharpshooter fired a pass that was off by a couple of inches. The football flew past his tight end's fingertips, and Longhorn back Tom Campbell swooped in for the game-ending interception. "Tom didn't even stop running and hand the ball to the referee," Freddie said. "He just headed straight for our bench, which had just become a wild tribal dance."

The victory sealed, the Longhorns were not only undisputed national champions in every poll, but they had also enshrined themselves in the annals of college football history, legend, and lore. Reporters on the sidelines rushed in to capture the joyous moment: "The Longhorns made another dramatic comeback to edge Notre Dame, 21–17, and nail down the undisputed national championship. Royal was standing near Steinmark when defensive back Tom Campbell preserved the Texas victory by intercepting a Joe

Theismann pass with less than a minute left. Royal responded by running to Steinmark and giving him a big hug. 'We got 'em, Freddie, we got 'em,' Royal said as he held Steinmark closely."

Freddie himself recalled, "Then everybody started grabbing me and throwing me around like a rag doll and Father Bomar and Dr. Healy and the police sergeant were trying to keep me upright." Eventually, Freddie and his small entourage managed to make it through the swarming crowds and back into the locker room for the postgame celebration, which included a lot of wound stanching, bandaging, and concussion testing after the incredibly tough game. The mood was raucous, however, and the atmosphere decidedly festive. After a short while, Coach Royal climbed onto a bench to deliver his congratulations to the team. Then, in a moment of great emotion, he delivered the game ball to Freddie. It was the ball that Tom Campbell had plucked out of the air in that final interception, and as he said, there was no question whom the ball was going to go to. Coach Royal held the ball over his head and proclaimed, "We've got a guy that we love a lot. Freddie, here it is for you." The room erupted. In the back of the locker room, Freddie bowed his head, overcome with emotion as his teammates mobbed him. They eventually ferried him to the front of the room. "Then [Royal] gave it to me and hugged me and kissed me and he had tears in his eyes," Freddie recounted. "A lot of people did. Me too."

Just across the way, in the Notre Dame locker room, Joe Theismann and his Irish teammates were very much aware of Freddie. As the *Washington Star* later reported: "Theismann said if Notre Dame had won he wanted the squad to give the game ball to Fred Steinmark. . . . 'He had a lot of courage and you've got to admire him for it,' Theismann said."

FREDDIE WAS EXHAUSTED. HE KNEW THAT HIS PARENTS, doctors, and pilots were all waiting for him, so after a brief conversation with former US president Lyndon Johnson, who had come to the locker room to congratulate the team and personally express his admiration for Freddie, Freddie slipped away, back to the limousine and the waiting Cessna Air King. He later recollected, "I meant it sincerely when a couple of young reporters came up to me immediately after the game and asked my reactions. I said it was the greatest day of my life."

Freddie found joy in his teammates' victory more than anything. The fact that he could be there with them to share it was just icing on the cake. He was happy for them and proud to have been a part of it. And it was this spirit that carried him into the next, remarkable phase of his life.

CHAPTER 15

ON THE ROAD AGAIN

REDDIE RECEIVED HIS PROSTHETIC LEG, "A $1,320 beauty," on the Monday after the Cotton Bowl. He endeavored to walk right away. "My incision wasn't fully healed," he recounts in *I Play to Win*, "but I strapped on the darn thing and I spent a couple of hours each morning and a couple of more in the afternoon, trying to learn how to swing it." It was more than tricky, but if Freddie meant to meet his goal of walking across the stage at the UT football awards banquet, he would have to learn how to walk all over again in under a week.

Meanwhile, this phase of Freddie's life took on tornadic qualities. Thousands of letters, all with good wishes, arrived. Invitations to events, to speak, to be a guest of honor, streamed in. It became overwhelming. That year, the Hula Bowl committee in Honolulu dedicated their game to Freddie. They invited Freddie, Linda, Gloria, and Big Fred to the island, but this created a tough decision for Freddie. He would miss precious rehab time and the chance to meet his goal. "I hated that my parents wouldn't get a trip to Hawaii," Freddie writes, "but I was mule-headed about the banquet."

On Friday, January 9, the M. D. Anderson doctors and therapists—much to their own surprise—gave their final approval of Freddie's use of the prosthesis, just in time for the banquet on Monday. This was several weeks ahead of the schedule the doctors had originally laid out. The *Houston Chronicle* reported: "An impish grin spread across Freddie Steinmark's face Friday afternoon. 'Golf anyone?' the former Texas Longhorns' star safety asked as he flipped his black cane over so it resembled a putter." A photograph accompanying the article shows a smiling Freddie, joking with his cane. Although a lighthearted moment, it presaged Freddie's summer, when he would learn to balance on one leg and swing actual golf clubs. During a nine-hole round with Tom Kite and Ben Crenshaw, two UT alumni who would become professional golfing champions, Freddie shot a 46, a good score for most amateurs on two legs.

Before Freddie's departure from Houston, he watched the Hula Bowl from his Mayfair apartment, along with Linda, Father Bomar, and his parents. During halftime, Freddie made a long-distance call to the stadium press box to express his gratitude for the game's dedication, and he spoke with ABC announcers Chris Schenkel and Bud Wilkinson—the pair that had covered Freddie's last football game, at Arkansas, just four weeks earlier.

THE BIG NIGHT WAS ELECTRIC. THE UNIVERSITY OF TEXas annual football banquet had been moved to the Municipal Auditorium in order to accommodate the overflow crowd of more than four thousand. It was a much different event from ones in years past. Freddie explained: "The Texas football banquet format was another example of Darrell Royal ingenuity. The Longhorn season had not been an ordinary season, so he didn't want to have an ordinary banquet, bloated with long, formal speeches and boring platitudes. Instead, he thought it should be a celebration, a fun night. So he hit on a novel idea—a western party, with everybody in boots and jeans, a string band picking and singing, a menu with barbecue and beans and onions and a lot of laughs. And the public invited at $5 a throw."

Those in attendance included former president Lyndon B. Johnson and his wife, Lady Bird. Cactus Pryor, one of Texas's leading humorists and political satirists, served as master of ceremonies, and he narrated a Longhorn blooper reel. As Freddie described it: "[They] had combed our game films and extracted the fumbles, the dropped passes, the slips and stumbles, the somersaults, and put them all on one reel and showed them in slow motion, interrupting with occasional shots of Coach Royal grimacing or muttering something under his breath, or turning away in disgust."

The evening culminated with the presentation of letter jackets to the Longhorn players, who each walked across the stage to receive his letter and shake Coach Royal's hand. The player announced right before Freddie was Cotton Speyrer, whose tremendous fourth-down catch in the Cotton Bowl had made that victory possible. As Speyrer approached the stage, Coach Royal folded his letter jacket into the size of a football and tossed it low and behind him, almost on the floor. Freddie writes, "Cotton dropped to his knee and caught it, just like he caught Street's pass in the Notre Dame game. The banquet crowd roared."

As Coach Royal gathered himself at the microphone, Freddie began his laborious journey to the stage with his new slow, mechanical walk. Scott Henderson was right behind him as a backup. One reporter described the scene:

> Amid the jokes, the laughter, the fun, the films, and the trophies there was one poignant moment when the crowd was hushed. Royal was handing out the letter jackets to the Longhorns. "The next two players," he said, "would come to the stage together . . . Scott Henderson and Freddie Steinmark."
>
> Unaided, a slim, cheerful, awesomely-courageous figure, face split by a grin, hobbled across the stage, big Scott Henderson at his side, and the applause started in the back of the big coliseum and it swept forward and it overshadowed anything else that drew applause Monday night. On and on the applause went, and there wasn't a dry eye in the house. The ovation for Freddy Steinmark continued until Royal held up a hand, so he could continue. Unforgettable.

In Freddie's words: "Naturally, I had a stomach full of emotions. I remember feeling bad about Scott Henderson giving up his solo appearance to be my bodyguard and consequently not getting recognition for himself." He goes on, highlighting the nature of his friendship with Henderson: "Of course [Scott] told me later that the applause was really for him, that he could hear people in the audience asking, 'Who is that guy limping across the stage with Henderson?'"

THAT WEEK, FREDDIE MOVED INTO A SPARE ROOM AT THE rectory of St. Peter the Apostle Catholic Church, at the invitation of Father Bomar. The church and its staff could provide additional support for Freddie as he continued with his course load and attended to the thousands of letters and many speaking invitations. An Austin furniture dealer, who insisted on anonymity, was kind enough to donate the furnishings for Freddie's room—a bed, a desk, and carpeting, as well as drapes in Longhorn burnt orange.

Because of the many generous donations, Freddie was also able to order a Pontiac Grand Prix with a metallic blue body and a white top. It had a special dashboard switch for the high-beam lights, replacing the floorboard switch operated by the left foot.

When Freddie went to secure his disability parking permit for the car, the clerk, unaware that Freddie was on crutches, his pants leg pinned up, asked him, "Is this a temporary disability?"

Freddie replied with a smile, "I would like to think so . . . but I'm afraid it's not."

After reevaluating himself and his purpose that semester, Freddie changed his major to prelaw, the same as Scott Henderson. Freddie envisioned that he might be more effective in society if he could navigate the law. And he most likely imagined that he and his good buddy Henderson might work together one day.

AS SPRING FOOTBALL PRACTICE NEARED, FREDDIE wished to remain somehow involved with the Longhorns. Although a newspaper article at the time mentions that Freddie spoke briefly with the baseball coach, it was Coach Ellington of the freshmen team who was quick to pick up on the idea of "Coach Steinmark." When asked why Freddie became a coach for the freshmen instead of the varsity defensive backs, Coach Akers said, "Because Ellington got to him first!"

Just after the semester started, Freddie received a powerful, emotional, handwritten letter. It came out of the blue from the former Chicago Bears running back Brian Piccolo, who had been stricken with cancer just a few months before Freddie. Piccolo wrote:

> I watched your game with Arkansas from my hospital bed while recovering from the [November 28] surgery and then read about your problems a few days later. I guess I, more than any other football player, knew how you must have felt. I spent a lot of time thinking about you and praying for you in those few days and that's when I decided I would write. . . . Fred, I guess I'd mainly like to share with you my feelings since my operation. Simply that our lives are in God's hands now just as they were before our illnesses were known, and I shall never stop praying to God for the strength and help to carry out the plan that he has laid out for me. I know you are a courageous young man and I hope this letter might be of some help to you. Perhaps maybe one day we will meet one another. I am sure we would have a lot to talk about. Best of luck to you, Fred.
> Your friend,
> Brian Piccolo

The speaking invitations came in fast and furious as the semester progressed. In late January, Freddie flew to Pennsylvania to receive the Philadelphia Sports Writers Association's Most Courageous Athlete Award, truly an elite honor, previously bestowed on the likes of Joe DiMaggio, Ben Hogan, and Steinmark personal hero Mickey Mantle. Freddie had prepared a dynamic reception speech. Accepting his award, Freddie said, "I'm awed to be considered to be with such a great group of previous recipients. I want to thank the dear Lord for giving me the opportunity to participate in football, baseball, and athletics and to learn the ideals so appropriate to life in general. I want to thank the dear Lord for giving me the chance to play under Coach Royal and the University of Texas. And I want to thank the dear Lord for making it possible for me to be here tonight. Thank you."

By early February, Freddie was feeling the burden of multiple, complicated stressors: learning about his cancer and its possible treatments; answering all the encouraging letters; deciding which speaking invitations to accept; juggling his studies with coaching duties; and adjusting to his new way of living. Unsurprisingly, all this pressure led to tension between Freddie and Linda—as it probably would have for any young couple. Things came to a head a week before Valentine's Day, and in an act of fairness and equity to each other, Freddie and Linda ended their relationship. She felt a need to consider her future, and Freddie needed to consider his.

Among other responsibilities, Freddie wanted to in some way thank the world that had supported him: his coaches, teammates, and the thousands of fans who had reached out. He wrote a long, grateful letter on February 15, 1970, that was copied and reprinted and shared. Among other things, Freddie wrote:

> I would be remiss if I did not single out Coach Darrell Royal, my Texas coaches, and high school coaches, and my truly great teammates. Only a team member understands what it means to have such great friendships; only members of a squad realize the affection that we share for one another after hundreds of hours of practice and then playing in game conditions where the result of our work is realized. My coaches and teammates are the greatest! Football and competitive sports have taught me invaluable lessons, but most of all, they have taught me the game of life. I am most grateful!

IN APRIL, TWO INTERESTING THINGS HAPPENED TO Freddie. First, on April 7, he signed a contract with the publisher Little, Brown to write an autobiography, with the assistance of the sportswriter Blackie Sherrod. Together, they began work on *I Play to Win*, meeting, recording interviews, and writing throughout the rest of the year. Second, President Nixon invited Freddie to the White House, and so Freddie journeyed to Washington on April 13 along with Coach Royal, Father Bomar, and Fess Parker, the actor. Parker, who was best known for having played both Davy Crockett and Daniel Boone in television series, served as chairman of the 1970 American Cancer Society Crusade. "I can't agree more that Fred is symbolic of the courage of hundreds of thousands of Americans afflicted with cancer. He is symbolic of those who have taken a real hard knock and come back," Nixon said. The president gave Freddie a scroll that read: "The American Cancer Society salutes Fred Steinmark for having met the challenge of cancer with the courage and spirit that marked his athletic career, for providing inspiration and hope to thousands of Americans whose lives have been touched by cancer; for his steadfast faith in God, his country and himself."

In Austin, the American Cancer Society asked Freddie to make a public-service film for cancer awareness, with Fess Parker as narrator. In *The Fred Steinmark Story*, Freddie outlined his vision for the future: "My outlook is one of hope that with more extensive research on cancer, that the ultimate cure will be found, where people won't have to die or lose an arm or a leg or an organ, in order to stop the spread of cancer."

As the spring semester came to an end, Freddie was going hard. To stay on track to graduate the following May, Freddie needed to make up some lost credits; he decided to attend the summer semester at UT.

During those early weeks of summer, assistant trainer Spanky Stephens had moved into the rectory as well, since he needed an apartment and Father Bomar was willing, at Freddie's suggestion, to give Spanky a discounted rent. Spanky later recalled how he would come into the rectory and find Father Bomar and Freddie sitting in Bomar's office, deep in conversation. One might imagine the philosophical questions they discussed—the mysteries of life, and what Freddie's future might hold.

Freddie's need to examine deeper mysteries coincided with the death of Brian Piccolo, on June 16, 1970. For Freddie, it was solemn and foreboding news, and he shared his feelings about it with Big Fred in a phone call that Sammy overheard. Big Fred had sent Sammy to Austin to spend the summer with Freddie. "Keep your dauber up, son," Big Fred said. "Everyone is different. You're taking care of yourself, and you're strong. Just keep praying." Years later, when Sammy was an assistant football coach at the US Air Force Academy, he visited Chicago to recruit a player named Jeff Johnson. Jeff's father, John, had been a defensive tackle for the Chicago Bears and was a friend of the Piccolos. When Sammy met the Johnsons for dinner, Brian's wife, Joy, came along. Joy reached out and hugged Sammy as if they had known each other their entire lives, though they had never met. They embraced each other, tears rolling down their cheeks, in shared memory.

In July, Father Bomar drove Freddie to M. D. Anderson for the first checkup and scan since his amputation. The results were disheartening. The cancer had spread—there were spots on Freddie's lungs. Freddie knew what they signified.

As they began the drive back to Austin, Freddie told Father Bomar to turn around. He asked Bomar to take him directly to the Houston airport so that he could fly to Denver that evening. He found an available seat on a cargo plane that would get him home at ten thirty that night.

P.K. went with her father to pick up Freddie. P.K. recalls how quiet the airport was that late at night, how deserted the terminal. She remembers a distant, rhythmic thump-clap-thump-clap, like the working of some lonesome machine. The sound was made by Freddie's crutches echoing through the empty concourse. P.K. and Big Fred met Freddie with tearful embraces.

At the house, Freddie explained the situation to his mother and father and informed them that he would start chemotherapy at the end of the month.

Gloria whispered, "God has the final say in everything."

Freddie whispered in reply. "I know, Mother."

AFTER FREDDIE RETURNED TO TEXAS, BIG FRED AND Gloria felt that it was important for each of the younger kids to spend some time with him in Austin. He would need help dealing with the chemotherapy, but they also suspected this might be the last real opportunity that GiGi, P.K., and Sammy would have to be alone with Freddie. GiGi settled into an apartment and with Freddie's help, got a job with Gus Mutscher, the Texas speaker of the house. P.K. drove down with their cousin Loretta, who began work with the Department of Transportation. These were reflective days. P.K. recalls going to mass at St. Peter's and discovering her brother already there, praying an early rosary in one of the pews.

At the end of July, Freddie was asked to give a speech at the annual Football Writers Association of America convention, during College All-Star Week in Chicago. With his thoughts now focused on so many of the larger questions in life, Freddie built the speech around issues of faith and life and teams. One sportswriter present, Verne Boatner, later wrote of Freddie's address, saying, "I have heard some eloquent testimonials to football in my time. But the most stirring speech I ever heard came from the lips of a young man . . . Freddie Steinmark." Boatner seemed to recognize how Freddie, in the face of his illness, had gained tremendous insight into the games of football and life, and quoted Freddie as saying, "I've really been fortunate to play on a winning team, as there is such a fine line between winning and losing."

AT THE END OF THE SUMMER, FREDDIE MOVED INTO AN apartment with Scott Henderson, in the same complex where GiGi lived, along with Cousin Loretta and Becky Sumner (Becky was a friend of GiGi's from Colorado who had a young baby, and she moved to Austin as well and spent a lot of time with Freddie). His treatment now had him in a full-court press. In 1970, chemotherapy regimens were far more toxic and far less precise than they are now. As a result, Freddie began showing signs of wear and tear. Chronicling these weeks, Blackie Sherrod later wrote:

"The chemo-therapy consisted of six days of shots that, hopefully, would kill or arrest any fast-growing cancer cells. They make the patient frightfully nauseous. But [Freddie] masked the trips and treatments from all save a precious few. Scott Henderson, the linebacker, and Freddie's apartment mate, knew but respected the confidence . . . [Freddie] guarded the news like the atomic secret. He wanted no one to know. It was almost as though Fred [worried] the news would bring pity from his teammates and friends, and above all, he didn't want that."

The fall semester began. Freddie had a full course load on top of his coaching and continued chemo. At the same time, an Austin Chevrolet dealer approached Freddie with a deal on a burnt-orange Corvette. After Freddie did a little horse trading that involved switching cars with his parents, trading in their car, and appearing in an advertising photo for the dealer, he made the deal, and that Vette was a sight to behold on the streets of Austin. Over the summer, Freddie had let his hair grow long, for the first time in his life, rounding out his new, stylish aura.

Once fall practice kicked off, the players ribbed Freddie about his hippie-like new do. It was all good natured, and Freddie had a comeback for everything. But one day, while combing his hair, he let out a shout. GiGi, next door, came running and discovered Freddie holding a fistful of his hair. It was the chemo. Freddie had always taken pride in his appearance, and he devised a way to mask his hair loss while also playing along with and inspiring the Yearlings. Blackie Sherrod later recapped the moment when Freddie addressed the freshman Longhorns: "Okay you guys, . . . just to show you how seriously I'm taking this job, I'll get rid of the hippie image. I'll get rid of all this hair. As a matter of fact, I'll just shave it all off, just to show you I'm not kidding." And during a little ceremony in the locker room, the team cheered as Bobby Wuensch shaved Freddie's head. When someone pointed out that Freddie looked like a pirate, with his bald head and missing leg, Freddie went a step further and had GiGi pierce his ear and add an earring. GiGi recalls that Freddie didn't like how painful the clothespin on his earlobe was. "It was funny," she recalls. "After all he had been through without ever complaining, yet that little clothespin got to him." Unfortunately, as a side effect of the chemo, his earlobe took a long time to heal.

With fall in full swing, Linda came to Freddie and pleaded for a reconciliation. The pain of betrayal had hurt him deeply, as it had his mother. But Freddie remembered that she had been able, somehow, to forgive his father, and he found it within himself to think of the future, not the past, and take Linda back. On September 11, Loretta's twenty-first birthday, Freddie surprised his cousin, GiGi, and Linda with front-row tickets to a Temptations concert. It was a night of happy togetherness and celebration.

As the days grew cold, Freddie's illness became a day-to-day struggle. He lost weight, and his skin took on a pallor. Freddie kept his spirits high, though, and looked forward to the end of final exams and returning to Denver for Christmas. But before returning to Colorado, Freddie and Linda attended Longhorn teammate Bill Zapalac's wedding. As Freddie and Linda sat at the reception and watched the happy young couple, thoughts of marriage crossed their minds. But given Freddie's prognosis, the right course for him and Linda to take couldn't be easily determined. They were back together, but what filled their minds was the looming uncertainty of Freddie's future.

CHAPTER 16

THE RAINBOW

HOLIDAYS WERE ALWAYS OCCASIONS FOR great feasts in the Steinmark-Marchitti community, and Gloria wanted the 1970 Christmas gathering of the families to be the biggest and best celebration ever. Freddie was coming home instead of going to the Cotton Bowl, where, for the second year in a row, the Texas Longhorns would meet the Fighting Irish of Notre Dame. Gloria told Big Fred, GiGi, P.K., and Sammy to plan on spending the week before Christmas in the kitchen, helping her. She would need all hands on deck, she informed them, because she wanted it to be a special time for Freddie. Scores of relatives and friends were told to come by anytime on Christmas Eve or Christmas Day, and all were advised to come hungry. The menu for Christmas Eve would be built around the traditional Catholic, Italian-American Feast of the Seven Fishes. Christmas Day visitors would be treated to turkey and ham, ravioli, spaghetti, and manicotti. As a special surprise for Freddie, Gloria planned to make the cheesecake she always made for Easter. Freddie loved it, and Gloria wasn't sure whether he would be home for Easter. She didn't know this yet, but Freddie was coming home with a surprise for her, too.

The shopping list of ingredients was lengthy. It took Gloria, GiGi, and P.K. two full days of running around town to Gloria's favorite Italian markets in order to obtain everything they needed.

196

Gloria cooked the way her mother and Mrs. Gomez had taught her to cook when she lived in the Bottoms—use the freshest ingredients possible, because it makes a difference, and if there is an opportunity to buy the Italian version of something—say, Italian, flat leaf parsley instead of common or curly parsley—go with the Italian option. For Italian sausage, ribs, and the meats for meatballs, as well as the cured meats, cheeses, and olives for the antipasti, they went to Balfiore's and Cerrone's in North Denver. They hit Leprino's Cheese for fresh Italian Romano cheese and ricotta cheese, and Carbone's Bakery for loaves of Italian bread. Along the way, if Gloria ran into family friends, she invited them to the gathering. Big Fred's assignment was to bring home the fish. "We couldn't afford lobster, and nobody liked smelts," Gloria says. "So we had five, not seven." To ensure that he got the freshest available fish, Big Fred waited until the last minute to make his annual run downtown to the Seattle Fish Company, where he exchanged season's greetings with the Iacino family and picked up restaurant-quality halibut, scallops, *baccalà* (salt cod), shrimp, and squid.

Freddie arrived home five days before Christmas. After Bill Zapalac's wedding he had gone to Houston for his third, five-day chemo treatment, then he recuperated in Austin for a few days before flying to Denver. Despite not feeling great, and looking as bad as he must have felt, he was excited to be home and happy to see everyone. Being with his family energized him, and he seemed to be his usual cheerful self even though the chemotherapy treatment had slammed him hard.

"Freddie never wanted anyone to worry about him," says Sammy, "especially our mother. We all knew he couldn't be feeling as good as he wanted us to think he was feeling. He put on a good front. If you didn't know better you would have thought he was just a bald guy who had one leg."

But there was an elephant in the room, and everyone could feel it. "There was some anxiety, sure," Sammy says.

It wasn't just how he felt physically that concerned us—think how he must have felt about Texas and Notre Dame meeting in the Cotton Bowl again. Texas was still undefeated, and the second meeting against Notre Dame would have been his last game as a collegian if he hadn't lost his leg. What do people do on New Year's Day? Watch bowl games. We knew that's what we'd be doing with all those people coming to the house. Imagine sitting in front of the television watching that game with Freddie and my dad. But you know Freddie—it was impossible to be down in the dumps around him. He wouldn't let you.

Coach Akers described it as Freddie's gift for "lighting it up." He recalled that whenever Coach Ellington was in his office wrestling with one problem or another and noticed Freddie walking by, he would call Freddie in to chat for a few minutes. "And the next thing you knew," Akers said, "Ellington was all lit up. Freddie had that effect on everyone."

Becky Sumner recalls his cheerfulness, even after a debilitating chemo treatment left him too weak to do anything but lean back on the sofa and suck on lime popsicles. "[He] made you feel like he knew something wonderful that you didn't know. I just always sensed that he wanted me to know everything was okay, no matter what. It was comforting."

Freddie's cheerfulness changed his cousin Janet's life that Christmas. His illness had made her deeply, existentially angry:

When my parents came back from seeing Freddie Joe after he first went to M. D. Anderson, I heard them talking, and they were saying they didn't know if Freddie was doing very well. I yelled, I really yelled, "If anything happens to Freddie Joe, I'll never believe in God again!" It just really broke my heart. I was really mad at God. How could something like this happen to *Freddie*?

Janet's anger intensified after the amputation. She was still angry at Christmas, but hoping it wouldn't show when she saw him.

I remember his head was all shaved, and he didn't look very

good, but his whole attitude was—I mean, he was laughing and acting like everything was fine, and it was as if he was saying, "This is my destiny, this is what I'm supposed to be doing." He gave you encouragement, you know? He just had this charisma about him that made you feel hopeful. He was talking, and I was feeling kind of bad, and I was listening to him, and all of a sudden I felt at peace. My whole personality changed. He brought me back. My anger vanished, and I believed again.

While Freddie didn't evangelize, he often said he found strength from reading his Bible. That he remained so cheerful after his amputation confused some people, but the answer for him was found in 2 Corinthians 6:8–10: "We are treated as imposters, and yet are true; as unknown and yet well known; as dying, and behold we live; as punished, and yet not killed; as sorrowful, yet always rejoicing; as poor, yet making many rich; as having nothing, and yet possessing everything."

SAMMY WAS GLUED TO FREDDIE FROM THE MINUTE HE came through the front door. They hadn't seen each other in nearly four months, and Sammy was eager to hang out with "the best brother in the whole world" and to do all the things they had talked about doing when Freddie got home. Freddie, over the summer, had mastered one-legged water skiing, and Sammy now hoped he could help his brother master one-legged *snow* skiing in Breckenridge. Freddie thought they should stay home and spend time together with their parents. Freddie told him, "Let's do some Christmas shopping and go to a movie or two." Freddie gently suggested that Sammy should invite GiGi and P.K. to come along. Sammy wasn't crazy about the idea. He remembers that he, Freddie, and P.K., went to a theatre downtown. Freddie drove, Sammy sat in the front with Freddie, and P.K. was in the back seat. They saw *The French Connection.*

What they all remember most is an incident that happened on the walk back to the car after the movie. A drunk lurching and weaving on the sidewalk in front of them suddenly lost his footing and fell hard. Freddie hopped quickly to the man and helped him get up. If that weren't kindness enough, Freddie reached into his pocket and pulled out a few dollars and some change, which he placed in the unsteady fellow's hand. Unsure of what was happening, the drunk looked at the money, then tried to focus on Freddie's face and said, "Thank you." Sammy and P.K. heard their brother say, "No, sir, thank you."

This was a manifestation of something Freddie realized after he lost his leg: what he wanted most in life was no longer to be a professional athlete but to help others. This deeply felt altruism included subjecting himself to experimental chemotherapy in the hopes that it would help many others down the road.

WITH THE PREPARATION OF FOOD FOR 100 GUESTS ABOUT to get into high gear, Freddie decided it was a good time to tell his mother the secret he had come home with. No matter how she reacted, she was too busy to stop working and discuss it.

"Linda and I are getting engaged, Mother." He delivered the news matter-of-factly.

Gloria's hands were in sticky dough. She flashed a big smile at Freddie. "That's nice, Freddie honey. Are you sure it's what you want to do? If you're sure, I'm happy for you."

GiGi and P.K. were happy for him, too. "We weren't surprised," P.K. says. "It seemed like everyone was doing it."

"We all just wanted him to be happy," Gloria says. "Anything that would make him happy, we were for it." Big Fred wasn't *against* it, Sammy says, but neither did he embrace the idea. "Freddie told Dad he was getting engaged, and that he had an appointment with Tommy—a jeweler—to pick out a ring. Dad said, 'Freddie Joe, let's get you healthy and then we can talk about marriage.' Dad always trusted Freddie Joe's judgment, but I think he thought Freddie Joe already had enough to deal with."

"That was quite a week," GiGi recalls. "I don't know how Mother did it all. I think we all just tried to work together and keep Freddie happy. We were all so young! Even mom and dad were young." And this, it seems, is a subtle detail that so often gets lost in the broader context that develops around stories like Freddie's, stories that capture a nation's attention and grow with time into near-mythic proportions. The central players here—Freddie and his family—were young people; they experienced titanic changes in the moment; and they didn't yet have the relative cushion of decades of experience to help guide them.

On Christmas Eve and Christmas Day, a steady stream of friends and relatives were in the house. The dozens of simultaneous conversations were loud and animated and overflowed with laughter and good cheer. Nana Marchitti and the first of her great-grandchildren were there, and it was evident that Freddie was enjoying every minute of everyone's company. There was no announcement about the engagement. At midnight on Christmas Eve the whole family went to mass at Risen Christ Catholic Church.

THE GAME PLAN IN THE STEINMARK HOME ON NEW Year's Day called for watching football. The Cotton Bowl in Dallas was one of the early games, and everyone hoped Texas would prevail and keep its winning streak alive. The Longhorns had already been named the 1970 national champions. Which was a good thing, because they lost the game.

Sammy recalls watching the whole game and listening intently to Freddie and Big Fred discussing every play, particularly the performance of Rick Nabors, who had taken Freddie's place at starting safety. Nabors played well and had an interception. Because Sammy had only recently started playing organized football, Freddie would never know how much Sammy had learned by watching him play over the years and by listening to the hundreds, maybe thousands, of hours of conversations Freddie and Big Fred had had about how to play the game. Freddie would never know that Sammy would be an all-state receiver at Cherry Creek High School. Freddie would never know that Sammy would form a lifelong friendship with Earl Campbell when they were freshmen Texas Longhorns, playing together in the Gator bowl against Auburn. Freddie would never know that Coach Akers would get the head coaching job at Wyoming and ask Sammy to transfer there to help him transform a 2–9 program into a winner, and that Sammy would go to Laramie with Coach Akers and perform so well that Wyoming would win the Western Athletic Conference Championship and play Oklahoma in the Fiesta Bowl. Freddie would never know that the little brother who went everywhere with him would be signed by the NFL's Minnesota Vikings and after two years there would be picked up by the Denver Broncos. Freddie would never know that although an injury would end Sammy's playing career, he would be with the Broncos long enough to set a strength record, bench-pressing 255 pounds twenty-nine times, and managing a one-time maximum of 440 pounds. Freddie would never know that Sammy would become an assistant coach at the US Air Force Academy for seventeen years, followed by another three years at the US Naval Academy before retiring and starting a new career in the oil business. Freddie would never know that Sammy would have a son named Freddie Joe.

FREDDIE AND LINDA RETURNED TO AUSTIN SOON AFTER the holiday festivities were over. Freddie was anxious to resume his studies so that he could graduate on time. They returned to Denver over spring break, when Gloria, GiGi, and P.K. threw a wedding shower for Linda. Seventy-five women came, and all but Linda and her own mother were Steinmark and Marchitti family members and friends.

Freddie did not feel well enough to greet anyone on the day of the shower, so he stayed in Gloria and Big Fred's bedroom. It was obvious he wasn't doing well, but there had been no second-guessing about the shower. Freddie was the leader everyone was following. He held fast to the hope he would get better and believed that to give up or quit was unthinkable. His life was in God's hands, he knew, and whatever happened was part of God's plan for him. Rather than waste time by feeling sorry for himself after the amputation, he had shifted gears, set new goals, and pursued a new course. Instead of having a future in chemical engineering, he would become a lawyer. Instead of football or baseball, he took up golf. Freddie was never one to sit around wondering what to do with his time—even as a young boy, he never sat still for long. "He was constantly on the move," P.K. says. "When I think about how Freddie always was doing *something*—reading a book, or writing, or working out—I wonder now if he somehow knew he didn't have any time to waste."

When it was time for Freddie and Linda to return to Austin, which Freddie was impatient to do so that he could finish his classes and get ready for graduation, he was too weak and too ill to travel. He sent Linda on and told her he would be there as soon as he felt better. Several days passed. He called his Longhorn teammate Jimmy Gunn, whose upcoming August wedding Freddie was supposed to be in. "He didn't sound great," Jimmy says. "We were in Bill Zapalac's wedding, in December. Freddie was going to be in mine. He said he was in Colorado, and was sorry to say he didn't think he'd be well enough to come, and he didn't want to leave me hanging out there."

GiGi describes those days after Linda returned to Austin without Freddie as "upside-down days." She recalls that "Freddie would be awake all night coughing, and then he would be marginally better during the day, and he'd sleep."

On Monday morning, April 19, Freddie told Gloria that he needed to go to M. D. Anderson as soon as possible. She called Big Fred at work and then made flight arrangements to Austin. Gloria told P.K. she could take the Grand Prix to school if she dropped Sammy off at his school and did not mention she was taking Freddie to Austin. As P.K. and Sammy were leaving, they stuck their heads into Freddie's room and told him good-bye. As P.K. recalls, "He kissed us good-bye, and we said we'd see him after school."

GiGi walked with Freddie to Big Fred's cruiser, which was idling in the driveway. Before he got in, she hugged him and tried to hold back her tears. "I'll pray for you, Freddie Joe," she said. He kissed her and said, "Thank you, Gloria Gene. Love you. I'll see you soon." It was the last time GiGi, P.K., and Sammy saw their brother.

When Gloria and Freddie got to the apartment he shared with Scott Henderson, it was too late to attempt the drive to Houston. After she got Freddie comfortable, Gloria washed, dried, and folded his and Scott's laundry as a way to keep her mind occupied. The next morning, she put Freddie in the passenger seat of his Corvette and set out for Houston. It was raining so hard that it reminded her of floods in the Bottoms when she was a little girl.

She could barely see over the steering wheel and the Vette's long, burnt-orange hood. The 454-cubic-inch engine had far more horsepower than she could handle, and she fishtailed repeatedly while trying to hurry to Houston and still keep the tires in contact with the road. She had just turned forty years old. Of this trip Gloria wrote:

> I had to drive Freddie Joe from Austin to Houston in a horrible rainstorm, and was in agony. He never, ever tried to let me know how much pain he had throughout all his suffering, because he was always thinking of me, wanting not to hurt me or have me worry because the summer he was home I had bleeding ulcers and was in intensive care for three days. I can still see him, so loving, through the window of the door, waiting patiently with Fred and the kids. He always worried over everyone and everything. I was trying to keep the back end of the Vette on the slippery, rain-filled roads and it was so terrifying about halfway down. He took my hand and said, "Mother, I'm not going to make it." I immediately said, "Yes, you are, Freddie! God will help you. Keep praying." His back was ready to burst with pain (so was everywhere else). I had called ahead to the hospital to let them know we were coming and how much pain he was enduring, and to please have his room ready. Well . . . we sat in the waiting room two hours. He sat on a bench next to the wall in complete misery. They just didn't . . . it was a nightmare from morning to . . . I guess they knew there was nothing more for them to do for him. Most of the doctors were scarce. I know Dr. Moreton did all he could for Freddie Joe. I think he sincerely cared for him.

When Gloria was sure that she couldn't take another minute of sitting in the packed emergency room waiting area with Freddie in so much pain, she told him she was going to get someone. He put his hand on her arm and said, "No, Mother. Everyone here is sick. Just like me. We can wait our turn." It was April 20.

Big Fred immediately flew to Houston, and for the next forty-eight days he slept on the couch in Freddie's room all night. Gloria sat in a chair beside the bed all day. Freddie was too weak to get up from the bed when he needed to use the bathroom, so Big Fred would carry him. Cousin Loretta, who had returned to Denver after the previous Thanksgiving to work for an oil company, miraculously found herself transferred to the company's Houston office in April. This meant that she was able to go to the hospital each evening after work, and on weekends, to sit with Freddie while Gloria and Big Fred got something to eat or did laundry or just went outside for some fresh air.

"I would sit with him and recall all the times he had tried to steer me in a good direction," Loretta says.

> I thought about what a great athlete he had always been, whether he was playing baseball or basketball or football or Wiffle ball in Nana's yard, and how our whole family went to all his games because it was so much fun to watch him play. I looked at him lying there so weak and asleep, and remembered how he looked on that run against Lakewood. It was hard at times. When Uncle Fred would get very sad, he'd go out to the hallway and walk. He was a pacer. Freddie would talk occasionally, but his voice was very weak. He'd ask me how I was doing, and I would say, "Okay. How are you doing?" And he would smile or wink and say, "I'm getting better."

P.K., Sammy, and GiGi would call Freddie to let him know that they were thinking about him and that they were saying prayers for him, but they knew to keep their calls short. In May, P.K. called him from a pay phone at Aurora Central High School, where the Centennial League track championship and state qualifying meet was being held.

"Freddie, guess what?" she shouted into the phone. "I qualified for state in the hundred and the four-forty and eight-eighty relays! I did it for you!" His voice was barely audible, and she pressed the phone hard to her ear so she could hear him say, "That's great, P.K. I'm really proud of you."

There were several Texas people who had become close to Big Fred and Gloria, and in her "driving to Houston" narrative, Gloria acknowledged how much their friendship meant:

> His last days in the hospital were overwhelming to me and Fred—except for (Freddie's) humble and loving attitude and his concern for us and everyone else. Dear friends from Baytown Texas Exes, who came everyday to see him and make sure we had dinner—David and Gladys Conway—were two angels in our sorrows. Freddie Joe asked to see David a few days before he died, and David leaned over to hear what he had to say because Freddie Joe didn't have any strength in his voice. David never told me what Freddie said. He just came out with tears and said, "Every time I think I'm going in to cheer him up, he does more for me than I could ever do for him." This is so difficult for me to write, because I don't want to think or dwell on the sad things that happen—every day, if Fred and I were not there.

On Sunday morning, June 6, 1971, Gloria entered Freddie's room and said, "Good morning," as she had every morning. He startled her by sitting bolt upright. He had been too weak to even speak the day before.

"Mother!" he said. "Get me my boot! I'm going home tomorrow!"

Gloria thought there had been a miracle. The next day was GiGi's birthday, and this was Freddie's gift.

"Hurry, Mother!" Freddie said. "Get me that at the end of the rainbow!"

Gloria looked around frantically, unsure of what he wanted. She asked him what she was supposed to get.

He smiled and settled back on his pillow, waved his hand across his face, and said, "Never mind, Mother."

At 10:58 p.m. Freddie exhaled for the last time and let go, freed finally from the cancer. Gloria was on one side of his bed, and Big Fred and Loretta were on the other. Linda was in her chair at the end of the bed.

On Monday morning, Big Fred, Gloria, Loretta, and Linda flew back to Denver. That afternoon, as sunset began to soften and cool Houston, a local television news crew showed Freddie's casket being loaded into an airplane, and the plane taking off into the setting sun. Freddie was going home.

CHAPTER 17

THIS ENDLESS LIFE

ALSO ON THAT MONDAY, TEXAS'S US SENA-
tors, Lloyd Bentsen and John Tower, delivered impas-
sioned addresses in Congress concerning the former
number 28 of the Texas Longhorns.

The depth of Tower's emotion at the loss of Freddie Steinmark
was unequivocal. One of the things he admired most was the brave
face Freddie maintained. In his speech, he acknowledged that
Freddie likely knew the score from the beginning of his diagnosis:

> Given the nature of the cancer, Freddie most probably knew that
> his days were numbered. Nevertheless, he faced this fact with
> the courage that he had always displayed on the gridiron. Never
> once did he complain about his situation; he went about his ac-
> tivities as a man of deep conviction. He appeared before many
> sports groups and many youth organizations urging that they
> renew their adherence to the principles that helped to make
> Texas a great State and this Nation a great country: honesty and
> courage. . . . I am also personally richer because of the fine ex-
> ample that Freddie set both in the face of victory and adversity.

Senator Bentsen spoke about bravery, his deeply personal feelings about Freddie, and a way for Freddie's example to live on, a

practical path forward. After mentioning the most moving aspects of Freddie's life and the ways in which he carried himself after his diagnosis, Bentsen addressed President Nixon with the following words:

> The death of Freddie Steinmark, reminds us further, Mr. President, that we in the Congress have a duty to act affirmatively on proposals to broaden aid for cancer research so that we will hasten the day when we can eradicate this dread disease from American life.
>
> It has been estimated that 34 million Americans will die of cancer if better methods of prevention and treatment are not discovered. The amount spent on cancer research today is grossly inadequate. In 1969, for every man, woman, and child in the United States, our Government spent $120 on the war in Vietnam, $19 on the space program, $19 on foreign aid, but only 89 cents on cancer research.
>
> If the method of funding increased cancer research is delayed for political purposes over the coming months, thousands of other Freddie Steinmarks will perish because of our delay. Let us make the passing of this fine young man a signal for action in this body, to move as expeditiously as possible to achieve a cure for this dread disease.
>
> I wish to express my condolences to the family of Freddie Steinmark and to all those who stood by him during his long and painful ordeal.

Part of Senator Bentsen's hope was that the recently introduced Senate Bill 1828, which was titled an "Act to Conquer Cancer," would not be stalled by political aims that ran counter to the collective good. The day after delivering this address, Bentsen sent the Steinmarks his speech, along with a letter that states in part, "[The speech] expresses my heartfelt sentiments and my hope that we will quickly find a cure that would prevent such tragic losses in the future."

His letter was one of thousands that expressed condolences and detailed the myriad ways in which Freddie and his example had enriched the lives of so many others.

One of those letters was from President Richard Nixon. Brief but heartfelt, it ends with this sentence: "The example [Freddie] leaves behind in courage, perseverance and good sportsmanship will be an inspiration throughout the country." And as can be seen in the two Texas senators' speeches, the lasting, tangible effects of Freddie's inspiration had already begun.

FREDDIE'S DEATH WAS HAVING AN IMPACT AROUND THE nation, but nowhere was the combination of inspiration and anguish more pronounced than back home in Colorado, where Freddie's funeral rites were being planned. On the day that President Nixon wrote his letter, the Steinmarks, along with extended family and friends, were gathered at their home in Denver. What happened next, according to members of the Steinmark family, was quite powerful.

While they congregated, thunderheads formed in the sky. As Big Fred pulled into the driveway after viewing Freddie's body at the funeral home, two lightning bolts collided and shot down the Steinmarks' chimney. Bricks went flying—injuring no one, thankfully—and the walls pulsated, bringing down pictures throughout the house, except for the portrait of Freddie. At that moment, an old family friend named Pete Ciancio was walking up the sidewalk to the front door, where Gloria had rushed to see what was happening. Pete, extending his arms, said to her, "Gloria, that lightning is God telling you Freddie is with him." Gloria smiled and looked at the sky, and before her a glorious double rainbow materialized. She started to cry. It was as if Freddie were smiling upon them, offering one last good-bye.

Later that day, family and friends gathered beneath the soaring modern architecture of Risen Christ Catholic Church for a rosary, led by Father Bomar. The church building, much like Freddie, was a marvel of ingenuity and inspiration. It had been completed in 1969, the year that Freddie helped take his team to the national championship, and less than two years later it was hosting the mournful, ritual ceremonies in honor of one of Colorado's favorite sons. By then, the family had some notion of how large a public figure Freddie had become, but as they gathered in the sanctuary of their faith and family ties, they didn't imagine the magnitude that Freddie's legacy would achieve.

The funeral was held the next day at Risen Christ, and thousands of people arrived from all over the nation to walk in procession past the closed casket and mourn the passing of Freddie Joe Steinmark. Many people wore white, at Gloria's request. She said that Freddie would have liked that better. He wouldn't have wanted the mood to be too solemn. As Coach Royal and the contingent from the Longhorn football squad arrived from Texas, they must have felt right at home in that day's uncommonly hot weather. The thunderstorms of the previous day had swept on across the Colorado plains, and the weather turned bright for the beautiful requiem mass held beneath the stunning high wall of stained-glass windows. Father Bomar, who had shared many experiences with Freddie over his last years, delivered a moving eulogy. "But we must all remember," he said to the assembled, "each of us, that the entries on the pages in the book of life are not made or calculated by the number of years; instead they are recorded as deeds accomplished. In this sense Freddie's was a full life—a life that leaves a meaning much greater than most people realize who live seventy and eighty years."

Meanwhile, all across the nation, many joined in the mourning. The United Press International ran an article with lines such as this: "Freddie was a courageous young man, and the example he set while on the campus of the University of Texas will be a guideline for others to follow for many years." The *Austin American-Statesman* ran a deeply personal editorial that read in part: "When death finally came, we said a prayer and knew that a great young man had passed on. No Gipper of Notre Dame ever exhibited more courage, more of the qualities of manliness than Freddie. We miss him. But we are richer for having known him."

Sports commentator Howard Cosell gave a fitting tribute as well:

There's a great sadness today in Austin, Texas. There's a sadness overwhelming the youngsters at the University of Texas. And I suspect that there is a great sadness everywhere in the country among sports lovers . . . in a sense he is representative of the very finest qualities that sport can bring to the human society: the qualities of courage, the qualities of self-sacrifice, the qualities of individual commitment to a group effort, the qualities of how to live with other men together. There's got to be sadness in this country today over the loss of such a great young man as Freddie Steinmark.

After mass, Gloria was in the car waiting for the procession to Mount Olivet Cemetery when someone knocked on the darkened window. She rolled it down and was surprised to see Frank Leahy, Notre Dame's greatest coach after Knute Rockne. Leahy and the Steinmarks had met when Frank and Freddie were both patients at M. D. Anderson.

"Hello, Coach," Gloria said. "You didn't have to come." She knew it had to be difficult for him, because of his health.

"I wanted to be here, Gloria," he said. "I wouldn't have missed it. Freddie Joe was a fine young man."

Among Freddie's pallbearers were Scott Henderson, Kent Cluck, John Brock, and his cousins Gregg, David Enarson, and Johnny-boy. The blue sky was filled with billowy white clouds—a perfect football day—but the gathering was somber as the final prayers were said and Freddie was lowered into the ground.

Following the ceremony, the Steinmark home welcomed Freddie's closest friends, coaches, and teammates to partake in a final Italian feast, in the tradition of all those grand Gloria and Nana Marchitti holiday spreads that Freddie had enjoyed with his family over the years.

Also in attendance was Jay Wilkinson, a top aid to President Nixon and the president's personal representative at the funeral. Jay's father, Bud, of course, was the television commentator who had called the Big Shootout. Jay Wilkinson expressed his and the president's sympathies, and he asked whether there was anything

President Nixon could do to aid her and her family in their time of need. Gloria replied, "Tell him to fight cancer just as he would fight any other war." Wilkinson promised that the president and his team would do everything they could.

Gradually, among the breaking of bread and telling of stories, the mood brightened. The house and the yard were filled with people conversing and laughing, sharing their favorite memories of Freddie Steinmark. Mourning and loss had slowly transformed into a celebration of life and spirit, just as Freddie would have liked.

THE LAST OF THE GUESTS EVENTUALLY LEFT, AND THE flowers eventually wilted. Freddie was gone. Except for one thing: he *wasn't*, not entirely. Freddie's legacy continued to grow.

True to his word, President Nixon worked with Congress to enact the "War on Cancer." Spurred in large part by Freddie's story, Senate Bill 1828 passed through Congress later that fall. The bill came before President Nixon in December. It sought to greatly bolster funding for the National Cancer Institute and its power to advance the cause of cancer research. Among other things, the bill mandated that the institute's budget be submitted for approval directly to the president in order to bypass the tiered approvals generally required, which often subjected the appropriation to political jockeying. In fulfillment of Gloria's wishes, President Nixon, with thoughts of Freddie surely on his mind, signed the National Cancer Act of 1971 into law on December 23, 1971.

Inspired by Freddie's story, communities and organizations around the nation began their own grassroots campaigns to support cancer research and treatments. Golf tournaments were started. Bookstores and publications began Freddie Steinmark funds, the proceeds going to cancer societies. The Wheat Ridge boys' basketball team attempted to break a world record by participating in a 100-hour-long basketball tournament as a way to raise money for the American Cancer Society in the name of Freddie Steinmark. After the team reached twice its original financial goal, and stole the hearts of thousands of people around the nation, its members were recognized by several congressmen, including Representatives Jack Kemp and Gerald Ford, for their efforts.

Freddie was inducted into the Colorado Sports Hall of Fame. The award for the top high school athlete in the state was named after him (eighty-seven winners to date, including a father and son—see the listing in the appendix). Scholarships bearing his name were created. Years after his death, his presence and indomitable spirit remained a source of inspiration, as can be seen in news articles that have appeared through the years. In 1986, the sports columnist David Flores wrote, "Fifteen years after his death, Steinmark is still remembered fondly by all who knew him and admired him for his courage in the face of insurmountable odds. For some, the pain of loss always will be fresh—as if it happened yesterday—but the hands of time have shifted attention from the way he died to the way he lived."

Freddie's memory was still very much alive when the *San Antonio Express-News* ran a profile, reporting, "Forty years later, former Texas Longhorns quarterback James Street says he 'still gets chills' thinking about former UT defensive back Freddie Steinmark."

In 2006, an article in the *Denver Post* by Terry Frei observed, "It happened again and again: Reminiscing former football players laughed and smiled through their memories of their younger days, and when the subject turned to Steinmark, a junior during that 1969 season, the words caught in their throats."

Jerry Izenberg used his column to memorialize a long quote by Freddie: "I must not be afraid because fear itself is more painful than any pain you fear. . . . To quit is unthinkable. . . . I have been wished well by millionaires, by paupers, by the President of the United States and by Johnnie's Used Car bowling team in Baltimore and the fifth grade of the Jackson School in Cedar Rapids, Iowa. In almost all ways, I've already won."

Perhaps one of the most enduring and well-known testaments to Freddie arrived soon after his death. In 1972, the University of Texas created a monument to Freddie in the form of the new Longhorn Stadium scoreboard, officially dedicated to Freddie in a touching ceremony. To this day, Longhorn football players touch the image of Freddie on that scoreboard as they stream out onto the field, in the hope that Freddie's example will help them on game days. The dedication itself was a fine remembrance of the fearless boy from Colorado, who was always known for his tenacious heart. The plaque reads: "Dedicated to the memory of Freddie Steinmark, 1949–1971, defensive back of the Texas Long-horns, national football champions of 1969, whose courageous fight against savage odds transcended the locker room, the playing field, the campus, the nation itself. The indelible memory of his indomitable spirit will ever provide an inspiration to those who play a game or live a life."

FREDDIE'S AUTOBIOGRAPHY, *I PLAY TO WIN*, WAS PUB-lished just two short months after his death. One of the last senti-ments that he expresses in the book, is this: "I wish this impossi-bility: that all cancer patients—and that figures to be one of every four people—could have the morale boost given me by all of the well-wishers. That's the reason I feel like taking every one of these 'courage awards' and giving them to someone who had my illness and my operation and faced it with much, much less support and attention than I received." It may be true that, as Freddie said, he had no choice but to face his tragic circumstances; however, the perspective he brought was a willful decision to choose a path of honor.

As Coach Royal put it, "[Freddie] met this traumatic experience head on, jaw to jaw, with the greatest of determination, just as he always met his football opponents. . . . I think there is a connec-tion." Since Freddie has become a source of hope for millions of people, spanning continents and generations, he has, in a man-ner of speaking, bestowed those "courage awards" upon people throughout society. Now, decades later, the thought of Freddie can be a comfort to people who find themselves in suddenly challeng-ing or terrifying situations.

There is a notion that you become that which you practice. By extension, you personify the way in which you play the game or practice, regardless of the endeavor. Whether in football, baseball, running, music, or chess, a person's nature is manifested in his physical actions and thunders over him all the while. Freddie did everything intensely, with faithful commitment and every ounce of his heart. These attributes became embodied in his being. During a moment of overwhelming grief, Big Fred blamed himself for Freddie's death, certain that God had taken the son to punish the father, and it was the grace with which Freddie had lived, and died, that allowed Gloria to absolve her husband once and for all, to remind him that God does not work that way. And now, having greatly assisted us in this endeavor—reliving unfathomable heartache and sorrow, but also the happiness of many joyful times—she feels able to let go, relieved of her duties, and offer the complete Freddie to everybody, with the wish that anyone needing inspiration will find it in his story.

In the span of his short life, Freddie offered much to his family, friends, teammates, coaches, teachers, advisers, and doctors. Freddie's magic was rooted in his ability to help family and friends carry their dreams until they could carry them themselves. He thrilled sports fans and people from all walks of life with his heart, both on the field and off. Now his tale is one that people tell and retell, hoping to capture some of that magic, hoping to capture some of the essence of his character.

But the telling and retelling of Freddie's story might have another important role: it helps channel all those good wishes he received, all those courage awards, all the astounding support, and pay it forward, helping others play to win. Freddie would want his story to remind people that they have greatness inside themselves. This would be Freddie's wish, for each of us to nourish that potential within, and in doing so to carry on in his spirit.

Freddie knew better than most how people are transformed every day into patients, victims, case numbers, subjects, and survivors. Freddie offers us hope in the form of a guide for meeting life's challenges, no matter how difficult, with grace and strength as a promise for the future.

EPILOGUE

SEPTEMBER 1, 2012

O N SATURDAY, SEPTEMBER 1, 2012, THE
Texas Longhorns opened their season against the
Wyoming Cowboys in Darrell K Royal–Texas Memo-
rial Stadium. Coach Royal, in attendance as an honorary coach,
participated in the coin toss, though by now his brilliant mind had
begun to withdraw into the infinite unknown resulting from Alzheimer's disease.

My wife, Suzanne, and I were also there, in the company of Gloria, GiGi, P.K., Sammy, and Sammy's son, Freddie Joe. Big Fred,
who passed away on February 6, 2000, was with us in spirit. It
had been forty years since Gloria was last in the stadium. She
watched quietly as the stands began to fill, and I imagined she was
recalling long ago days when she, Big Fred, and the kids would
drive all night from their new home in South Denver—where she
still lives—to be here and see Freddie play. So much had changed.
She was now a grandmother to Sammy's four children and GiGi's
three, and a great-grandmother to three.

Gloria, Big Fred, and P.K. were here in 1972 when the University of Texas unveiled the Freddie Steinmark Memorial Scoreboard.
P.K. was a UT student then. The marching band spelled "FRED"
on the field that night, and Father Bomar delivered a nice tribute to Freddie over the public-address system. She and Big Fred
witnessed Texas's Billy Schott—who, as a young equipment man-

ager in 1969, had known Freddie—kick a field goal and put the first points on the board. Big Fred loved the idea of a scoreboard dedicated to Freddie. He remembered well the old advice he had frequently given his son: "If you aren't going to keep score, don't play." And Freddie always played to win.

Assistant athletic director Christine Plonsky had given us tickets for the game, and she told Gloria there might be an opportunity to say hello to Coach Royal when he came off the elevator on the way to his box after the coin toss. After the pregame festivities, we anxiously watched the crowd-energizing video as it flashed on the massive screen over the end zone. The last image in the video was a picture of Freddie, emblazoned with the word "Heart."

The elevator doors opened, and Coach Royal emerged. He was in a wheelchair, pushed by his wife, Edith. When Royal saw Gloria and her children, his face lit up with recognition, and he called them each by name. Gloria hugged and kissed him. "Hello, Coach," she said.

Soon, Edith had to get the coach moving so that he could be in his box by kickoff. Gloria watched them go. Just as Gloria was about to turn away, Coach Royal glanced at her over his shoulder and smiled, acknowledging their connection and shared love for an unforgettable boy named Freddie Joe Steinmark.

Acknowledgments

"Freddie Joe, if you were here, we wouldn't be doing this," Gloria said one afternoon, mostly to herself.

By "this," she meant writing this book. Gloria had been thinking for some time that an accurate biography of Freddie should be written, because without it, her grandchildren and great-grandchildren would never know who their Uncle Freddie really was. It was a bittersweet but necessary endeavor. As we began to discuss the project, we came to understand why it had taken her so many years to get to this point: while everyone who knew Freddie has fond and fun memories of him, Gloria's mind goes first to his end days, especially the last forty-eight, at M. D. Anderson, when his body was ravaged by cancer and he endured terrible suffering. Tom and I were initially concerned that reliving those memories might be too much for her; yet it was she who buoyed us when occasionally it became necessary. We could not have done this without Gloria's faith and strength always guiding us.

This biography could not have been written without the tremendous effort, continuous support, and unwavering commitment of a great many people who assisted us in both small and large measure. For all their insight, talent, energy, and faith, we are truly grateful. To each and every one we express our deep appreciation. We voice special and profound thanks to the Steinmark children, GiGi, P.K., and Sammy, who for the past four decades have endured the absence of their brother and worked unselfishly in their own ways to protect and serve his legacy. For years, P.K. was the driving force behind the golf tournaments that honored her brother and raised money for cancer research. She dove into every task we gave her with the same enthusiasm that made the tournaments so successful. She was always there to help us, no matter the request. GiGi gave us great insight into the evolution of the Fred Steinmark Award and shared many stories about its recipients and what winning it means to them. Sammy's discussions with Denny Aldridge, Tom Campbell, Bobby Mitchell, Billy Schott, David McWilliams, and Glenn Halsell were enlightening and helpful, and his memories of nearly continual companionship with Freddie explained for us the meaning of the sentiment "We had the older brother all kids wish they could have." The countless hours we spent discussing Freddie and his life with Sammy, GiGi, and P.K. brought us all an endless ebb and flow of tears and laughter.

In many ways, the production of this book has been a collaborative effort, something Freddie Joe would surely have appreciated. Our expanded team consisted of invaluable members Jack Dusendschon, Nick Mainieri, and David Parker—to each of you our heartfelt thanks for your time, research, writing, and editing contributions; we are truly indebted. And we extend our thanks to Pete Brown for his enthusiasm in collecting, refining, and editing the photographs presented.

To all the Steinmark-Marchitti family members who shared their memories with us, especially cousins Loretta Young Willis, Janet Duncan Wyche, Gregg Duncan, Mike Marchitti, and Johnnyboy Marchitti, we thank you, knowing that our thanks are hardly enough. You know how much we appreciate the time you gave us. We extend our thanks to GiGi's daughter-in-law, Magan Kunz, an excellent photographer who gave her time and expertise, and GiGi's daughter, Shawnee, whose research was invaluable. We must express our special thanks to Sammy's son, Freddie Joe Steinmark, for always going the extra mile when we needed his help in researching the extensive family archives that P.K. has collected, catalogued, and maintained for many years. Freddie Joe is the embodiment of, and a testament to, his Uncle Freddie's spirit. He is even quiet like Freddie was.

Our special thanks go to Sandy Watkins, Big Fred's sister, who helped us appreciate not only the difficult circumstances of their childhood but also the healing power of this family's love and togetherness. Her recollections of the happy teenage years she spent living in Nana Marchitti's basement with Fred and Gloria and the four kids, and of being head girl and cheerleader at North High, where her brother was a legend, and of having five-year-old GiGi beside her as the mascot cheerleader at all the games, was a delightful trip down memory lane.

We are indebted to all the people who shared with us personal stories about Freddie, and very much wish we could have included every one of them in this biography. All the stories are indicative of the powerful effect Freddie had on people, and some must be considered evidence that there are mysteries yet to be understood. Shawnee, who was born two years after Freddie was gone, shared her vivid memory of a day when she was a small girl playing by herself in Gloria's basement. It touched us deeply. She told us how, suddenly,

"Freddie was there, and I was sitting on his lap. He only had one leg, and he smelled like Papa [Big Fred]." Both Freddie and his father wore the same aftershave. "He kept looking at me and smiling, and after a minute or so he said, 'Oh, how sweet. Everything is going to be okay.' Then he was gone." Shawnee, herself, is a cancer survivor. Gloria treasures this story and others that are similar.

There are many others we must thank for taking the time to speak with us and share their memories. All of you helped us with your input and encouragement, especially Joe Fanganello, the late Ron Himstreet, and Don Westbrook, for bringing the North Denver of the 1940s and 1950s to life; Suzanne Gammage, Patricia Myer, Jeanine Solomon, Thomas E. Maloney, Audrey Dusendschon, Tina Yousse-Wheeler, and Debbie Waitkus, for reading and rereading the manuscript and offering editorial suggestions; and Amy Waitkus and Martha Trello, for taking notes and transcribing interviews. Our tremendous appreciation and thanks go to all the high school players who relayed their remembrances of Freddie, especially Roger Behler, Kent Cluck, Stan Politano, Mike Rich, Lenny Losasso, Bobbi Himes, and Mike Schnitker. And we extend deep thanks to the University of Texas players, staff, supporters, and coaches who shared their thoughts, emotions, and memories, including Scott Henderson, Ted Koy, Bob McKay, Rick Nabors, Fred Akers, Jimmy Gunn, Bill Zapalac, David "Cat" Ballew, Brad Knippa, Spanky Stephens, and Bill Little. Thanks to Freddie's friends Rocco Rofrano, Binny Droll Howard, Ann Morrison Michener, Lindi Coulter, Bitsy Ray Blakely, Leigh Ann Iannacito Brewer, Tony Garramone, Bruce DeCook, Ralph Hinst, and Robert Linnenberger for answering endless questions and sharing their memories. Thank you to Dr. Joel Brill and Dr. Xiaodong Wu for helping us understand Freddie's cancer and how it was treated, and to Danny Akers for showing us the power of prayer and faith in God.

Additionally we extend our sincere thanks to Bud Brigham for his commitment to and support of this book; the entire staff of the H. J. Lutcher Stark Center for Physical Culture and Sports for their help with research; Christine Plonsky and her staff in the UT Athletic Department; and the entire staff at the University of Texas Press, especially David Hamrick and Robert Devens, who embraced and encouraged this book from the outset, taking extraordinary measures to make this a timely reality. We are grateful to our families for their understanding, patience, and encouragement, for without them this book would not have been possible. Finally, we acknowledge that this work is our own, and any errors or omissions that may exist are our responsibility.

BOWER YOUSSE
THOMAS J. CRYAN

APPENDIX

THE FRED STEINMARK AWARD

The Fred Steinmark Award was started in 1972 by Scott Stocker, a Colorado sportswriter who covered high school competition for the *Rocky Mountain News* and also published his own newspaper, *Colorado Sidelines.*

This prestigious award is now sponsored by the Colorado High School Coaches Association. It is presented annually to the Colorado high school senior boy and senior girl who best exemplify Freddie's high standards for excellence in the classroom, athletics, and school, along with community involvement. Student-athletes must meet four requirements to be considered for the award: be a senior in high school; maintain at least a 3.0 grade-point average throughout high school; participate in a minimum of two sports each year; and be selected all-state in one sport and at least all-league in another.

Over the years, in a testament to family ethos, a father and son (Mike Hendricks, 1977, and Brian Hendricks, 2007), two brothers and two sisters (Jeff Singleton, 1992, and Kevin Singleton, 1999; Rebekah McDowell, 1996, and Mary McDowell, 2001), and two cousins (Tom Hubbard, 2001, and Dex Cure, 2006) have won the award. A member of Freddie's family has been present at every award ceremony since its inception.

STEINMARK AWARD WINNERS, 1972–2016 (91 WINNERS)

BOYS (47 WINNERS; COWINNERS IN SOME YEARS)

1972	Dave Logan	Wheat Ridge High School, Wheat Ridge
1973	Gary Washington	Colorado School for the Deaf and the Blind, Colorado Springs
1974	Daryl Monasmith	Burlington High School, Burlington
1975	Tim Roberts	Arvada West, Arvada

1976	Mike Edwards	John F. Kennedy High School, Denver
	Tom Reed	Fruita Monument High School, Fruita
1977	Mike Hendricks	Burlington High School, Burlington
1978	Steve Needens	Brush High School, Brush
1979	Kevin Baird	Cherry Creek High School, Greenwood Village
	Craig Kaiser	Merino High School, Merino
1980	Jerry Kersey	Rye High School, Rye
1981	Tom Southall	Steamboat Springs High School, Steamboat Springs
1982	Stein Koss	Durango High School, Durango
1983	Rick Wheeler	Cherry Creek High School, Greenwood Village
1984	Todd Tyrell	Arvada West, Arvada
1985	Terry Taylor Jr.	Rangeview High School, Aurora
1986	Pat Manson	Aurora Central High School, Aurora
1987	Brett Quigley	Lakewood High School, Lakewood
1988	Fred Harris	Montbello High School, Denver
1989	Scott Phillips	Lewis-Palmer High School, Monument
1990	Kent Kahl	Fort Morgan High School, Fort Morgan
1991	Justin Armour	Manitou Springs High School, Manitou Springs
1992	Greg Jones	John F. Kennedy High School, Denver
1993	Jefferson Singleton	Broomfield High School, Broomfield
1994	Scott Elarton	Eaton High School, Eaton
1995	Brad Schick	Gunnison High School, Gunnison
1996	Matt Rillos	Golden High School, Golden
1997	Kyle Howell	Kent Denver School, Cherry Hills Village / Central High School, Grand Junction
1998	Derek Applewhite	Brighton High School, Brighton
1999	Kevin Singleton	Broomfield High School, Broomfield
2000	Martin 'M.J.' Flaum	Northglenn High School, Northglenn
2001	Tom Hubbard	Limon High School, Limon
2002	David Hall	Akron High School, Akron
2003	Dustin Sprague	Holyoke High School, Holyoke
2004	Jeff Byers	Loveland High School, Loveland
2005	John McGuire	D'Evelyn Junior/Senior High School, Denver
2006	James 'Dex' Cure	Wray High School, Wray
2007	Brian Hendricks	Burlington High School, Burlington
2008	Kevin Williams	D'Evelyn Junior/Senior High School, Denver

2009	Bryan Peters	Rocky Mountain High School, Fort Collins
2010	Kyle Pollock	Wiggins High School, Wiggins
2011	Connor Medbery	Loveland High School, Loveland
2012	Canyon Barry	Cheyenne Mountain High School, Colorado Springs
2013	Koby Close	Buena Vista High School, Buena Vista
2014	David Sommers	Holy Family High School, Broomfield
2015	James Willis	Lutheran High School, Parker
2016	Chance Canty	Sanford High School, Sanford

GIRLS (44 WINNERS; COWINNERS IN SOME YEARS)

1974	Anne Vento	Centennial High School, Pueblo
1975	Donette Fischer	Alameda International High School, Lakewood
1976	Mary Lou Piel	Prairie High School, New Raymer
1977	Brenda House	Wray High School, Wray
1978	Jayne Gibson	Arvada West High School, Arvada
1979	Janet Winter	Windsor High School, Windsor
1980	Tanya Haave	Evergreen High School, Evergreen
1981	Armella Kanski	Bishop Machebeuf High School, Denver
1982	Deana Simpson	Highland High School, Ault
1983	Tracy Hill	Ridgway High School, Ridgway
1984	Michelle Bostrom	Brush High School, Brush
	Sheila Quillen	Fowler High School, Fowler
1985	Katie Salen	Pomona High School, Arvada
1986	Lori Shalberg	Plainview Junior/Senior High School, Sheridan Lake
1987	Cindy O'Connor	Lyons Middle/Senior High School, Lyons
1988	Jen Tubergen	Denver Christian High School, Denver
1989	Dee Binning	Cherry Creek High School, Greenwood Village
1990	Cruz Zarco	Sargent High School, Monte Vista
1991	Tricia Bader	Roaring Fork High School, Carbondale
1992	Kayci Emry	Lewis-Palmer High School, Monument
1993	Wendy Braye	Arvada West High School, Arvada
1994	Shelly Greathouse	Rocky Mountain High School, Fort Collins
1995	Jennifer Coalson	Ellicott High School, Calhan
1996	Rebekah McDowell	Wheat Ridge High School, Wheat Ridge
1997	Sarah Law	Ponderosa High School, Parker
1998	Britt Hartshorn	Lamar High School, Lamar
1999	Ashley Augspurger	Wheat Ridge High School, Wheat Ridge

2000	Cari Jensen	Fowler High School, Fowler
2001	Mary McDowell	Wheat Ridge High School, Wheat Ridge
2002	Laura Probst	Arvada West High School, Arvada
2003	Jasmine Oeinck	Arapahoe High School, Centennial
2004	Sara Hunter	Rocky Mountain High School, Fort Collins
2005	Maddie McKeever	Heritage High School, Littleton
2006	Danielle Kachulis	Kent Denver School, Cherry Hills Village
2007	Annie Perizzolo	Smoky Hill High School, Aurora
2008	Stephanie Pepper	Cherry Creek High School, Greenwood Village
2009	Laura Tremblay	Thompson Valley High School, Loveland
2010	Claire Gallagher	Cherry Creek High School, Greenwood Village
2011	Annie Kunz	Wheat Ridge High School, Wheat Ridge
2012	Janae VanderPloeg	Cheyenne Mountain High School, Colorado Springs
2013	Sidney Merrill	Akron High School, Akron
2014	Elise Cranny	Niwot High School, Niwot
2015	Jordan Baer	Akron High School, Akron
2016	Tara Traphagan	Yuma High School, Yuma

NOTES

All letters to or from Freddie Joe Steinmark, or to or from his family members, as well as diaries, are from the Steinmark Family Archives unless otherwise noted.

All quotations and reprinted sections from *I Play to Win* are the property of the Freddie Joe Steinmark Estate, managed by the Steinmark family.

All interviews were conducted by the authors unless otherwise noted.

AUTHORS' NOTE

xi   *This bill*: *National Cancer Act of 1971*, Public Law 92–218, 97th Cong., 1st sess. (December 23, 1971).

CHAPTER 1

3   *The third time*: Gloria Steinmark interview, September–December 2014.

3   *The headline read*: Chet Nelson, "Steinmark Selected All-American Boy: North Side Youngster Picked Unanimously," *Rocky Mountain News*, June 30, 1946.

3   *Gloria rolled over*: Gloria Steinmark interview.

3   *Baseball fans rejoiced*: *Wikipedia*, s.v. "Ted Williams."

4   *On the morning*: Gloria Steinmark interview.

4   *The article read*: Nelson, "Steinmark Selected All-American Boy."

5   *Fred Steinmark had thick*: Gloria Steinmark interview.

5   *He had more or less*: Sandra "Sandy" (Steinmark) Watkins, interview, November–December 2014.

6   *At thirteen, he was playing*: Gloria Steinmark interview.

7   *"My mother worked eighteen hour days"*: Gloria Steinmark interview.

7   *She was alone too*: Gloria Steinmark, personal memorandum, Steinmark Family Archives.

7   *By the time she was fourteen*: Gloria Steinmark interview.

8   *"It's what everybody did"*: Gloria Steinmark interview.

9   *When Fred, wearing number 1*: Gloria Steinmark interview.

13   *"Boy, he was a good kisser"*: Gloria Steinmark interview.

15   *Of Fred's ninety-seven teammates*: "Fred Steinmark," Baseball -Reference.com.

15   *He underperformed his first year*: "1947 Green Bay Bluejays," Baseball -Reference.com.

15   *His second year*: "Fred Steinmark," Baseball-Reference.com.

16   *The long-distance relationship*: Gloria Steinmark interview.

16   *What Gloria heard shocked her*: Gloria Steinmark interview.

17   *Fred was batting .361*: "Fred Steinmark," Baseball-Reference.com.

17   *But Gloria didn't share his enthusiasm*: Gloria Steinmark interview.

Chapter 2

18   *Dr. Benjamin Spock*: Benjamin Spock, *Baby and Child Care* (New York: Duell, Sloan and Pearce, 1946).

18   *"I wouldn't have had time to read that book"*: Gloria Steinmark interview.

19   *Monroe's "Ballerina"*: "Best Sellers in Stores-1948," *Billboard*, 1948.

19   *"Sometimes it meant putting Freddie Joe"*: Gloria Steinmark interview.

19   *In March 1908*: Steinmark family tree and genealogy, Steinmark Family Archives.

19   *Sometimes called the "first world war"*: *Wikipedia*, s.v. "Seven Years' War."

20   *After their voyage*: *Wikipedia*, s.v., "Globeville, Denver."

21   *"You could see it from the start"*: Gloria Steinmark interview.

22   *When he talks about Freddie*: John "Johnnyboy" Marchitti, interview, October–November 2014.

22   *"Fred's [semi-pro and softball] games"*: Gloria Steinmark interview.

23   *"If you screwed up in the drills"*: Gregg Marchitti, interview, November 2014.

24   *One of those diamonds was where I met Freddie*: Bower Yousse, interview, September–December 2014.

25   *Gloria doesn't remember Freddie crying*: Gloria Steinmark interview.

26   *"The way you guys talked"*: Kent Cluck, interview, November 2014.

26   *"Freddie and Frankie"*: Gloria Gene "GiGi" Steinmark, interview, September–December 2014.

27 *But suddenly, Big Fred wasn't there*: Gloria Steinmark interview.

27 *"I think we all had a pretty good idea"*: Stan Politano, interview, November 2014.

CHAPTER 3

29 *Boys hoping to make*: Yousse interview.

30 *"That's it. You guys"*: Yousse interview.

31 *In a newspaper story*: Undated, unidentified newspaper clipping, 1966.

31 *Their winning tradition had started*: Yousse interview.

31 *He was determined to restore*: *Jefferson Sentinel*, 1966.

31 *When it was officially announced*: Yousse interview.

32 *At the end of every summer*: Sammy Steinmark, interview, September–December 2014.

33 *Always one to look*: Yousse interview.

34 *To paraphrase*: Tom Robbins, *Still Life With Woodpecker* (New York: Bantam, 1980).

34 *Six months later*: Yousse interview.

35 *"Gather 'round!"*: Yousse interview.

35 *When half the team*: Sammy Steinmark interview.

36 *After the coaches led*: Roger Behler, interview, November 2014.

36 *Coats got his first look*: Politano interview; Cluck interview; Dave Dirks, interview, November 2014; Bob Himes, interview, November 2014; Mike VanMaarth, interview, November 2014.

37 *"Doesn't he ever get tired?"*: Politano interview.

37 *Freddie spoke to Coats about Sammy*: Sammy Steinmark interview.

38 *"How much do you weigh"*: Yousse interview.

38 *Four co-captains*: Politano interview.

38 *During the second week*: Yousse interview.

40 *Knowing that Freddie and the Farmers*: Gregg Marchitti interview.

40 *"Steinmark is gifted"*: "Look, Fans, Look: Tigers Done In by Farmers," *Rocky Mountain News*, October 8, 1966.

40 *Stan Politano's parents were so giddy*: Yousse interview.

41 *The minute the game was over*: Sammy Steinmark interview.

CHAPTER 4

42 *The first time they spoke*: Yousse interview.

42 *"Wheat Ridge was always"*: Mike Schnitker, interview, November 2014.

43 *When Hancock's call rang*: Yousse interview.

43 *His track record of winning*: Yousse interview.

44 *Perhaps the only person*: Gloria Steinmark interview.

44 *Sometime during the two weeks*: GiGi Steinmark interview.

44   *The thing that had got under*: Yousse interview.

45   *"I saw your coach today"*: Gloria Steinmark interview.

46   *Mike Schnitker recalled*: Schnitker interview.

46   *Coats prepared us for the game*: Yousse interview.

47   *"We use the best players"*: *Rocky Mountain News*, 1966.

47   *Coats called the team together*: Yousse interview.

49   *Later that night*: Sammy Steinmark interview.

49   *He would meet Sammy there*: GiGi Steinmark interview.

49   *The locker room was quieter*: Yousse interview.

50   *Sammy emerged from the training room*: Sammy Steinmark interview.

50   *Traffic crawled*: Yousse interview.

51   *"Throw that damn thing away"*: Sammy Steinmark interview.

51   *Freddie always was first*: Yousse interview.

52   *As one reporter wrote*: "Look, Fans, Look: Tigers Done In by Farmers," *Rocky Mountain News*, October 8, 1966.

52   *The Tigers responded*: Yousse interview.

53   *The next morning*: Irv Moss, "Wheat Ridge Spills Lakewood in Thriller 19–13," *Denver Post*, October 8, 1966.

53   *The article went on to say*: "Look, Fans, Look."

54   *A full week after the game*: Irv Moss, "Steinmark Feat Still Talk Topic," *Denver Post*, October 1966.

54   *Lakewood coach Hancock*: "Farmers Wreck Tiger Homecoming," unidentified newspaper clipping, October 1966.

54   *One article carefully*: "Look, Fans, Look."

54   *"What play should we run"*: Behler interview.

55   *GiGi was so proud*: GiGi Steinmark interview.

CHAPTER 5

59   *By Monday morning*: Yousse interview.

59   *Freddie arrived at school*: Behler interview; Cluck interview; Loretta Young, telephone interview, September–December 2014.

59   *Freddie might have a new*: Yousse interview.

60   *One local sportswriter*: Unidentified newspaper clipping, October 1966.

60   *It is important to remember*: Yousse interview.

61   *While we raced up the Hill*: Mike Rich, interview, September–December 2014.

62   *Freddie was the silent heart*: Yousse interview.

62   *In the paper the next morning*: Unidentified newspaper clipping, October 1966.

63   *Practice in the days leading up*: Yousse interview.

64   *"Certainly," Irv Moss went on*: Irv Moss, *Denver Post*, December 1966.

64 *This reality was slowly dawning*: Yousse interview.

65 *Freddie ranked 25th*: Freddie Steinmark, high school academic ranking, May 1967, Steinmark Family Archives.

65 *As Freddie's cousin*: Johnnyboy Marchitti interview.

65 *Everybody knew that Notre Dame*: Yousse interview.

66 *As the holiday season arrived*: GiGi Steinmark interview.

66 *And, of course, Freddie*: Gloria Steinmark interview.

66 *GiGi discovered Notre Dame's reply*: GiGi Steinmark interview.

67 *One day at school*: Yousse interview.

68 *University of Texas assistant coach*: Bill Ellington Jr., interview, December 9, 2014.

68 *"Oh my goodness"*: Fred Akers, interview, December 9, 2014.

68 *"Freddie," Koy recalls*: Ted Koy, interview, December 2014.

69 *"The head coach doesn't overwhelm you"*: Freddie Steinmark, *I Play to Win* (Boston: Little, Brown, 1971), 186–187.

69 *Freddie observed the painting*: Ibid., 186.

69 *Royal likely told*: Yousse interview; Akers interview.

70 *Once Freddie was back in Wheat Ridge*: Yousse interview.

70 *Family dinners had always been*: Gloria Steinmark interview.

71 *I'm so happy*: Freddie Steinmark to Linda Wheeler, June 26, 1967.

71 *Moreover, the Steinmark family*: Gloria Steinmark interview.

72 *In June, Freddie received*: Cincinnati Reds, draft notice, June 1966, Steinmark Family Archives.

72 *GiGi and P.K. hadn't been*: Paula Kaye "P.K." Steinmark interview, September–December 2014.

72 *Gloria started to well up*: Gloria Steinmark interview.

73 *Sammy cried out*: Sammy Steinmark interview.

73 *Gloria hid a smile*: Gloria Steinmark interview.

CHAPTER 6

74 *Freddie woke on his hard mattress*: Sammy Steinmark, telephone interview, October 10, 2014.

74 *The Republic of Texas*: UT History Central: Explore, TexasExes.org.

76 *Freddie was curious about everything*: Yousse interview.

76 *I remember an August night*: Ibid.

77 *At football orientation*: Spanky Stephens, telephone interview, November 18, 2014.

77 *Earl Campbell would give*: Sammy Steinmark interview.

78 *Passing by the varsity practice*: Freddie Steinmark, *I Play to Win*, 190–191.

78 *Meanwhile, back in Denver*: Gloria Steinmark, telephone interview, October 1, 2014.

79 *Don't worry about the bad day*: Fred Steinmark to Freddie Steinmark, September 27, 1967, Steinmark Family Archives.

79 *"Don't forget, you have"*: Fred Steinmark to Freddie Steinmark, September 26, 1967, Steinmark Family Archives.

79 *"He played to win"*: Blackie Sherrod, *Dallas Morning News*, 1996.

79 *"Oh, yes"*: Johnnyboy Marchitti interview.

80 *I recall something similar*: Yousse interview.

80 *In one of Freddie's letters*: Gloria Steinmark, telephone interview, October 2014.

80 *"We recruited athletes"*: Akers interview.

80 *"Come on, you kids"*: GiGi Steinmark, telephone interview, October 4, 2014; P.K. Steinmark, telephone interview, October 5, 2014; Gloria Steinmark, telephone interview, October 2014.

81 *Sammy ran for his brother*: Sammy Steinmark, telephone interview, October 6, 2014.

82 *How are your grades*: Sammy Steinmark to Freddie Steinmark, February 6, 1968, Steinmark Family Archives.

82 *Alternatively, Bob Mitchell*: Leigh Ann Iannacito Brewer, telephone interview, October 6, 2014; Sammy Steinmark interview.

82 *The last thing Mark told him*: *The Big Shootout: The Life and Times of 1969*, documentary, directed by Mike Looney and George Francisco (Heroes are Hard to Find, LLC, 2013).

83 *Dick Collins, an Austin sportswriter*: Dick Collins, "Clean Bill UT's Aim," *Austin American-Statesman*, November 22, 1967.

83 *Texas, however, as he later said*: Ed Spaulding, "Yearlings Glad Steinmark Decided against Air Force," *Daily Texan*, undated [November 1967].

83 *The game has no time limit*: John Margolis, "The Sweet Spot: How the Baseball Diamond Has Captured the Hearts of American Artists," *Chicago Tribune*, July 2, 1989.

84 *The expansive Longhorn tradition*: *Wikipedia*, s.v. "University of Texas Baseball."

84 *Freddie, early in practice*: Stephens, telephone interview.

84 *By the end of the season*: *Wikipedia*, "University of Texas Baseball."

84 *Well, I don't know*: Martin Luther King Jr., "I've Been to the Mountaintop" (speech), Mason Street Temple, Memphis, Tennessee, April 3, 1968.

84 *On the next evening, while King*: Stephen J. Spignesi, *In the Crosshairs: Famous Assassinations and Attempts from Julius Caesar to John Lennon* (New York: Barnes & Noble Books, 2003).

85 *When Freddie returned to Denver*: Gloria Steinmark interview.

CHAPTER 7

87   *"The most punishing part"*: Freddie Steinmark, *I Play to Win*, 106.

88   *"I know this is tough"*: Ibid.

88   *"I worked harder"*: Ibid., 200.

88   *"I* had *to be in shape"*: Ibid., 154.

89   *In a moment of great personal triumph*: Ibid., 200.

89   *The Longhorns under Royal*: TexasSports.com: The Official Website of UT Athletics.

89   *The UT administration*: Jim Adkinson, "Texas Primer: The Wishbone Offense," *Texas Monthly*, October 1985; Sammy Steinmark interview.

90   *The gruesome memories*: "The UT Tower Shooting," TexasMonthly .com.

90   *"The cover of* Life*"*: Pamela Colloff, "96 Seconds," *Texas Monthly*, August 2006.

91   *"Freddie Steinmark, the rookie safety"*: Ed Fowler, "Run Fast, Horns Say," *Austin American-Statesman*, September 17, 1968.

91   *September 21, 1968*: Bill McCurdy, "Gilbert vs. Gipson, a 1968 Clash of Champions," *The Pecan Park Eagle* (blog).

92   *Murray Chass*: Murray Chass, "Simpson, Gilbert, Gipson Praised," Associated Press, September 23, 1968.

92   *Most notably, Freddie came up*: Jerry Wizig, "Cougars Bitter over Longhorn Play for Tie," *Houston Chronicle*, September 22, 1968.

92   *Then, in the final minutes*: "Cougars Fall Just Short of Victory," *Houston Chronicle*, September 22, 1968.

92   *The press corps certainly took notice*: Lou Maysel, "Those 'Out-of-Staters' Pay Dividends for UT," *Austin American-Statesman*, undated [September 1968].

93   *One week later, the Longhorns*: Ted Koy, "T for Texas, T for Togetherness," Cotton Bowl Classic program, January 1, 1970.

93   *This time, the wishbone*: "Texas vs. Texas Tech, Sep 28, 1968," TexasSports.com.

93   *Scott Henderson, sitting next to Freddie*: Scott Henderson, telephone interview, September 9, 2014.

93   *Standing on the sideline*: Jenna Hays McEachern, with Edith Royal, *DKR: The Royal Scrapbook* (Austin: University of Texas Press, 2012), 92.

94   *During the previous summer*: Bruce Weber, "Emory Bellard, Creator of Wishbone Offense, Dies at 83," *New York Times*, February 20, 2011.

95   *Texas, over the 1965–1967 seasons*: TexasSports.com.

95   *Bellard and Royal never officially*: Weber, "Emory Bellard, Creator of Wishbone Offense."

97   *As Lou Maysel declared*: Lou Maysel, "Steers Rebound, Rout OSU," *Austin American-Statesman*, October 6, 1968.

97   *Freddie's big plays*: Associated Press, "Longhorns Overpower Razorbacks by 39–29," October 22, 1968.

98   *The Longhorns tallied*: Lou Maysel, "Explosive Steers Saddle Mustangs with 38–7 Loss," *Austin American-Statesman*, November 3, 1968.

98   *As Gloria worked*: Gloria Steinmark, telephone interview, December 2014.

99   *Ed Fowler of the* Austin Statesman: Ed Fowler, "As It Was Last Year," *Austin Statesman*, November 12, 1968.

99   *Blackie Sherrod of the* Dallas Times Herald: Blackie Sherrod, "Texas, SMU Break the Bank," *Dallas Times Herald*, November 10, 1968.

99   *Andy Yemma of the* Austin American-Statesman: Andy Yemma, "Steers Not Cooperative," *Austin American-Statesman*, November 10, 1968.

100 *The piece highlighted*: Austin Bureau of the News, "Steinmark Won't Miss White Yule," undated [December 1968].

CHAPTER 8

101 *The previous year*: *Wikipedia*, s.v. "1968 in the Vietnam War."

101 *Freddie, Bobby, and the rest*: Henderson, telephone interview.

102 *For example, Freddie had no idea*: Yousse interview.

102 *Upon hearing of Mark's death*: *The Big Shootout: The Life and Times of 1969*.

102 *As the Longhorns' athletic trainer*: Stephens, telephone interview.

103 *Bobby himself would recall*: *The Big Shootout: The Life and Times of 1969*.

103 *"I was upset with the way"*: Terry Frei, *Horns, Hogs, and Nixon Coming* (Lanham, Md.: Taylor Trade Publishing, 2002), 73.

103 *Despite his strong play*: Freddie Steinmark, *I Play to Win*, 189.

103 *This was a comfortable situation*: UT 1969 Baseball Media Guide.

104 *As Ed Fowler pointed out*: Ed Fowler, "Spring Grid Drills vs. Baseball," *Austin American-Statesman*, undated [1969].

104 *Lou Maysel observed*: Lou Maysel, "Royal's Grid Plan Up to Weatherman," *Austin American-Statesman*, March 11, 1969.

105 *Baseball, however*: Freddie Steinmark, "What I Learned from My Loss," *Guideposts*, October 1970, 23.

105 *Freddie continued to trigger*: James Gallagher, Office of the Commissioner of Major League Baseball, to Freddie Steinmark, May 5, 1969, Steinmark Family Archives.

105 *Still, it was premature*: Ed Fowler, "Carry-Over Value Shows in Longhorns' Grid Drills," *Austin American-Statesman*, undated [March 1969].

105 *The local media wrote*: "Gridders Open Final Drill Week," unidentified, undated [August 1969] clipping.

106 *When Ed Fowler*: Ed Fowler, "UT Secondary Starting Over," undated [1969] clipping, *Austin American-Statesman*.

106 *Back home, Freddie again*: Freddie Steinmark, *I Play to Win*, 189.

106 Texas Football, *the cherished publication*: Untitled, undated [1969] article, *Texas Football*.

106 *The* Dallas Times Herald'*s sports editors*: "1969 Times Herald Players' All-SWC," *Dallas Times Herald*, undated [1969].

107 *On one clear July night*: Sammy Steinmark interview.

107 *First, Frank Caputo*: Freddie Steinmark, *I Play to Win*, 105.

107 *In the waning days*: Scott Henderson, telephone interview, September 9, 2014.

108 *First, Freddie took Scott*: Freddie Steinmark, *I Play to Win*, 105.

108 *As the trainer*: Stephens, telephone interview.

108 *Soon, Scott noticed the limp*: Henderson, telephone interview.

108 *"In retrospect"*: Freddie Steinmark, *I Play to Win*, 106.

CHAPTER 9

113 *They began the year*: TexasSports.com.

113 *As Darrell Royal put it*: Lou Maysel, untitled article, *Austin American-Statesman*, September 7, 1969.

113 *A seasoned veteran*: Roger Stanton, untitled article, *Football News*, September 6, 1969.

113 *"I've got a lot of work"*: Ed Fowler, "Anything Goes," *Austin American-Statesman*, August 16, 1969.

114 *It is essential to remember*: Fred Steinmark to Freddie Steinmark, September 26, 1967, Steinmark Family Archives.

114 *That year, in seven*: TexasSports.com.

115 *Nevertheless, Freddie indicates*: Freddie Steinmark, *I Play to Win*, 106.

115 *The coaches observed*: Ibid., 112.

115 *Nearly two months earlier*: Fred Bomar, with Michael Rutland, *Faith, Ministry, and the Modern World: A Texas Priest Reflects on 50 Years of Service*, 3 vols. (Buda, Tex.: Texas Bindery Services, 2009), 1:74.

116 *The history of the Catholic Church*: AustinDiocese.org; *Wikipedia*, s.vv. "Roman Catholic Diocese of Austin," "Roman Catholic Archdiocese of Galveston-Houston," "Spanish Missions in Texas"; Catholic-Hierarchy. org, "Archdiocese of Mexico."

117 *Bomar had become a good friend*: Bomar, *Faith, Ministry, and the Modern World*, 1:74–75.

117 *Spanky Stephens recalls that Freddie's leg*: Stephens telephone interview.

118   *"Looks to me"*: Freddie Steinmark, *I Play to Win*, 116.

118   *Scott Henderson recalls frequent*: Henderson, telephone interview.

118   *"Sometimes," Freddie said*: Freddie Steinmark, *I Play to Win*, 105.

118   *And so although Freddie's stats*: Henderson, telephone interview.

118   *Freddie's backup, Rick Nabors*: TexasSports.com.

119   *One of his favorite anecdotes*: Freddie Steinmark, *I Play to Win*, 103.

119   *"Athletes are supposed to play"*: Ibid., 100.

119   *Texas still sat firmly*: *Wikipedia*, s.v. "1969 Texas Longhorns Football Team."

120   *"But," Freddie writes*: Freddie Steinmark, *I Play to Win*, 31.

120   *November 27, 1969*: Ibid., 119.

CHAPTER 10

122   *The United States had been increasing*: "The Vietnam War: The Bitter End, 1969–1975," HistoryPlace.com.

122   *At 8:00 CST*: "The Draft Lottery," report by Roger Mudd, CBS News, December 1, 1969, YouTube video, www.youtube.com/watch?v=-p5X1FjyD_g.

123   *Representative Alexander Pirnie*: *Wikipedia*, s.v. "Draft Lottery (1969)."

123   *In the lobby of Jester Hall*: Henderson, telephone interview.

123   *Freddie Steinmark didn't stay*: Freddie Steinmark, *I Play to Win*, 66.

123   *Freddie had played in eighteen*: TexasSports.com.

123   *Last year, Texas had triumphed*: Associated Press, "Longhorns Overpower Razorbacks by 39–29," October 22, 1968.

124   *The rosary beads*: Father Gerard Cryan, telephone interview, September 2014; *Wikipedia*, s.vv. "Rosary Devotions and Spirituality," "History of the Rosary."

125   *"The first question"*: Freddie Steinmark, *I Play to Win*, 67.

125   *"So that was my exciting routine"*: Ibid., 74.

125   *"I didn't tell Mr. Medina"*: Ibid., 71.

125   *"I wore full pads"*: Ibid., 74.

126   *GiGi ran to the receiver*: GiGi Steinmark interview.

126   *"Freddie Joe!"*: P.K. Steinmark, telephone interview, September 2014.

126   *He had been considering*: Gloria Steinmark, telephone interview, September 2014.

127   *Freddie later wrote*: Freddie Steinmark, *I Play to Win*, 75.

127   *Gloria remembers her husband*: Gloria Steinmark, telephone interview, September 2014.

127   *Scott Henderson recalls*: Henderson, telephone interview.

127   *James Street addressed the crowd*: Freddie Steinmark, *I Play to Win*, 76.

127 *"This is the most important"*: Frei, *Horns, Hogs, and Nixon*, 180.

128 *Enthusiastic telegrams*: Freddie Steinmark, *I Play to Win*, 76–77.

128 *Freddie writes in*: Ibid., 80.

128 *As Freddie would later write*: Ibid., 77.

CHAPTER 11

129 *Freddie stood in the back*: *1969: The Game of the Century—Texas Longhorns*, documentary, ESPN: The Greatest Games series (ESPN and Virgil Films and Entertainment, 2009).

129 *Texas linebacker Scott Henderson*: Henderson, telephone interview.

129 *Arkansas, leading 14–8*: *1969: The Game of the Century*.

130 *Freddie cheated backward*: Henderson, telephone interview.

130 *So far, Montgomery*: *1969: The Game of the Century*.

130 *Air Force One*: *The Big Shootout: The Life and Times of 1969*.

131 *"It was an unreal atmosphere"*: Henderson, telephone interview.

131 *As Nixon disembarked*: *The Big Shootout: The Life and Times of 1969*.

132 *Arkansas, with the benefit*: *1969: The Game of the Century*.

132 *Henderson recalls similar moments*: Henderson, telephone interview.

132 *It was the culminating game*: *The Big Shootout: The Life and Times of 1969*.

133 *To the surprise and relief*: *Wikipedia*, s.v. "Dixie (song)."

133 *The visitors' locker room*: Jimmy Gunn, telephone interview, December 16, 2014; Bob McKay, telephone interview, December 17, 2014.

134 *Scott Henderson recalls*: Henderson, telephone interview.

134 *"The Razorbacks were playing"*: Freddie Steinmark, *I Play to Win*, 86. Freddie was incorrect on one account. At this point, Texas had lost only three fumbles; the fourth fumble (and sixth turnover) would come in the fourth quarter. Regardless, the point is well made. A team with a 0–5 turnover ratio could plausibly (and frequently would) be losing by five scores.

134 *Street dropped back*: *1969: The Game of the Century*.

135 *Before the game, Royal*: Freddie Steinmark, *I Play to Win*, 84.

135 *Chris Schenkel, announcing*: *1969: The Game of the Century*.

136 *Later, he would speculate*: Sammy Steinmark interview.

136 *Henderson got the defensive signal*: Henderson, telephone interview.

136 *Big Fred stared*: Sammy Steinmark, telephone interview, September 2014; GiGi Steinmark interview; P.K. Steinmark interview.

137 *After his discussion with Broyles*: *1969: The Game of the Century*.

138 *"No, no"*: Sammy Steinmark, telephone interview, September 2014.

138 *"A marker is down"*: *1969: The Game of the Century*.

138 *Big Fred later recalled*: Sammy Steinmark interview.

138   *Hearing her husband's concern*: Gloria Steinmark, telephone interview, September 2014.

138   *The referee paced off*: 1969: The Game of the Century.

139   *Big Fred looked at Gloria*: Gloria Steinmark, telephone interview, September 2014.

139   *ABC didn't go to*: 1969: The Game of the Century.

139   *"We went for"*: Freddie Steinmark, I Play to Win, 92–93.

139   *"They'll be expecting"*: Ibid., 91–92.

140   *Street returned to the huddle*: Henderson, telephone interview.

140   *A national television audience*: 1969: The Game of the Century.

141   *Cheers filled the Steinmark living room*: Gloria Steinmark, telephone interview, September 2014.

141   *On second and three*: 1969: The Game of the Century.

142   *If you've ever been*: Freddie Steinmark, I Play to Win, 97.

142   *Coach Royal was so full of emotion*: The Big Shootout: The Life and Times of 1969.

143   *"Frank Medina somehow waded"*: Freddie Steinmark, I Play to Win, 99.

143   *The Longhorns—number one*: Ibid., 120–122

143   *Coach Royal said it was*: Ibid., 122.

144   *There was a big buffet*: Ibid., 123–124.

CHAPTER 12

145   *"Sunday was a bad day"*: Freddie Steinmark, I Play to Win, 124.

146   *"My knee is hurting"*: Ibid.

146   *"[I] had x-rays taken"*: Freddie Steinmark, "What I Learned from My Loss," 24.

146   *"I'll take the pictures"*: Freddie Steinmark, I Play to Win, 125.

147   *"Got to go get the verdict"*: Ibid., 126.

148   *"They think I have a tumor"*: Ibid., 127.

149   *Restless, his mind racing*: Ibid., 128–129.

149   *The first thing Dr. Julian did*: Ibid., 129–130.

150   *When Freddie entered the dorm*: Stephens, telephone interview.

150   *When Freddie told him*: Gloria Steinmark interview.

150   *Hurriedly, Spanky drove with Freddie*: Bomar, Faith, Ministry, and the Modern World, 1:93.

151   *Back on campus, Spanky*: Freddie Steinmark, I Play to Win, 130–132.

152   *In the early evening, Freddie*: Gloria Steinmark interview.

152   *First, they marked Freddie's body*: Freddie Steinmark, I Play to Win, 134–135.

153   *After finishing their explanation*: Ibid., 135–136.

154   *Now I got to tell you about Henderson*: Ibid., 137.

155 *"What are you doing in a hospital?"*: Ibid., 141.

156 *Back in Austin, Coach Royal*: Gunn, telephone interview; Henderson, telephone interview; Koy interview; McKay, telephone interview; Rick Nabors, telephone interview, December 2014.

156 *"I was just numb"*: Nabors, telephone interview.

156 *Koy recalls*: Koy interview.

156 *"I was worried mostly"*: Freddie Steinmark, *I Play to Win*, 142–144.

157 *Bomar offered to hear*: Bomar, *Faith, Ministry, and the Modern World*, 1:80–81.

158 *"As a kid," Freddie explains*: Freddie Steinmark, *I Play to Win*, 144.

158 *Bomar walked across the room*: Ibid.

158 *"I remember trying to reach down"*: Ibid., 206.

159 *Bomar details the scene*: Bomar, *Faith, Ministry, and the Modern World*, 1:80–81.

Chapter 13

163 *A surgical biopsy*: Freddie Steinmark, *I Play to Win*, 205.

164 *In fact, when Dr. Martin*: Gloria Steinmark, telephone interview, September 2014.

164 *Ted Koy, when asked*: United Press International, untitled article, December 14, 1969.

164 *Texas A&M sent him*: Texas A&M, telegram, December 12, 1969, Steinmark Family Archives.

164 *Rice University sent a note*: Rice University, telegram, December 12, 1969, Blackie Sherrod Papers, SMU.

165 *"No one ever got"*: Freddie Steinmark, *I Play to Win*, 212–213.

165 *In fact, his room became*: Ibid., 221.

165 *In fact, President Nixon*: Ibid., 208.

165 *Gloria, for her part*: Gloria Steinmark, telephone interview, September 2014.

165 *"Honestly," he writes*: Freddie Steinmark, *I Play to Win*, 208.

166 *When his beloved cousin*: Johnnyboy Marchitti interview.

166 *Freddie, sitting for the first time*: Freddie Steinmark, *I Play to Win*, 222–223.

166 *"He is a fine boy"*: Associated Press, untitled article, December 16, 1969.

167 *Big Fred and Father Bomar*: Freddie Steinmark, *I Play to Win*, 223.

167 *Upon arriving at M. D. Anderson*: Gloria Steinmark, telephone interview, September 2014.

168 *On December 23, Dr. Healey*: Freddie Steinmark, *I Play to Win*, 224.

168 *There are photographs of Freddie*: United Press International, "Astrodome Lights Up for Freddie," December 24, 1969.

168   *"This," Freddie told reporters*: Freddie Steinmark, *I Play to Win*, 225.

169   *Freddie was to be discharged*: Ibid., 226.

169   *"I'm not that tough"*: Ibid., 227.

CHAPTER 14

171   *On New Year's Day 1970*: Freddie Steinmark, *I Play to Win*, 14–15.

171   *"The doctors told Coach Royal"*: Ibid., 228.

172   *"There was this nagging feeling"*: Ibid., 18, 20.

172   *Father Bomar sensed much*: Bomar, *Faith, Ministry, and the Modern World*, 3:13.

173   *"Everything was real quiet"*: Freddie Steinmark, *I Play to Win*, 19.

173   "I was happy they dedicated": Ray Didinger, "Freddie's Walk across Stage Is a Lasting Memory," *Philadelphia Bulletin*, January 27, 1970.

173   *"He came over and we said"*: Freddie Steinmark, *I Play to Win*, 19.

173   *Ted Koy later recalled*: Koy interview.

173   *I don't think any of us trusted*: Freddie Steinmark, *I Play to Win*, 19.

174   *"Why did they only put"*: Sammy Steinmark, telephone interview, September 2014.

174   *"In those final moments"*: Freddie Steinmark, *I Play to Win*, 21–22.

175   *"When you come out of that tunnel"*: Ibid., 8.

175   *As he later recalled*: Bomar, *Faith, Ministry, and the Modern World*, 1:82.

176   *"Your courage has inspired"*: Joe Cipriano, telegram, December 13, 1969, Blackie Sherrod Papers, SMU.

176   *"In great crises"*: Brigadier General James Cross, letter, December 12, 1969, Steinmark Family Archives.

176   *Even during the buildup*: University of Notre Dame, letter, December 12, 1969, Steinmark Family Archives.

176   *In other words, as Father Bomar*: Unidentified article, *Fort Worth Star-Telegram*, January 1970.

176   In Making Cancer History: James S. Olson, *Making Cancer History: Disease and Discovery at the University of Texas M. D. Anderson Cancer Center* (Baltimore: Johns Hopkins University Press, 2009), 4.

176   *Further, Olson describes*: Ibid., 7.

177   *Cancer is an insidious*: Xiaodong Wu, president and CEO, Biophysics Research Institute of America, Albert Einstein College of Medicine, New York, and Mansoor Ahmed, program director, Radiation Research Program, Division of Cancer Treatment and Diagnosis, National Cancer Institute, Rockville, Maryland, telephone interview, January 3, 2015.

177   *"That kind of thing"*: David Flores, untitled article, *San Antonio Express-News*, January 1970.

178 *Over the weeks*: Associated Press, "Fred Steinmark: Symbol of Courage," February 15, 1970.

178 *"Steinmark said he wanted"*: United Press International, "Steinmark Gets Dome Salute, Plans to Attend Cotton Bowl," December 1969.

178 *"I won't get a chance to play"*: Jack Agness, "Steinmark Deluged with Gifts," *Houston Post*, December 1969.

179 *As James Olson recorded*: Olson, *Making Cancer History*, 5.

179 *Texas was riding the longest*: Freddie Steinmark, *I Play to Win*, 25–26.

179 *Irish defensive tackle Mike McCoy*: Cotton Bowl program, January 1, 1970, 27.

180 *In response, however*: McEachern, *DKR*, 96.

180 *Finally, kickoff arrived*: The Big Shootout: The Life and Times of 1969.

181 *"Everybody had tried to throw"*: Freddie Steinmark, *I Play to Win*, 43.

181 *At the end of the third quarter*: The Big Shootout: The Life and Times of 1969.

182 *Freddie, hovering nearby*: Freddie Steinmark, *I Play to Win*, 43.

182 *When Street dropped back*: The Big Shootout: The Life and Times of 1969.

182 *"Tom didn't even stop"*: Freddie Steinmark, *I Play to Win*, 45–46.

182 *"The Longhorns made another dramatic"*: Unidentified clipping, January 2, 1970.

183 *"Then everybody started grabbing me"*: Freddie Steinmark, *I Play to Win*, 46–47.

183 *"Theismann said if Notre Dame"*: "Street Earns Respect of Theismann," *Washington Star*, January 2, 1970.

184 *"I meant it sincerely"*: Freddie Steinmark, *I Play to Win*, 50.

CHAPTER 15

185 *Freddie received his prosthetic leg*: Freddie Steinmark, *I Play to Win*, 229.

185 *"I hated that my parents"*: Ibid.

185 *On Friday, January 9*: Ibid., 231.

185 *"An impish grin spread"*: Mary Jane Scher, "Freddie Walks on New Leg," *Houston Chronicle*, January 10, 1970.

186 *During a nine-hole round*: Sammy Steinmark interview.

186 *Before Freddie's departure*: Freddie Steinmark, *I Play to Win*, 232.

186 *"The University of Texas annual football banquet"*: Ibid., 233–236.

187 *Amid the jokes, the laughter*: Dave Campbell, "On Second Thought," *Waco News-Tribune*, January 12, 1970.

187 *"Naturally, I had a stomach full"*: Freddie Steinmark, *I Play to Win*, 236.

188 *That week, Freddie moved*: Ibid., 232–233.

188 *"Is this a temporary"*: Ibid., 233.

188 *When asked why Freddie*: Akers interview.

189 *I watched your game*: Brian Piccolo to Freddie Steinmark, January 19, 1970, Steinmark Family Archives.

189 *"I'm awed to be considered"*: Paul Giordano, "Steinmark 'Awed' by His Company," *Bucks County (PA) Courier Times*, January 27, 1970.

190 *By early February*: GiGi Steinmark interview.

190 *I would be remiss*: Freddie Steinmark, letter, February 15, 1970, Steinmark Family Archives.

191 *Second, President Nixon invited*: Freddie Steinmark, *I Play to Win*, 237–238.

191 *"I can't agree more"*: United Press International, "President Nixon Honors Coloradan Steinmark," April 14, 1970.

191 *"The American Cancer Society salutes"*: Freddie Steinmark, *I Play to Win*, 240.

191 *"My outlook is one of hope"*: *The Fred Steinmark Story*, narrated by Fess Parker (American Cancer Society, 1970).

191 *During those early weeks*: Stephens, telephone interview.

192 *"Keep your dauber up, son"*: Sammy Steinmark interview.

192 *In July, Father Bomar drove Freddie*: Gloria Steinmark, telephone interview, September–December 2014.

192 *P.K. recalls how quiet*: P.K. Steinmark, telephone interview, September–December 2014.

192 *Gloria whispered*: Gloria Steinmark, telephone interview, September–December 2014.

193 *P.K. drove down with their cousin*: Loretta Young, telephone interview, September–December 2014.

193 *P.K. recalls going to mass*: P.K. Steinmark, telephone interview, September–December 2014.

193 *One sportswriter present*: Verne Boatner, "First and Goal," *Arizona Republic*, August 1, 1970.

194 *"The chemo-therapy consisted of"*: Blackie Sherrod, "Freddie's Courage," *Dallas Morning News*, May 1971.

194 *At the same time, an Austin*: Sammy Steinmark interview.

194 *GiGi, next door*: GiGi Steinmark interview.

194 *Blackie Sherrod later recapped*: Sherrod, "Freddie's Courage."

194 *"It was funny"*: GiGi Steinmark interview.

195 *But before returning to Colorado*: Bill Zapalac, interview, December 2014.

196 *Holidays were always*: Gloria Steinmark, telephone interview, September–December 2014.

197 *"Freddie never wanted"*: Sammy Steinmark interview.

198 *Coach Akers described it*: Akers interview.

198 *Becky Sumner recalls*: Becky Sumner, interview, December 15, 2014.

198 *When my parents came back*: Janet Marchitti, interview, December 2014.

199 *Sammy was glued to Freddie*: Sammy Steinmark interview.

199 *What they all remember most*: GiGi Steinmark interview; P.K. Steinmark interview.

200 *With the preparation of food*: Gloria Steinmark interview.

200 *GiGi and P.K. were happy*: P.K. Steinmark interview.

200 *"We all just wanted him"*: Gloria Steinmark interview.

200 *Big Fred wasn't against it*: Sammy Steinmark interview.

200 *"That was quite a week"*: GiGi Steinmark interview.

201 *Sammy recalls watching the whole game*: Sammy Steinmark interview.

201 *Nabors played well*: Rick Nabors, telephone interview, December 15, 2014.

201 *Freddie would never know how much*: Akers interview.

202 *Freddie and Linda returned*: GiGi Steinmark interview.

202 *"He was constantly on the move"*: P.K. Steinmark interview.

203 *He called his Longhorn teammate*: Gunn, telephone interview.

203 *GiGi describes those days*: GiGi Steinmark interview.

203 *On Monday morning*: Gloria Steinmark interview.

203 *"He kissed us good-bye"*: P.K. Steinmark interview.

203 *"I'll pray for you"*: GiGi Steinmark interview.

203 *When Gloria and Freddie*: Gloria Steinmark interview.

204 *I had to drive*: Gloria Steinmark, journal entry, 1971, Steinmark Family Archives.

204 *When Gloria was sure*: Gloria Steinmark interview.

205 *Cousin Loretta, who had*: Young, telephone interview.

205 *"I would sit with him"*: Young, telephone interview.

206 *"Freddie, guess what?"*: P.K. Steinmark interview.

206 *His last days*: Gloria Steinmark, journal entry, 1971, Steinmark Family Archives.

206 *On Sunday morning, June 6*: Gloria Steinmark interview.

CHAPTER 17

208 *Given the nature of the cancer*: *Congressional Record*, June 7, 1971.

209 *The death of Freddie Steinmark*: Ibid.

209 *Part of Senator Bentsen's hope*: Office of Government and Congressional Relations.

209 *"[The speech] expresses"*: Lloyd Bentsen to the Steinmarks, June 8, 1971, Steinmark Family Archives.

210   *"The example [Freddie] leaves"*: President Richard Nixon to the Steinmarks, June 9, 1971, Steinmark Family Archives.

210 *While they congregated*: GiGi Steinmark interview.

210 *At that moment, an old*: Gloria Steinmark interview.

211 *"But we must all remember"*: Father Bomar, handwritten speech, June 1971, Steinmark Family Archives.

211 *"Freddie was a courageous"*: United Press International, "Steinmark, a Profile in Courage, Dies at 22," June 7, 1971.

211 *"When death finally came"*: Editorial, "Passing of Freddie Steinmark," *Austin American-Statesman*, June 10, 1971.

212 *"There's a great sadness today"*: Howard Cosell, radio broadcast, June 1971.

212 *After mass, Gloria*: Gloria Steinmark interview.

213 *"Tell him to fight"*: Gloria Steinmark interview.

213 *In fulfillment of Gloria's wishes*: National Cancer Act of 1971.

213 *The Wheat Ridge boys' basketball team*: Unidentified article, *Rocky Mountain News*, June 1971.

214 *"Fifteen years after his death"*: David Flores, unidentified article in an unidentified publication, 1986.

214 *Freddie's memory was still*: Jerry Briggs, "The Off-Speed Pitch: These Athletes Live Strong," *San Antonio Express-News*, July 9, 2009.

214 *"It happened again"*: Terry Frei, "Steinmark Lives On in Memories," *Denver Post*, January 2, 2006.

214 *"I must not be afraid"*: Jerry Izenberg, "At Large: Death Be Not Proud," *Newark Star-Ledger*, June 1971.

215 *"Dedicated to the memory"*: University of Texas at Austin, plaque, 1972.

215 *"I wish this impossibility"*: Freddie Steinmark, *I Play to Win*, 264.

215 *"[Freddie] met this traumatic"*: Darrell Royal, introduction to Freddie Steinmark, *I Play to Win*, ix.

Epilogue

217 *My wife, Suzanne*: Bower Yousse, telephone interview, December 18, 2014.

INDEX

Single capital letters indicate photos in the first unnumbered section. Double capital letters indicate photos in the second unnumbered section.

Campbell, Earl, 77, 201
Campbell, Mike, 67, 126–129, 134, 136. *See also* Longhorn football
Campbell, Tom, 130, 136, 141, 172, 182–183. *See also* Longhorn football
Caputo, Frank, 71, 107
Carpenter, Mark, I
Catherine the Great, 19
Catholic Church, 16, 48, 116–117, 124–125. *See also specific churches; specific people*
Chass, Murray, 92
Ciancio, Pete, 21, 210
Cincinnati Reds, 72
Cipriano, Joe, 176
Clark, Harley Jr., 75–76
Clark, R. Lee, 166
Cleveland Indians, 13
Cluck, Kent, I, 26, 37, 55, 212
Coats, John W. "Red," I; and Big Fred, 44–45, 46; and Mike Campbell, 67; and corporal punishment, 61; and football practice strategy, 47; on Freddie's defensive play, 64; and Tom Hancock, 42–43; as high school football coach, 29, 31, 35–41; and Lakewood game, 50–51, 52–53, 54, 55, 60; on Ranum game, 62. *See also* Wheat Ridge Farmers
Cobb, Ty, 4–5
Collins, Dick, 83
Conway, David, 206
Conway, Gladys, 206
Cormier, Jay, FF
Cosell, Howard, 211–212
Cotton Bowl (1969), 100, BB
Cotton Bowl (1970): and Freddie's determination to attend, 169, 171; as Freddie's dream game, 151, 153; and Freddie's popularity, 175, 178, 179; and Longhorns playing without Freddie, 164; and Longhorn victory, II, EE, FF; and President Nixon's call to Freddie, 165; and Notre Dame's regards for Freddie, 176; and Coach Royal, 145, 156; and Cotton Speyrer, 187, HH
Cotton Bowl (1971), 196, 197–198, 201
Covello, Gene, I
Crenshaw, Ben, 186
Cross, James, 176

Dale, Billy, 182
Davis, Derek, 99
Dean, Mike, 179–180
Dearinger, Ted, 97
Dicus, Chuck, 127, 129, 130, 134, 135–136, 138
Dill, Ted, 52
DiMaggio, Joe, 189
Dirks, Dave, I, 37, 38, 53
Duncan, Gregg, D, 21, 23, 34, 40–41, 212
Duncan, Joe, 3–5, 21, 34
Duncan, Lena Marchitti, 3–4, 12, 21

Ehrig, Ronnie, 97. *See also* Longhorn football
Ellington, Bill, 68, 81, 188–189, 198. *See also* Longhorn football
Enarson, David, 212
Enid Buffaloes, 17
Ewing, Finley, 171
Ewing, Gail, 171
Ewing's sarcoma, 177

Fallico, Gary, 52
Feller, Happy, 141
Field, Bobby, 131
Fighting Irish, 146, 164, 181, 196. *See also* Notre Dame

52–53; and Longhorn football, 70, 83; and scholarship offers, 64; and Texas recruitment, 67, 68

Mitchell, Mark, 82, 101, 102

Monroe, Vaughn, 19

Monson, Scott, 46

Montgomery, Bill: and Longhorns–Razorbacks game (1968), 97; and Longhorns–Razorbacks game (1969), 129, 130, 132, 134, 135–136, 137–138, 141; as Razorback quarterback, 124

Monzingo, Scooter, 88

Moore, Jerry, 140

Moreton, Bob, 151–152, 158, 204

Moss, Irv, 54, 64

Mudd, Roger, 122

Mutscher, Gus, 193

Nabors, Rick, 118, 156, 172, 201, HH

Newman, Joe, I

Nixon, Richard: and draft lottery, 123; and Freddie, 165, 191, JJ; on Freddie's example, 210; and Longhorns–Razorbacks game (1969), 130–132, 142; and protesters, 133; and War on Cancer, 212–213

Nobis, Tommy, 89

Notre Dame, 65, 66–67, 180. *See also* Fighting Irish; *specific coaches*; *specific players*

Olson, James, 176–177, 179

Owens, Steve, BB

Palmer, Scott, 119, 144, FF

Panek, Pat, 13

Parker, Fess, 191

Peschel, Randy, 103, 140–141

Phillips, Eddie, 173

Piccolo, Brian, 189, 191–192, GG

Pitts, Henry, 75

Plonsky, Christine, 218

Politano, Stan, 27, 31, 37, 38, 40–41. *See also* Wheat Ridge Farmers

Pryor, Cactus, 186

Pueblo Central Wildcats, 41

Raugh, Bob, I

Ray, James Earl, 85

Rees, John, 130, 132, 135–136, 141

Reicher, Louis Joseph, 116

Reneau, Joe, 146, 147, 150

Rich, Mike, 61

Risen Christ Catholic Church, 201, 210

Risoli, Harry, 23

Robbins, Tom, 33–34

Robichau, Paul, FF

Royal, Darrell K.: and Alzheimer's disease, 217; and attitude toward pain, 118–119; and awards banquet (1971), 186–187; and Baylor Bears game (1968), 99; and Father Bomar, 117; and Cotton Bowl (1970), 181–183; and Freddie, II, CC, JJ; on Freddie's courage, 215; and Freddie's diagnosis, 150, 152–154, 156; and Freddie's funeral ceremonies, 211; and Freddie's gratitude, 190; on Freddie's heart, 164, 178; and Freddie's recruitment, 69–70; on Freddie's return after amputation, 173–174; on Freddie's running, 100; and Gloria, 218; and Longhorns–Razorbacks game (1969), 135, 139–140, 142; and loss to Red Raiders (1968), 93–94; and President Nixon, 191; and record as Longhorn coach,

hopes, 65; and competitive spirit, 26; and Cotton Bowl (1970), 182, 183–184; and Cotton Bowl (1971), 201; and departure for Austin, 72–73; and diagnosis, 145–148, 152–154, 163–164; endurance of, 37; and faith, 49, 124–125, 149, 157, 193, 199; on fear and pain, 214; final days of, 206–207; and final return to M. D. Anderson, 203–205; and first signs of cancer, 107–108; and flight to M. D. Anderson, 150–151; and growing pressure, 123; and helping others, 199–200; on Scott Henderson, 154–155; and high school football, 28, 40–41, 44, 47–48, 52–55, 59–60, 64; and high school graduation, I; and hopes for cancer patients, 215; legacy of, 216; and legacy of cancer research, 213–214; as Longhorn, II, CC, DD, AA, BB, EE, FF, HH; and Longhorn baseball, 83–84, 103–105; and Longhorn football, 74, 88–89, 99–100, 113–114; and Longhorns–Baylor Bears game (1968), 99; and Longhorns–Houston Cougars game, 91–92; and Longhorns–Oklahoma State game (1968), 96–97; and Longhorns–Razorbacks game (1969), 129–130, 132, 133–134, 135–136, 137–138; and Longhorns–Red Raiders game (1968), 94; as Longhorn Yearling, 77–78, 81, 82–83; and Loretta, 27; mental abilities of, 76–77; and Mark Mitchell's death, 102–103; and Most Courageous Athlete Award, KK; and nationwide popularity, 175–176, 178–179, 189–190;

and President Nixon, 165; and Notre Dame, 66–67, 179; on Ohio State–Michigan game (1969), 119–120; and playing through pain, 50, 127; as point guard, F; and post-surgery attitude, 168–170; and prosthetic leg, 185–186; and rehab, 166–167; and release for Cotton Bowl (1970), 171–173; and Mike Rich, 61–62; on Coach Royal, 69; and Sammy, 35–36; in SMU game (1969), 118; and spread of cancer, 192; and stats (1968 versus 1969), 114–115; and Larry Stegent collision, 120–121; on Gloria Steinmark, 156; and summer activities, 32–34; and Texas heat, 87; and Texas recruitment, 67–70; and wedding shower, 202; and Linda Wheeler, 70, 85–86, 195; on winning national championship, 142, 143–144; on wishbone offense, 181

Steinmark, Freddie Joe (Sammy's son), 217

Steinmark, Friedrich (Big Fred's father), 6, 20

Steinmark, Friedrich (Big Fred's grandfather), 19–20

Steinmark, Gloria Gene "GiGi," A, B; on Big Fred's talk with Red Coats, 44; birth of, 17; and Christmas 1970, 196–197; in early childhood, 18–19; and Freddie's cancer, 126, 194; and Freddie's departure for Austin, 72; and Freddie's engagement, 200; and Freddie's last days, 203, 205; and Freddie's laundry, 59; and Freddie's Notre Dame rejection, 66–67; and high school, 55, 78; and Longhorn game (2012),